D0195166

Wyoming

Nathaniel Burt
Updated by Richard Anderson
Photography by Don Pitcher

COMPASS AMERICAN GUIDES
An Imprint of Fodor's Travel Publications

917.87

Compass American Guides: Wyoming

Editors: Kit Duane, Sarah Felchlin, Jennifer Paull
Designer: Christopher Burt
Photo Editor: Christopher Burt
Map Design: Mark Stroud, Moon Street Cartography

Copyright © 2008 by Fodor's Travel, a division of Random House, Inc.
Maps Copyright © 2008 by Fodor's Travel, a division of Random House, Inc.

Fodor's is a registered trademark of Random House, Inc.

All rights reserved. Published in the United States by Fodor's Travel, a division of Random House, Inc., and simultaneously in Canada by Random House of Canada Limited, Toronto. Distributed by Random House, Inc., New York.

No maps, illustrations, or other portions of this book may be reproduced in any form without written permission from the publisher.

Fifth Edition
ISBN 978-1-4000-0737-0
ISSN 1539-3283

Although all prices, opening times, and other details in this book are based on information supplied to us at press time, changes occur all the time in the travel world, and the Publisher cannot accept responsibility for facts that become outdated or for inadvertent errors or omissions. So always confirm information when it matters, especially if you're making a detour to visit a specific place.

All photographs are by Don Pitcher unless otherwise credited below.
Compass American Guides acknowledges the following institutions and individuals for the use of their photographs: American Heritage Center, University of Wyoming, Laramie, p. 161 (neg. #1265); Arizona Historical Society, Tucson, p. 27 (AHS#51035); Buffalo Bill Historical Center, Cody, pp. 21 (Vincent Mercaldo Collection; P.71.143A), 74 (Gift of Olive and Glenn E. Nielson; 1.69.2725), 163 (Vincent Mercaldo Collection; P.71.728.7), 186 (Cody Manuscript Collection; MS6.1.D.MC1), 187 (1.69.26), 193 (P.6.156), and 279 (Vincent Mercaldo Collection; P.71.1246); Carbon County Museum, Rawlins, p. 164; Gilcrease Museum, Tulsa, pp. 20 (watercolor; 4776.5.68), 76 (oil on canvas; 0126.727), and 194 (watercolor; 0226.1457); Dr. George Gill, p. 272; Homesteader Museum, Powell, p. 166; Hot Springs County Museum, Thermopolis, p. 176; Jackson Hole Historical Society and Museum, pp. 225, 245, 246, and 250; John Wesley Powell River History Museum, Green River, Utah, p. 312 (photo by E. O. Beaman, U.S. Geological Survey); Johnson County Jim Gatchell Memorial Museum of the West, Buffalo, p. 151; Kansas State Historical Society, Topeka, p. 85; Library of Congress, p. 153; Montana Historical Society, Helena, p. 154 (photo by L.A. Huffman); National Park Service, Yellowstone National Park Collections, pp. 198 and 224; Telluride Ski & Golf Company, p. 243 (photo by Prescott Jones); Wyoming State Archives, Department of State Parks and Cultural Resources, Cheyenne, pp. 32, 44, and 262.

Compass American Guides, 1745 Broadway, New York, NY 10019
PRINTED IN CHINA BY TWIN AGE LIMITED
10 9 8 7 6 5 4 3 2 1

To my father and my son,
both full of Wyoming experiences.

C O N T E N T S

continued on following page

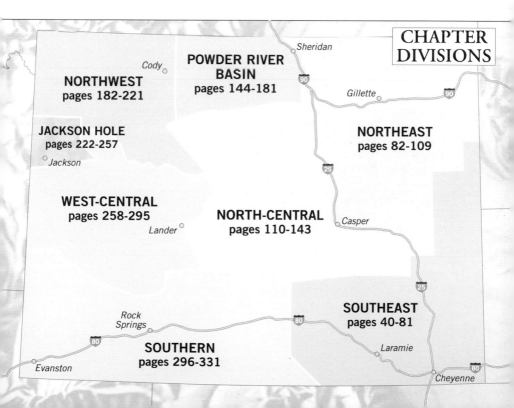

Maps

Literary Extracts

Topical Essays

O V E R V I E W

THOUGH WYOMING IS AMAZ-
INGLY COHESIVE, the geometric
boundaries do cut across some
natural sub-areas, notably the
Black Hills and the midwestern
plains. However, it is remarkable
how many self-contained regions
the state embraces. Moving generally from southeast to northwest, and back again, you can
broadly distinguish at least eight
such regions. Each is dealt with in

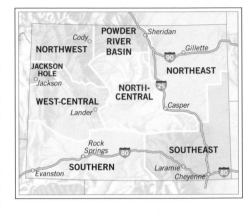

a separate chapter of the book, and their organization is based on the assumption
that you are driving an automobile. The following list describes those regions,
while the map on page 7 shows the boundaries we've assigned them.

SOUTHEAST: OLD WYOMING & STAGECOACH CORRIDOR
pages 40–81

Old Wyoming consists of the southeastern
corner of the state, including Cheyenne,
the capital city, and Laramie, the university town. Between them can be found the
bizarre Vedauwoo; the Medicine Bows
stand farther west. The Stagecoach Corridor lies along the state's eastern border.
With its rangeland and plains, the area
resembles the Great Plains states—the
Dakotas and Nebraska—more than it does
the rest of the state.

NORTHEAST CORNER: BLACK HILLS & THUNDER BASIN
pages 82–109

The Northeast covers the north-easternmost corner of the state, a region of low mountains encompassing the western extension of the Black Hills. Thunder Basin comprises the corridor of plains south from Montana to the North Platte River.

NORTH-CENTRAL: PLAINS & BIGHORN BASIN
pages 110–143

The plains district extends west from the bend of the North Platte and its mountains toward the Wind River Basin. The Bighorn Basin is a valley of badlands and farmland which lies between the Owl Creeks, the Big Horn Mountains, and the Absarokas.

POWDER RIVER BASIN   *pages 144–181*

Two county seats —Buffalo (Johnson County) to the south, and

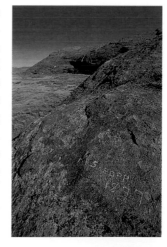

Sheridan (Sheridan County) to the north—are the civic centers of the Powder River Basin, the area east of the Big Horn Mountains, including the actual watershed basin of the Powder River. Historically, these two towns represented the two factions of the Johnson County War. The Northern Wyoming Farmers and Stock Growers' Association was based in Buffalo, while Sheridan was dominated by big cattle owners.

Northwest Corner: Absarokas & Yellowstone *pages 182–221*

The Absarokas are one of the country's most formidable mountain ranges—a barrier of seemingly random peaks occupied largely by bear, moose, and elk. Cody is a favorite gateway to Yellowstone National Park, but may be better known as the birthplace of Buffalo Bill Cody. This chapter also includes the first national park in the United States, Yellowstone, an embarrassment of riches with hundreds of geysers and hot springs, dozens of waterfalls, and countless bear, bison, and elk.

Jackson Hole & Grand Teton National Park *pages 222–257*

Jackson Hole begins where the Snake River runs into Jackson Lake, at Grand Teton National Park's northern boundary, and includes the Teton and Gros Ventre Ranges. In the summer visitors come to hike and raft; in fall, they come to fish and hunt; in winter, skiers come for the thick blanket of powdery snow. Jackson is the lake and town, Jackson Hole the valley and the area. No wonder people get confused.

WEST-CENTRAL: WIND RIVER & STAR VALLEY LOOP *pages 258–295*

The Wind River Basin extends east from the Wind River Mountains. The Wind River Reservation, home to members of the Shoshone and Arapahoe tribes, covers a flat, green valley that broadens into plains. Trapper Land commences on the western flanks of the mountains and continues on to the Green River Basin, a land of sagebrush-covered plains and badlands. Star Valley begins in the north near Jackson Hole, at the spectacular Grand Canyon of the Snake River, then continues along the state's western border.

SOUTHERN WYOMING: FOSSIL COUNTRY, GREAT BASIN, & COPPER COUNTRY

pages 296–331

Fossil Country covers Wyoming's southwestern corner, and is a land of dry open spaces broken by buttes, cliffs, and ridges. Here can be found historic mining towns, as well as Fossil Butte, a quarry of ancient sea creatures. The Great Basin consists of Sweetwater County and the Great

Divide Basin, where wild horses roam with antelope among ancient teepee rings and Oligocene petrified forests, and where mining has long been the dominant industry. Copper Country includes the aspen-covered Sierra Madre, where copper miners built towns a century ago. Ranches and old cowtowns can be found in the mountains' foothills; surrounding these lie wide-open rangelands.

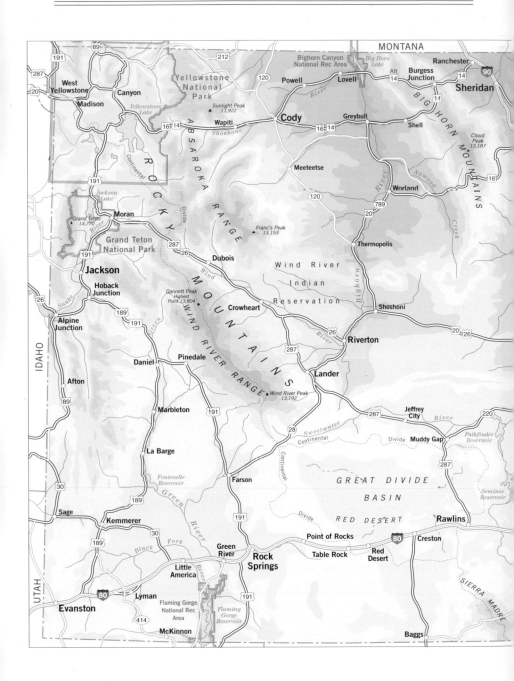

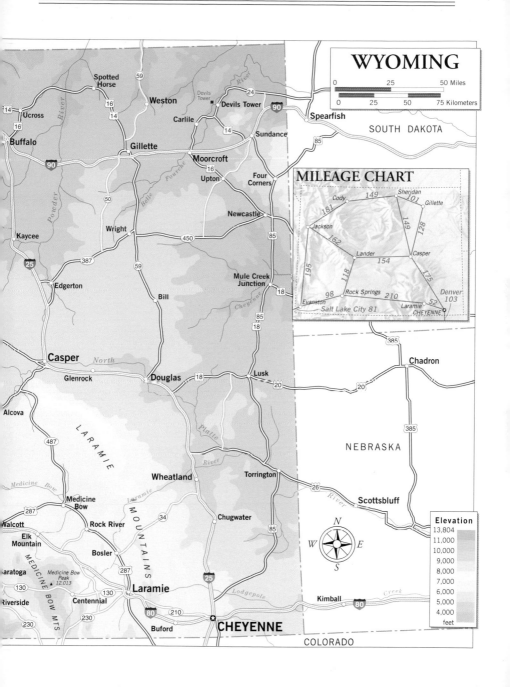

WYOMING

| 0 | 25 | 50 Miles |
| 0 | 25 | 50 | 75 Kilometers |

MILEAGE CHART

Cody — 149 — Sheridan
Cody — 181
Sheridan — 101 — Gillette
Jackson
Gillette — 181
Jackson — 162
149 — Casper
Lander — 154 — Casper
Jackson — 195
Lander — 118
Casper — 175
Rock Springs — 210 — Denver
Evanston — 98
Salt Lake City 81
Rock Springs
Laramie
Denver — 103
Laramie — 52
CHEYENNE

Elevation
13,804
11,000
10,000
9,000
8,000
7,000
6,000
5,000
4,000
feet

INTRODUCTION

WYOMING: "HIGH, WIDE, AND HANDSOME"; THE STATE that has a bucking horse on its license plate; where it is boasted that one of its native rivers, the Powder, is "a mile wide, an inch deep, and runs uphill all the way"; the state where the myth of the cowboy was born.

Bucking horses are not exclusive to Wyoming, and rodeos, where horses buck in public, are native to the West from California to Kansas, Washington to Texas. Cattle roam all over this wide region. Indians, sagebrush, mountains, forests, and open spaces are commonplace all over the Far West. Just the same, Wyoming *is* special, and most certainly high, wide, and, in its various ways, superbly handsome. For the outdoor enthusiast, Wyoming is indeed paradise.

To see it properly one has to get off the main drag, which in this case is Interstate 80. This over-traveled route goes right across the bottom of the state, roughly along the historic Overland Trail. For much of the way it is pretty dreary—unmitigated brown badlands. Unfortunately, the vast majority of motorists who go through the state see this and judge Wyoming by it. In this way Wyoming is like its exact opposite—the country's most densely inhabited state, New Jersey, with its industrialized turnpike by which most people misjudge that state. It ain't necessarily so. As soon as you get off this western version of the New Jersey turnpike, things improve. The purpose of this book is to guide the traveler away from Interstate 80 and on to better things.

The beauties of Wyoming are largely scenic. The permanent rancher-farmer settlement of the state goes back barely more than a hundred years. Wyoming is still predominantly uninhabited; it is, after a brief spurt of oil boom-and-bust influx and exodus, the least populated state in the Union. Lots of Wyoming natives and visitors like it that way. Wyoming has few of the historic artifacts (such as Indian and Spanish remains) found throughout the Southwest. It has few quaint mining ghost towns like those of Colorado. There are no big urban centers like Denver and Salt Lake City, no striking man-made silhouettes. Wide, open spaces, mountains, forests and lakes, antelope and elk, buffalo and bear, hot springs and waterfalls—these are what the traveler comes to see.

While Wyoming remains the least populated state in the U.S., its character is rapidly changing. Urban transplants with incomes exceeding that of the average

Wyomingite are buying up choice land, especially in places like Jackson Hole and Cody, often pricing locals out of the market. Cattle are giving way to condos, beef buffets to bistros, and the vast wilderness that was once void is becoming overrun with eager recreationists. But by and large, Wyoming is still a far cry from modern America.

Wyoming is basically a flat oblong, 250 miles north to south and 350 miles east to west. It is like a table with protrusions up under its tablecloth: a high plateau, seldom much less than 4,000 feet, punctuated all over by various self-contained mountain ranges. There are not many places in Wyoming from which you can't see a mountain (the midpoint of Interstate 80 being one notable exception). From most of the mountains, in turn, you get expansive views of plains or wide valleys.

The essential and specific beauty of Wyoming, then, is one of open spaces culminating in mountain ranges. A bare, harsh Spanish type of beauty, rather than a fertile green Anglo-French one, makes it a world that either exhilarates or depresses—sets the spirit soaring or seems forbidding and oppressive. There are numerous cozy pockets, but if you're to take Wyoming as a whole, it is spaciousness you have to take.

It is over this spaciousness that Indians, emigrants, cowboys, and soldiers moved—and made Wyoming's history. And it is this vast landscape that mountain climbers, kayakers, bikers, anglers, backpackers, and sportsmen revel in today. If such spaciousness, relieved and exalted by mountains, exhilarates you, this is certainly the place for you. (If not, roads lead on to virgin forests and indigo lakes.) Wyoming is truly the land of sagebrush rangelands, where the cows and the cowboys work, and the deer and the antelope play.

■ THE LAND AND THE SEASONS

Despite an overall uniformity of plains punctuated by mountains, the landscape of Wyoming is rather complicated. There are, in fact, huge areas of nothing but plains, and also of nothing but mountains. With its odd geology and unique plants, Sweetwater County is more or less open semi-desert filled only with livestock, game, and wild horses. Yet the northwest corner is almost all peaks and forests, parks and wilderness, boasting the only intact ecosystem left in the lower 48 states, meaning that all species present before the white man arrived still thrive there—a truly wild stretch of country and the farthest you can get from a road in the continental U.S. The contrast between the two is extreme. None of the state is real desert, such as one finds in the Southwest, but the Great Divide Basin certainly comes close. Nobody lives there; no rivers go through it; there are no good roads into it. Some of the mountain country is equally forbidding. The summits of the Wind River Mountains are sprinkled with glaciers. Some forests in the Absarokas are so thick you can barely get through them, and people have been lost there for good. But for those intrepid souls who do venture forth into Wyoming's backcountry, mystery and awesome discovery await with beauty at every turn.

Summer in the mountains is glorious—brilliant skies and wonderful cloud effects, and riotous wildflowers from June into August. September, too, is spectacular, with turning aspens and pellucid atmospheres. (Of course, a few little snowstorms may come up.) Steady long rains are unusual except in the spring, but thunderstorms abound in summer particularly in the mountains during the afternoons. On the plains, summer can get pretty dry and hot. Mosquitoes and flies are common in wet, wooded places. January to April is for winter sports. Fall is for hunters. And the locals love it all year round. From June to September is the usual tourist season, popular with hikers, climbers, dudes, boaters, and anglers.

Since Wyoming is up high and up north, winters are rough. Below-zero temperatures, deep snows, and deadly blizzards can appear at any time from September to June. In mountain areas, six feet or more of snow falls before winter sets in. (Skiers rejoice in this.) On the plains, winds of 60 mph or more drive along blizzards that can and do kill people. (One of these killed more than a hundred emigrants in the covered-wagon days.) In the Red Desert, stock can be wintered because the wind is so fierce it keeps the range relatively free of that extra-dry snow. In the summer the desert is too hot to handle, yet when night falls it can go down to freezing. Which all gives you some idea of Wyoming's climate.

Wyoming, then, is a place of extremes: extremes of open bareness and mountain fastness, of summer heats and winter freezes. You don't fool around with Wyoming. It is exalting, but dangerous. Lightning strikes, bears roam, floods wreck, snows bury, dust storms obliterate, fires rage—all almost as a matter of routine. On the other hand, the air and altitude invigorate and intoxicate; the vastness and beauty uplift; the oddities and grandeur intrigue and awe. It's almost never dull or humdrum. It is—for residents of most of the rest of the country—no place like home.

■ THE PEOPLE

This all affects the people who inhabit the landscape, the people who put up with the treacherous nature of life there. As anywhere, there are all sorts, but nowhere are extremes of personality more evident and tolerated. Wyoming is a democracy of people who are, above all, individuals. The ethnic composition is also varied: Native Americans, Central Europeans, Latin Americans, Chinese (perhaps a few descended from those who built the railroads), a few African-Americans, even some Basque sheepherders and descendants of British aristocracies. Basically, though, the state is dominated by immigrants from the Midwest and the South, most with British (English, Scotch-Irish) and northern European (Dutch, Scandinavian, German) backgrounds.

The archetypal Wyoming citizen is characterized by the various meanings of the word "ornery": obstinate, cantankerous, nonconformist. He might be polite, even jovial, but there's hard rock underneath. And loyalty, respect, and reliability in the face of disaster are also embedded in the rock.

■ WYOMING HISTORY: BOOM AND BUST

Part of Wyoming's ornery character comes from its thoroughly outrageous, relatively short history. It has really only been settled since the Civil War, and it has never truly settled *down*. Throughout the state's past, people have learned to expect the worst, and they've usually been right. Like its landscape, Wyoming's past cannot be called dull. The year 1990 marked the centennial of the state's entry into the Union; considering what's happened there, it's a wonder the state has survived its first hundred years.

From the very beginning, the story of Wyoming has been one of boom and bust; history and economics have, as always, been closely connected. Each boom brought with it a new wave of immigrants.

The first boom took place before recorded Wyoming history. In the late 17th or early 18th century, the North American Plains Indians were introduced to the horse. The Spaniards brought the beast to the New World, and so impressed and intimidated the natives with their horsemanship that they conquered large parts of Central and South America in no time at all. The descendants of these horses gradually worked their way northward, either as wild strays or brought across the Rio Grande by settlers. When, where, and how the natives of the north met and mastered them is another story, but their mastery was complete. Over the next century, these horseback Indians developed one of the most successful non-agrarian civilizations in the world.

The West was teeming with another four-footed friend: bison, or buffalo. Men on horseback, with primitive but effective weapons (bows and arrows, spears, knives) hunted buffalo for food, clothes, and shelter. In summer they hunted; in winter they holed up in their camps. No fences, no boundary lines or landed property, no towns or taxes, no lawyers. Rival tribes engaged in summer battles—often man-to-man, often based on ritual horse-stealing. A chief badge of honor was striking an enemy during battle. Prestige, first access to buffalo grazing grounds, above all *face*—this was what one fought for. Not for king or county, not for walled-off territory or gold, not for religious or dynastic disputes. It was a nice boom while it lasted, and might possibly have gone on forever.

Some of these Indian horsemen were themselves immigrants to the area. It's possible that all the Wyoming plains dwellers the white men first met were interlopers, and not direct descendants of the prehistoric inhabitants who left all sorts of artifacts, such as arrowheads and awe-inspiring murals on cliffs and caves. The Sioux, the most active, warlike, and prominent tribe the white settlers encountered, were definitely outsiders. Originating down the Mississippi, they gradually moved north on foot or by river into Minnesota in the early 18th century. Along the way they adopted the horse and became what has been called the finest cavalry in the world. They drove the Crows off the Powder River and into the Bighorn Basin, and ended up with control of an area stretching from the Dakotas and the Black Hills to the Big Horn Mountains.

The next boom was based on beaver skins. Adventurous trappers from French Canada first began to penetrate the Far West in the mid-18th century. Sieur de la Verendyre actually saw either the Black Hills or the Big Horns, and recorded the sighting. Beginning in the early 19th century, the first trappers pushed farther and farther into the vast, remote, beaver-rich area of the Rockies. Wyoming became the center stage of the thriving new industry, under the sponsorship of distant capitalists—notably John Jacob Astor, one of the earliest and most successful of these moneymen. (Bas-relief beavers adorn the walls of the Astor Place subway station in New York.) The beaver dams of Wyoming and its forested neighbors made many other fortunes as well.

In 1825 Astor's main competitor, William H. Ashley, arranged to meet and resupply his trappers—"mountain men"—at Green River on the Wyoming-Utah border. Thus began the annual Mountain Man Rendezvous, a three-week-long affair where trappers, both white and Indian, and their backers would gather to tell stories, debauch, and trade furs for supplies and women. These gatherings continued until 1840, by which time the beaver boom had collapsed. Gentlemen in London gave up beaver hats and took to wearing silk toppers. The beaver trappers found themselves unemployed.

Fortunately for many of them, a third Wyoming boom occurred just in time. Drawn by hopes of free land in Oregon, gold in California, and freedom in Utah from religious persecution, great mass migrations across the continent began in the 1840s. The ex-trappers were there to act as guides, hunters, and shopkeepers along the new emigrant trails. Between 1845 and 1865, hundreds of thousands of farmers, Mormons, and gold seekers crept across Wyoming, first up the North Platte River and along the Sweetwater that ran into it from the west, then over the relatively low and easy South Pass, and then south and west into what are now Utah and Idaho. This was the Oregon Trail. Later, another pass was developed that was closer to the present southern border of Wyoming—and safer from Indian attack: the Overland Trail.

This invasion brought a sudden, hectic sort of prosperity, along with devastation and danger, to the region. Indians who resented the intrusion on their hunt-

George Catlin's watercolor Buffalo Hunt under White Wolf Skins *(1832–33) shows how Indians used the skins to approach bison more closely. (Collection of Gilcrease Museum, Tulsa)*

ing grounds took out their irritation on these unwelcome tourists. The army came to protect the emigrants, fought the Indians, and stayed to establish permanent forts. Buffalo were slaughtered as only 19th-century Americans could slaughter game. Soon the buffalo, like the beaver, was on the road to extinction. (Buffalo Bill alone killed over 4,000 buffalo to provide meat for the later railroad workers.)

Trappers had brought guns into the Indian world; Indians quickly adopted them. Indians didn't make guns or powder; traders easily supplied them. They also eagerly supplied whiskey, which proved disastrous to many Indians who had

Famed guide Kit Carson, about 1850. (Courtesy, Buffalo Bill Historical Center, Cody)

never tasted it before. The Indian warfare tactics of lightning surprise attack and mysterious disappearance were terribly effective at first, but not in the end.

Like the buffalo and beaver booms before it, the emigrant boom collapsed suddenly. Then came a fourth boom: the railroad. The westward-moving leg of the country's first transcontinental railway arrived in Wyoming in 1867. The covered wagon became obsolete. With the railroad came a horde of adventurers: gunmen, gamblers, prostitutes, shady entrepreneurs, and—at last—permanent settlers. All along the route of the old Overland Trail, now the Union Pacific Railroad, towns exploded into existence virtually overnight as the tracks crept west. Cheyenne, Laramie, Rawlins, Rock Springs, and other towns sprang up to the sound of gunfire and the roars of lynch mobs. Wyoming was settled, so to speak.

Likewise, the railroad construction boom turned out to be short-lived. The golden spike joining the transcontinental railroad's east and west legs was driven (at Promontory Summit, Utah) on May 10, 1869. But the effect was permanent; the presence of the railroad spurred the fifth boom, the one that had the biggest impact on the character of Wyoming: cattle.

The end of the Civil War had brought prosperity to cattle owners in Texas. Cattle drives from Texas to the new railheads in Kansas for shipment to the new stockyards in Kansas City and Chicago had become yearly epics. Gradually, Texas longhorns were driven farther north into Wyoming for summer feeding and fall shipment east on the new Union Pacific. Starting in the early 1870s, for a short and vivid period of less than two decades, the seemingly endless richness of grass in eastern Wyoming nurtured a cattleman's paradise. Younger sons of English titled families, hard-bitten Texans, and restless farm boys from farther east all flocked to Wyoming to try their luck with cows. On the open ranges was created Wyoming's heroic embodiment: the cowboy.

Cowboys had worked long before in Mexico and the Southwest, as well as in Texas, but they were more or less peons. The Wyoming cowboy was restively independent. The heady glamour and high living of the cattle barons rubbed off on their cowhands, who developed their own brand of glamour and high living. The romance of the great cattle spreads, with their lavish, often baronial ranch headquarters and surrounding wilderness of far horizons, and the dash of young horsemen in their chaps and spurs and hats, all struck adventurous and impressionable young visitors from the East as a sort of sun-baked version of Camelot. Theodore Roosevelt, Owen Wister, Frederic Remington, and many others were smitten by this brand-new type of chivalry, and survived to tell about it.

So it was in the area from the Big Horns to the Black Hills—eastern Wyoming, southeast Montana, and the western Dakotas—that the myth of the American cowboy came to fruition. Of course, this is rather unfair to the American Southwest, where it all started, and to the cattle kingdoms of Texas in particular. But that didn't stop the public at the turn of the century from identifying the Wyoming cowboy with those earlier heroes of the frontier: James Fenimore Cooper's Natty Bumppo, the Indian scout, and the real-life Buffalo Bill, also of Wyoming. To this day, the glamour of the horseman—memorialized on the state's license plate—pervades the psychology of Wyoming.

But with this significant boom also came a cropper. Success brought the disasters of overcrowding and overgrazing. The big owners got careless, spending less and less time on their ranches. Finally, the desperate blizzard in the winter of 1887–88, with the terrible loss of cattle, brought the boom to its end. Many of the big cattlemen were ruined. Homesteaders began to invade the cattle range. Overgrazing by sheep ruined the rangeland for cattle. All through the next two decades, cattlemen fought "grangers" (homesteaders) and sheepmen in a series of violent and bloody engagements. Cowboys out of a job turned into outlaws, and picturesque figures such as the lawbreaker Butch Cassidy and the more sinister Tom Horn continued the tradition founded by earlier robbers of stagecoaches.

No sooner had the cattle and sheep boom simmered down and adjusted itself to normal living than still another boom-and-bust cycle struck the state: oil. This one was neither as glamorous nor as specifically Wyoming as the earlier cycles. It produced a few high-placed villains, but they were hardly romantic figures (even if they did become nationally known).

Oil spouts in many places in the West, but Wyoming was one of the first states to take advantage of it. The center of the boom was the town of Casper, on the North Platte River, in mid-state. The oil business started in Wyoming in 1883, when a well was drilled up on Dallas Dome (Fremont County)—just as the country's first oil boom (in Pennsylvania) began to die down. It didn't amount to much; too far from transportation, for one thing. But beginning in the early 20th century, a frenzy of exploitation and prosperity struck Casper and its fields. As frantic real estate promoters got to work, the town doubled in size. The demands of the First World War brought the boom to its crest, and it continued through the Roaring Twenties. But the Depression and scandals attached to the Teapot Dome drillings brought it to an end. For a while, Wyoming was in the national headlines daily, and "Teapot Dome" was a byword (also see page 117).

When this boom collapsed, Casper lost half its population. But then came another war, another boom. And since then the pattern of boom and bust has continued regularly. In the seventies, it was boom time once more. With the '80s came another collapse of oil prices. In the 1980 census, Casper had outstripped Cheyenne as the state's largest city, though it didn't stay there.

There have been other booms. Hard-coal mining brought a boom to the area of Newcastle, near the Black Hills. Copper had a wild fling in the Sierra Madre, based on the mushroom city of Encampment. There was a short spree of gold mining in South Pass City. There was a boom of dry farming at the turn of the 19th century when homesteaders, lured by free land, broke the soil of the grasslands and watched their soil and savings blow away in the wind.

Abandoned hotel in Hudson.

The latest boom is tourism. Millions of travelers a year have been going through Jackson Hole and Yellowstone for the last couple of decades. Today, tourism is perhaps the main industry that can be called booming in Wyoming. The problem now is how to control this flood without stopping it, and how to preserve the things that have caused it: the scenery and character of Wyoming. Hard-headed stockmen and businessmen find themselves facing the issues of conservation and environmentalism as a matter not of morality, but of money. One hopes that Wyoming's boom-and-bust history will have taught people the need to diversify the state's economic base.

■ THE MYTH CREATORS

Wyoming is hardly an important center of the arts. No nationally famous, native artist, such as John Steinbeck in California, has made his or her home state the scene of a classic work. Abstract expressionist artist Jackson Pollock was born in Cody, but he sure didn't work there.

This does not mean that Wyoming is artless, or that the arts haven't been important in creating an *image* of the state. In fact, few other states in the Union

Agricultural elevator in Greybull.

have been so influentially presented and characterized by artists of national fame. The fact that these artists weren't native by no means alters their impact.

Two writers and three artists have, between them, virtually created the popular image of the state; their works have spelled "Wyoming" to millions of Americans. It was one novel in particular—*The Virginian*, by the very Philadelphian Owen Wister (1860–1938)—that by its wild success at the turn of the century established once and for all the character of the cowboy-as-hero, and Wyoming as his proper setting. Like its counterpart *Uncle Tom's Cabin*, it may not be a model of academic literature (though it is in fact very well written) and can be accused of being melodramatic and sentimental. But as a myth-creator in America, like *Uncle Tom's Cabin* and the more academically revered *Scarlet Letter* and *Huckleberry Finn*, *The Virginian* is a regional epic. There are other more grubby, graphic, and authentic portraits of the West and the cowboy, but none has so captured the national fancy and fixed the national stereotype. The handsome, polite, handy, soft-spoken and laconic, humorously menacing ("When you call me like that, *smile*"), deadly marksman who has ridden through almost a full century of print and film was first introduced to the world by Wister.

No one could have been a less obvious person for this role. Wister was a neurotic, class-bound, talented but frustrated intellectual and well-born gentleman who wanted to be a serious musical composer. (He once played his compositions for Franz Liszt in Germany.) His mother was the daughter of the beautiful, scandalous Fanny Kemble, last of England's greatest theatrical family. She had shocked the Victorians by publicly deserting her raffish husband, planter Pierce Butler, and then—even worse!—by publishing poems about her unhappiness. *Not* done, particularly in Philadelphia. Fanny's daughter, Owen's mother, was a beautiful, intellectual snob, and an intimate of Henry James. Owen's father was a stuffy German doctor from one of Philadelphia's most prestigious medical families. The supercilious put-downs of his mother, and his father's insistence that he give up music and become a proper Philadelphia lawyer, drove young Owen to a nervous breakdown. His doctor advised him to go west as a cure. It worked. He began writing Western short stories, and then *The Virginian*. It was an immediate success and, over the years, sold *millions* of copies. It was dramatized in a Broadway hit, and later in a long-lasting TV serial. *The Virginian* can be called the ancestor of the pulp novel and the Hollywood Western.

One of Wister's best friends at Harvard was the equally frustrated New Yorker, Theodore Roosevelt. He, too, had suffered from all sorts of youthful traumas. He,

Owen Wister, author of The Virginian. *(Courtesy, Arizona Historical Society, Tucson)*

too, went west to find himself. In the process he, too, became a profuse and popular writer about the West; later, he also became one of the country's most flamboyant presidents. But it was on the basis of his Western experience, and his image as cowboy, ranchman, and Rough Rider, that he developed into a national idol.

Between the two of them, in fiction and nonfiction, Wister and Roosevelt presented a view of the Wyoming-Dakota plains and its cowboys that, along with the equally horsey exploits and showmanship of contemporary Buffalo Bill, put the area, and the state, on the map.

Both Wister and TR were active big-game hunters and lovers of the wilderness, and both men presented and popularized the beauty of Wyoming's mountains and

Horse packer Jeff Bernkowsky dries out after a summer squall in the Bridger-Teton National Forest's Teton Wilderness.

forests, as well as the glamour of its plains. Roosevelt in particular, from his position as president, can be considered a prominent founder of the conservation movement. In 1906 Roosevelt—the first truly nature-loving president—designated Devils Tower, in the Black Hills of Wyoming, the country's first national monument.

The third member of this trio of friends who helped create the image of the cowboy was the artist Frederic Remington. He was a native of upstate New York and an accomplished realist painter who specialized in the American outdoors and outdoorsmen—including cowboys. As a painter and sculptor, he captured them in violent, cinematic exuberance. In the process, he made his fortune, fostered a cult following, and ruined his reputation among "serious art" lovers. (Wister was similarly sneered at by "serious" literary critics.) That's cowboy art for you.

Nonetheless, Wister and Remington enjoyed the rewards of their popular success; and they created, in prose and paint, the quintessential image of the wild, wild West—an image squarely framed by the plains and ringed by the mountains of the Wyoming grasslands and badlands.

Two other artists, Thomas Moran and William Henry Jackson, also did much to open the eyes of their countrymen to Wyoming's glories. With his vivid first paintings of the amazing, colorful scenery of Yellowstone, Moran became a pioneer in the endlessly profitable vein of landscape art. He did not specialize in Wyoming: he also painted the Grand Canyon and other such scenes. Few have improved upon them.

As staff artist on the first Hayden survey of Yellowstone in 1871, Moran was joined by Jackson, the staff photographer. They became bosom friends and together brought the wonders of the place to the attention of the public. More to the point, they got the attention of Congress. Besides the support of the railroad industry and the writings of early explorers advocating the area's preservation, it was the two artists' eye-opening revelations of beauty that prompted Congress to create Yellowstone National Park on March 1, 1872. Thus began the amazing process of the governmental preservation of nature. It would be hard to think of two visual artists who had a more overwhelming effect on political events.

(preceding page) Female moose in Grand Teton National Park, Mt. Moran in the background.

In 1877, Jackson came back to the area and took the first pictures of Jackson Lake, spread at the feet of Mount Moran in the Tetons. Mount Moran had been named after the artist by Hayden on his later expedition to Jackson Hole. Moran never saw his mountain. (Jackson Lake is not named after W.H. Jackson, though it should have been. Davey Jackson, after whom the valley and the lake are named, has had more than enough honor done him. Perhaps a simple ceremony by the Park Service of rededicating the lake to the later Jackson would be sufficient; with photographs, of course.)

Ever since Jackson's visits, Wyoming has been increasingly overrun by photographers as well as landscape artists. One of the most famous of all American photographs is Ansel Adams's picture of the Tetons from the northeast over the Snake River and Deadman's Bar.

During the 1820s and '30s, visual interpreters such as George Catlin, the German-Swiss Karl Bodmer (accompanying his patron, the Prince of Wied), and especially Alfred Jacob Miller left an unforgettable record of the world of the plains, distant mountains, trappers, Indians, and the game the Indians pursued, notably the buffalo. Two later, more academically accomplished artists—Albert Bierstadt and Worthington Whittredge—celebrate the landscape of Wyoming and of the West in general.

The most famous nonfiction writing about Wyoming from this era, and among the earliest, was that of Francis Parkman, infatuated Bostonian, whose *The California and Oregon Trail* is the most vivid firsthand account of the Sioux and of Wyoming before large-scale development began. His rigorous expedition of 1846, based from Fort Laramie when it was just a trading post, ruined his health, but started him on his long career as an American historian.

■ WYOMING WRITERS

Most of the people mentioned so far weren't actual residents of the state, though Owen Wister spent many summers there. Culture *in* Wyoming, unlike works *about* the state, presents no very grandiose panorama. But it has existed, and with both national reputation and Wyoming flavor. One could say without much argument that writing of a literary sort began in the state with the humorist Edgar Wilson "Bill" Nye. He was actually a professional newspaperman and columnist, but his great popularity came as a writer of books. Like Wister, Nye began his career in Wyoming, and his works became best-sellers. He wandered out west with the new railroad and came to roost in the brand-new, raucous town of Laramie. He was postmaster there, and eventually started his own newspaper. He called it the *Boomerang*, after his pet mule, and it exists to this day. (Not many university towns have a newspaper named for a mule.) He wrote an awful lot, much in the vein of the early Mark Twain (also a newspaperman in the old West), and generally in that tone of satiric exaggeration that was the trademark of early Western writing. A lot of Nye's work—and there was indeed a lot of it—is tedious now, but he was enormously popular then, and is sometimes very funny still. He left Wyoming in 1887 and went on to New York and to fame and riches; but he emerged from Wyoming as its first literary lion, and the frontier gave him his style and subject matter.

Nye came and went. One of the truly indigenous writers was the cowboy-artist-writer Will James. He flourished in the 1920s and 1930s in both Wyoming and Montana, under the editorship of Max Perkins at Scribner's. He wrote authentic cowboy vernacular, as unreformed as it was spoken, and illustrated his books with his own vivid drawings of riders and horses, using himself as a model. His handsome books—*Cowboys North and South* (1924), *Cow Country* (1927), *All in the Day's Riding* (1933), and others—give a far less varnished and more genuine view of cowboy life than Wister did. His most famous work is the self-illustrated children's book *Smoky* (1926). His books were, like those of Nye, immensely popular at the time, but don't seem to be as well remembered now as they ought to be.

Not native like James, but closely identified with the state, have been various writers settled in Jackson Hole. Struthers Burt (born in Baltimore in 1881 but a native of Philadelphia), his wife Katherine Newlin Burt (born in New York in 1882), and son Nathaniel Burt (actually born in Jackson Hole) have written 60 books over a period of 70 years; some are squarely focused on Wyoming—notably Struthers Burt's

Humorist and newspaper publisher Bill Nye, in 1880. (Courtesy, Wyoming State Archives)

BILL NYE: LARAMIE MAILMAN

When Bill Nye resigned as postmaster of Laramie, he supposedly drafted the following letter to President Chester A. Arthur. It is a representative example of the Nye style.

Laramie, Oct. 1, 1883
To the President of the United States:

Sir:

I beg leave at this time to officially tender my resignation as postmaster of this place, and in due form to deliver the great seal and key to the front door of this office. The safe combination is set on numbers 33, 66 and 99, though I do not at this moment remember which comes first, or how many times you revolve the knob or which direction you turn it at first to make it operate.

You will find the postal cards that have not been used under the distributing table and the coal down in the cellar. If the stove draws too hard, close the damper in the pipe and shut the general delivery window. Acting under the advice of General Hatton, a year ago, I removed the featherbed with which my predecessor, Deacon Hayford, had bolstered up his administration by stuffing the window, and substituted glass. Finding nothing in the book of instructions which made the featherbed a part of my official duties, I filed it away in an obscure place and burned it in effigy, also in the gloaming.

I need not say that I herewith transmit my resignation with great sorrow and genuine respect. We have toiled together month after month, asking no reward except the innate consciousness of rectitude and the salary fixed by law. Now we are to separate. Here the roads seem to fork, as it were, and you and I, and the cabinet, must leave each other.

You will find the key under the door-mat and you had better turn the cat out at night when you close the office. If she does not go readily, you can make it clearer to her mind by throwing the cancelling stamp at her. If Deacon Hayford does not pay his box rent, you might as well put his mail in the general delivery, and when Bob Read gets drunk and insists on a letter from one of his wives every day in the week, you can salute him through the box delivery with an old Queen Anne tomahawk, which you will find near the Etruscan water pail. Mr. President, as an official of the government, I now retire…"

—Bill Nye

Diary of a Dude Wrangler (1924) and his *Powder River* (1938). All three Burts were, like James, published by Scribner's and edited by Perkins. Famous naturalists such as Olaus Murie and his wife Margaret or Mardy (*Wapiti Wilderness* and others), the Craighead brothers, and many more have centered their prestigious careers in the Hole. The humorist Donald Hough settled into Jackson bars before World War II and wrote amusingly about what he saw from that vantage point.

Writers identified with the southeast of the state have made a national impression, notably Mary O'Hara with her *My Friend Flicka* (1941), and Thurman Arnold with his New Deal sarcasm in *The Folklore of Capitalism* (1937). More recently, Gretel Ehrlich (originally from California) gained national acclaim for *The Solace of Open Space,* with its rich details of ranch life in the Bighorn Basin. But there still has not been a writer who holds the position of local champion as A.B. Guthrie of Montana does with his novels *The Big Sky* and *The Way West,* even though Emerson Hough's *The Covered Wagon* (1922), an immensely popular emigrant epic set in Wyoming, was made into a movie.

■ WYOMING ARTISTS

The list of native Wyoming artists may not be prestigious, either, but it *is* truly characteristic of Wyoming. Will James, of course, was an artist as well as a writer. Jackson Hole has been as full of active painters (notably landscapist Conrad Schwiering) as it has of moviemakers; but, once again, nobody like Charles M. Russel of Montana has risen to national prominence.

The state does have two art locales of national reputation: the Buffalo Bill Historical Center in Cody, and Jackson Hole's National Museum of Wildlife Art. No fewer than four separate museums celebrate Buffalo Bill Cody, and the state and region where his adventures were set. The Whitney Gallery of Western Art is one of the most prestigious of its kind in the country. Remington, Russell, and others are represented, but there is no special concentration here on Wyoming artists. Jackson's National Museum of Wildlife Art has gained a reputation for excellence, and in 2007, its "national" designation was made official by an act of Congress.

The most distinguished of Wyoming's resident artists is the once-neglected but increasingly appreciated Bill (christened Emil) Gollings. Born in Idaho in 1878 and schooled in Chicago, Gollings came west after eighth grade to work as a cowhand and horse wrangler. After a return to Chicago and art school, he settled in Sheridan in the 1920s. There he was patronized by art lovers such as Bradford

Brinton and received commissions for works at the capitol in Cheyenne. His art is gradually emerging from the genre of "cowboy art," for, unlike many such artists, he can be appreciated as a master of form and color and as a dynamic realist in the vein of John Sloan or George Bellows.

Another such artist was Archie Teater, of a slightly later period. He, too, was a ranch boy who somehow got to New York. There he studied under Thomas Benton and became a modestly well-known member of the school of American native realism—represented by Grant Wood, John Steuart Curry, and Benton himself—that was so popular in the 1930s. This movement was eclipsed after World War II by the overwhelmingly popular new school of abstract expressionism, of which Wyoming-born Jackson Pollock was a major figure. Teater settled in Jackson and became a local lion; like Will James, though, he seems to have been undeservedly lost in the shuffle of artistic fashion. Alas, Wyoming has not done much to save the reputations of her truly indigenous talents.

■ OTHER WYOMING ARTS

As for music, it's hard to pin down anything as specifically "Wyoming." Cowboy songs originated throughout the West and were sung all over it, though some do have references to Wyoming, such as "Goodbye Old Paint, I'm leaving

Some architecture of the Old West is preserved at Trail Town, near Cody.

Cheyenne," with its slow, loping rhythm. And there have always been such cheap, sentimental, and commercial songs as "In the Gloaming of Wyoming" and "Home on the Range."

In contrast has been the growth of serious music in Wyoming, most notably the annual season of the Grand Teton Music Festival in Jackson Hole. A splendid symphony orchestra, famous soloists, a rich series of chamber music performances, and big, enthusiastic audiences make this one of the important musical events of the West. Casper's Wyoming Symphony Orchestra traces its origins to the 1920s.

You wouldn't suppose that such a recent settlement would produce a native architecture. There are no 17th- or 18th-century Spanish adobes or ancient Indian cliff dwellings. Teepees were native, but impermanent. The true native architecture of later settlement was the log cabin, and if anything can be called typical of Wyoming, that's it. Of course, it's typical of most northwestern states, too. But in Wyoming's rural and small urban settings close to timber, a character-istic style of residential log cabin developed: cabins with low, broad roofs (originally sod), lazy windows (that is, sliding horizontally, not sash windows), and usually with a porch out front. Many examples can still be found in less modern rural areas, and even in towns like Jackson and Pinedale. The style remains de rigueur for dude ranches. Many handsome ranch houses and summer places, some pala-tial, were built of logs, and still are. It's an appropriate, beautiful, cozy, and *local* product that is in contrast to the Californication of most modern mountain villas and town subdivisions.

■ SPACES

Despite all the influx of summer trippers and winter snow-lovers, despite the persis-tence, waxing and waning, of oil and uranium, mining and logging, cattle and sheep, beets and alfalfa, the real secret of Wyoming's fascination is still basically *emptiness.* There are square miles and miles of Wyoming where nobody lives at all. You can drive, for instance, from Jackson Hole into Colorado and beyond, via Pinedale and Rock Springs, and not see more than a ranch house and a filling station or two for hundreds of miles. This is beginning to change, but promises to be a slow process. To some, who find large-scale urbanization claustrophobic, this openness alone gives a wonderful feeling of release and relief; just to go along seeing nothing is a pleasure. But this vast sense of elbow room is varied by tantalizing distant heights and awe-some valleys. There is always the lure of distances: What's in them thar hills? What's down that there river? This call of distance no doubt motivated explorers of the region. For others, in whom a corresponding fear of openness prevails, there is the lure of the densely packed mountain-forest areas.

To fully appreciate the state of Wyoming you should ideally be receptive to both the plains and the mountains. As said before, the essence of Wyoming scenery is a combination of both—mountains seen over a vast distance, coming closer and closer, and finally revealing their contrasts of lower forests and higher glaciers. The Tetons, for instance, wouldn't be properly visible without the flats at their feet, nor would the flats be as beautiful without the interruption of the swath of the riverbed and cottonwoods down the middle of them. And even in the unrelieved desert, the state, at its high altitude, responds wonderfully to changes in weather and times of day. What can seem utterly dreary in drizzle, or hard and mean at blazing noontime, can become a fairy-tale scene under cumulus clouds and blue sky, or as evening comes on. Above all, those clouds build up magnificently in midsummer, when the storms are as grand as they are scary.

Wyoming is a state of vast spaces. It is fundamentally neither an urban nor a cultivated state; rolling farmlands and quaint old villages are not its specialty. While this guide takes you through all the major towns and cities, they're not necessarily what the traveler should come to see. Wyoming's towns are for use rather than show. It is in the empty areas beyond where Wyoming's beauties and curiosities lie.

This guide is designed to take you through the most exciting of these spaces, by car, and driving *toward* the best views. (Whenever possible, travelers should take advantage of Wyoming's views by driving in the direction suggested.) Except for a few bottlenecks such as the approaches to Yellowstone, the highways of Wyoming are smooth, pretty empty, and as wide open as the landscape. (For those who love driving, they can be a special pleasure.) Much of Wyoming is visible from these highways. Some areas are not and must be seen on horse or foot; but open or secluded, the state is always worth exploring.

Drifting through this vast landscape and worth uncovering, too, are the great stories of Wyoming's colorful past. The state is saturated with tales, some true, others doubtful, but all an integral part of Wyoming's personality. To ignore them is to dismiss a basic part of the Wyoming character. So take the stories as repeated in this work with the same grain of salt as you would the words of any Wyoming old-timer. There are some odd corners of the state and some pretty odd things have happened in them, but some wonderful things, too, in wonderful Wyoming.

(following pages) Cirque of the Towers, in the Wind River Mountains,
reflects off the surface of the North Popo Agie River.

SOUTHEAST
OLD WYOMING & STAGECOACH CORRIDOR

Map page 54

Laramie

Cheyenne

♦ AREA OVERVIEW

The southeastern corner of Wyoming, including Cheyenne and the mountain territories to the west of it, is the most densely settled part of the state: "Old Wyoming." That doesn't mean it's so very settled or so very old. Cheyenne, the capital, and Laramie, the university city, are the preeminent centers of power (political) and influence (educational). The country roundabout this corner, west of Cheyenne and Laramie, is some of the most beautiful in the state.

The landscape and historical background of Wyoming's southeast corner make it the proper introduction to any overview of the whole state: mountains, cities, plains, rivers, history, wildlife, dinosaurs, sports, even some industry—and lots of ranching. The same can't really be said of the central eastern border. It has its own regional features and lots of history; but to some extent, it's the least characteristic area of the state—an eastern frontier that is more like the true Plains states, Nebraska and the Dakotas, than like the rest of Wyoming.

Weather: Southeast Wyoming is said to have "300 sunny days a year," with temperatures during the summer days in the 80s and 90s. Temperatures at night will drop to 50 degrees F. Winters tend to be cold, dry, and windy.

Food & Lodging: Three of the most famous and historic hotels are found in this corner of the state. Reservations are recommended in Cheyenne and Laramie. The college town of Laramie has several creative and surprisingly reasonable restaurants, including vegetarian places.

■ CHEYENNE   *map page 43*

Cheyenne remains the chief city of Wyoming, with its population hovering around 54,000. It is physically at the end of the intrusion of the Great Plains into Wyoming. From Pine Bluffs on the Wyoming-Nebraska border—the first sight of a significant ridge as you come westward—Interstate 80 drives arrow-straight for 40 miles to Cheyenne. After that the land begins to break and ripple significantly, the road sways a bit, and the Laramie Mountains block the way. Cheyenne is another of the many "gateways to the West," and is certainly the principal gateway to Wyoming. That's where—psychologically, at least—Wyoming and the Far West begin.

There's nothing particularly Wild West about Cheyenne now. It's no longer the frontier. It's a well-settled, spruce, staid, but impressive small city dominated by the golden dome of its capitol. Most U.S. state capitols pay homage to the big one in Washington, D.C., and especially to its St. Peter's–like dome. Wyoming's doesn't, for though it has a dome, it's a small, rather pretty gilded one. Construction started in 1886, four years before Wyoming achieved statehood. It remains the dominant feature of Cheyenne.

Perhaps the most striking decorations of the building are the **memorial to Esther Hobart Morris,** of South Pass City, who served as the very first female justice of the peace in the United States in 1870, and the splendid statue by native Ed Fraughtoll of a wickedly bucking horse, designated *The Spirit of Wyoming.* (The rider has lost one stirrup—will he be thrown? The suspense is permanent.) These two works of art define Wyoming as both "the Cowboy State" (an unofficial but much-loved title), where men are men, and "the Equality State" (the official designation), where women are officeholders. Women had the vote here before anywhere else in the United States. Nellie Tayloe Ross, whose elegant portrait greets visitors to the governor's office, reigned as the first female state governor in the nation, elected in 1924. (There has not, incidentally, been another one in Wyoming since, but Thyra Thompson was Secretary of State from 1962 to 1986, and the position now seems to be traditionally filled by a woman.)

The interior of the capitol is an odd blend of sophistication and wildlife, formality and informality—just like Wyoming itself. Architecturally it's very imposing and chaste. The office doors of high dignitaries, however, use nicknames—Governor "Dave" Freudenthal, Treasurer "Joe" Meyers. You'll find some stuffed animals—a bison, a wildcat, an elk—as well as some newer, elegant decorations in the dome and murals in the legislative chambers. The paintings in the Senate Chamber—

COTTAGE GROVE PUBLIC LIBRARY

ESTHER HOBART MORRIS
PROPONENT OF THE LEGISLATIVE ACT WHICH
IN 1869 GAVE DISTINCTION TO THE TERRITORY OF

WYOMING

AS THE 1ST GOVERNMENT IN THE WORLD TO GRANT

WOMEN EQUAL RIGHTS

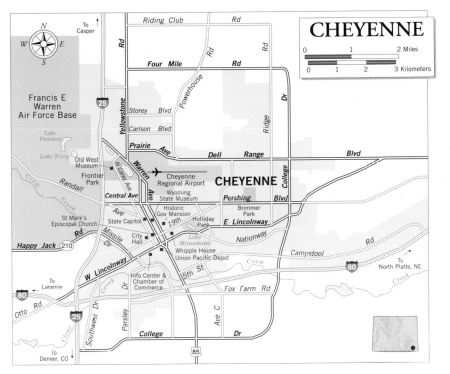

especially those by Emil Gollings, Wyoming's best native painter—are of particularly high quality. (Wyoming art, however unfortunately neglected, is not to be sneezed at.)

Plaques on the downstairs walls of the central rotunda commemorate the state's earlier great patrician-politicians, whose names are remembered all over Wyoming: Joseph M. Carey, Francis E. Warren, and John B. Kendrick. All three were big cattlemen of the plains areas. Between the three of them they held some office or other almost continuously from 1869 to 1933.

Carey Street (once called Ferguson) was the Fifth Avenue of Cheyenne when the city settled down, about 1880, as the state's metropolis. Cattle grandees and other such personages built splendid late-Victorian Italianate villas side by side near the Cheyenne Club, where they entertained lavishly. At dances, champagne flowed, the halls were wreathed with flowers, and the local belles wore gowns

(opposite) Esther Hobart Morris, the nation's first woman justice of the peace, guards the entrance to the state capitol in Cheyenne.

shipped out for the occasion from New York on the railroad. Even the haughty wives of senior officers at the fort were impressed. The villas on Carey Street are now all gone—liquidated by "progress"—and the street itself is a wasteland of parking lots interspersed with large institutional structures. But the memory lingers on. A very New York woman recently described how she impulsively drove up from Denver to Cheyenne, hoping to see cow ponies hitched to rails along the streets. Cheyenne probably hasn't seen a cow pony hitched to a rail since the early 20th century.

◆ THE FOUNDING OF CHEYENNE

Certain state capitols are an index of that state's general atmosphere. But Cheyenne's capitol is relatively modest and discreet, which most certainly does not describe the character of Wyoming as a whole. One thing is sure: the capitol is no proper memorial to the city's exceedingly raucous beginnings in 1867. Cheyenne owes its birth to the swift progress of the Union Pacific (U.P.), the eastern arm of the first transcontinental railroad. The town site was picked by Maj. Gen. Grenville M. Dodge, a U.P. planning engineer, who was prospecting for a good railroad route across the mountains. He had first camped on Crow Creek in 1865, and in 1867 he chose the site to be a terminal town for the railroad construction. Dodge named it for the Cheyenne Indians, who ranged in this area and who actually attacked him during his prospecting. (The name is a French trapper adaptation of the Sioux term *Shaiyena*—"People of a Strange Tongue"— and is a good deal closer to the original than some adaptations. It's now pronounced "shy-ANN.")

Soon afterward, the army established Fort D.A. Russell (later called Fort Warren) northwest of the town. Then came the raffish population preceding the first train westward, known as "Hell-on-Wheels" for its unsavory passengers. Speculators, gamblers, shopkeepers, craftsmen, prostitutes, and preachers soon made up the motley citizenship. A charter was adopted in that same year of 1867, and H.M. Hook, owner of the Pilgrim House Hotel, was elected mayor. That charter was accepted by the Dakota Territorial Legislature, which then controlled the area, and Cheyenne was in business.

The town was fraught with peculiar difficulties. For instance, the new transcontinental telegraph, one of the town's principal lifelines, was constantly disrupted by buffalo. Herds used the poles as scratching posts; they could rub a pole out of the ground in a few hours. Preventive spikes did no good. The buffalo loved the spikes, and thirty or more scratch-hungry animals would line up at any pole between Omaha and Cheyenne.

The lid blew off when the first train arrived on November 13. It came piled high with the "rubbish of a mushroom city": frames for shacks, boards, furniture—and more derelicts. When the locomotive came to a wheezing stop, a guard jumped off his van and shouted, "Gentlemen, here's Julesburg!" Julesburg was, of course, some 150 miles east. That month, Cheyenne's population hit 4,000. Lots that sold originally for $150 were now going for $2,500, and the place was littered with an unsightly and disorganized mess of some 3,000 shacks, "a standing insult to every wind that blew." Regardless, life went on. John Shaughnessy and the aptly named John Hardy fought a 126-round prizefight on the same day that the first public school entered the official planning stage.

By the summer of 1868, the town was in full swing. There were 300 businesses that catered to trappers, hunters, trainmen, engineers, and a whole transitory population of cardsharps, promoters, professional gunmen, and unattached (but easily attachable) ladies. Cheyenne soon ranked with that far eastern Colorado railroad station, Julesburg, in its bad reputation. As of 1868, the undoubtedly appalled founder, Maj. General Dodge, called it the "gambling center of the world." At the same time, the Reverend J.W. Cook organized an Episcopal congregation and built perhaps the first Protestant church in Wyoming; other denominations followed fast. The local cemetery was considered as essential as the post office. Both came second to the saloons. "Hell must have been raked to furnish the inhabitants," noted one critic, "and to Hell they must return after graduating here." Vigilante justice was the only (partially) effective law, and when the log cabin jail got too full, prisoners were simply told to get out of town—or else. Col. Luke Murrin, first mayor of incorporated Cheyenne, added 25 cents to each fine he imposed for his own use and (liquid) pleasure; law was "such dry work," he found.

As early as 1867, dreams of capitalization were budding, although there was nothing yet to be capital *of.* Wyoming hadn't even become a territory. By 1868, however, Laramie County was organized. Wyoming Territory, approved by Congress in 1868, began to function in 1869. Brigadier Gen. John A. Campbell,

(opposite) Cheyenne in 1867 was a wild and woolly town. (Courtesy, Wyoming State Archives)

assistant secretary of war under Ulysses Grant, was named governor. Cheyenne, the largest and just about the only town in the new territory, was now a capital.

In the 1870s and 1880s, Cheyenne also became the cow capital of the state. The coming of the railroad meant that cattle could be shipped east directly from Wyoming. In the southeast corner, but particularly up in the Bighorn and Powder River grasslands, the flamboyant era of the cattle boom began. Cheyenne was where the cowboys celebrated after driving their herds to the railhead. The big ranchers celebrated at the elegant Cheyenne Club. Here they sat in winter, "sipping rich wine, playing Boston, and settling cattle policy for the West." The Wyoming Stock Growers' Association ruled the range, and those sons of titled English families came down from their big ranch houses to disport themselves.

When the Black Hills gold fields officially opened in 1875, Cheyenne also became the outfitting center for miners. Stages left from Cheyenne for the boom in Deadwood, carrying thousands of passengers and enriching scores of holdup men on the way.

Over the years, the population doubled and tripled. In the two decades between 1880 and 1900, it exploded from 3,000 to 16,000. Cheyenne was one of the first cities in the country to have electric lights, as of 1882. Streets were paved in the

Rodeo queens. . .

1890s. Newspapers flourished. (As soon as a Western town started, a couple of rival editors would typically fight it out. In this case, it was the *Wyoming Eagle* against the *Wyoming State Tribune-Leader,* both of which survive as the *Wyoming Tribune-Eagle.*)

The blizzard of 1887–88, followed by the end of the Black Hills gold rush, brought hard times to Wyoming, but by then Cheyenne was established. The cattlemen in the south survived the blizzard; many to the north did not. Cheyenne remains Wyoming's "cow capital" and center for cattle organizations, policy makers, politicians, and shipping companies—with the focus on politics. Since 1890, this has been where state leaders get together and where native politicians have graduated from local lawmaking to national prestige. Wyoming's two senators and one representative have wielded influence out of all proportion to numbers, and often go on to higher pursuits. Vice President Dick Cheney (previously secretary of defense and a Wyoming representative) and the powerful past Wyoming senator Alan Simpson are two recent examples. Cheyenne is where the power gathers. Rustlers and gunmen, such as the notorious Tom Horn, are no longer executed there as celebrities, but the stakes can still be pretty high in Cheyenne. All the paths of political glory in the state lead there—and on to Washington.

. . . and deputy sheriffs brighten up Cheyenne Frontier Days.

◆ Visiting Cheyenne

After decades of devotion to progress (and its consequent destruction of the past), Cheyenne is now full of nostalgia for the great days of the 1880s, when the city was built up on the debris of Hell-on-Wheels. The façade of this boom town remains pretty well intact along the central blocks of 16th Street ("Main Street"), the city's business center. Rows of handsome buildings from that period face one another, or look across a plaza at the grandiose Union Pacific Depot, now a railroad museum.

The **Plains Hotel** dates from 1911 and is one of the few fine old hostelries still functioning in the state. It continues to flourish, flamboyantly and atmospherically, as a focus of downtown life. *1600 Central Avenue; 307-638-3311.*

The glorious town houses of the cattle barons have pretty much disappeared, but the massive churches they once surrounded still stand along the route north toward the capitol. Most notable are the Gothic Catholic **St. Mary's Cathedral,** the Romanesque redstone **Methodist Church,** and **St. Mark's Episcopal Church** of 1886 (on the site of Reverend Cook's original of 1868).

One remnant of Cheyenne's former residential elegance is the fine old **Whipple House,** built in 1883 at 300 E. 17th Street. Otherwise, this once "best part of town" is notable only for scattered big government buildings and banks. The more prosperous residential section doesn't begin until about 20th Street, closer to the capitol.

Near the capitol itself is the **Historic Governor's Mansion**, an imposing, porticoed, 1905 affair. The governor doesn't live there anymore. *300 E. 21st Street; 307-777-7878.*

The fine **Wyoming State Museum** stands at 24th and Central. It is a recapitulation, on a rather grand scale, of all the things you see in the local museum of every town in the state—exhibits on the old days of trappers, cattle, and mining; prehistoric aboriginal items; and lots about Indians. It lacks the quirky local color that makes the lesser museums so amusing, nostalgic, and evocative. *Barrett Building, 2301 Central Avenue; 307-777-7022.*

The **Cheyenne Frontier Days Old West Museum,** at the northwest end of Carey Avenue in Frontier Park, portrays the growth of that annual extravaganza from a small, local, bucking-bronc affair to the great civic event that it is now, full

(opposite) A teepee at the Fort Bridger Rendezvous, an annual event celebrating the gatherings that used to take place here among trappers and frontiersman in the 19th century.

of parades, beauty queens, dignitaries—and still, basically, bucking horses. Though most contestants are nationally famous professionals, there's still plenty of Wyoming and Cheyenne feeling to Cheyenne Frontier Days. Though every other town in the state has rodeos and similar events, this, marking its 112th year in 2008, is unquestionably Wyoming's biggest celebration, and it really packs them into Cheyenne in the last week of July. The museum also has more than 40 old carriages on display, along with changing historical exhibits, and (at the entrance) a statue of Lane Frost, a top bull rider who was killed at Frontier Days in 1989. *4610 N. Carey Avenue, Frontier Park; 307-778-7290.*

The huge **F. E. Warren Air Force Base** lies west of town, beyond the barricade of Interstate 25. It's now actively devoted to nuclear missiles, which are dotted around the nearby prairies. The base is open only to those with military ID or their guests, except in late July, during Fort DA Russell Days. Then guests may tour the Warren ICBM and Heritage Museum, visit historic homes, and even peek into missile silos. 7405 Marne Loop, Building 210; 307-773-2980.

A supersize boot planted in downtown Cheyenne's Depot Square

The **Cheyenne Area Convention and Visitor's Bureau** is located near the interesting red brick Victorian survivors, downtown, where you can get details on these buildings as well as the many other things to see and do around town. One thing you won't see is a cow pony hitched to a rail. *121 W. 15th St.; 800-426-5009.*

■ WEST TO LARAMIE   *map page 43; and 54, C/D-4*

There are two ways for the motorist to get from Cheyenne to Laramie: Interstate 80 and Happy Jack Road (Wyoming State Highway 210).

Though the 46-mile route on the interstate may lack any special interest, there are two curious detours off it. The first goes south to the ghost town of **Sherman,** once a busy Union Pacific depot. When the railroad line was moved south, the town was deserted. Nearby is a forlorn memorial, the **Ames Monument,** erected in honor of Oakes and Oliver Ames, two New England capitalists who backed the Union Pacific via the Credit Mobilier. The monument, a stern rock pyramid, was designed by the famous architect H. H. Richardson, and the portrait plaques of

Laramie, a short trip from Cheyenne, is one of the prettier towns in Wyoming.

CHEYENNE FOOD & LODGING

Albany Restaurant. Historic political gathering place across from old railroad depot. Hearty food. *1506 Capitol Avenue; 307-638-3507.*

Carriage Court. Where lobbyists take legislators they want to impress. An elegant place with fine traditional food. *At the Hitching Post Motel, 1700 W. Lincolnway; 307-638-3301.*

Senator's Steak House & Brass Buffalo Saloon. Sample buffalo and beef dishes in an Old Wyoming atmosphere. *Terry Bison Ranch, 10 miles south of town on I-25; 307-634-4994.*

A. Drummond's Ranch B&B. Adjacent to Curt Gowdy State Park is this 120-acre ranch, whose owners offer cross-country skiing, rock climbing, hunting, and fishing. Some guests bring mountain bikes, others horses. *399 Happy Jack Road; 307-634-6042.*

Plains Hotel. Built in 1911 and refurbished in 1986, this hostelry and its bar were for years the real political center of the state. Take note of the mosaic of Chief Little Shield on Central Avenue just outside. *1600 Central Avenue; 307-638-3311.*

Porch Swing Bed & Breakfast. The 1917 prairie-style bungalow is within walking distance from downtown and serves a delightful breakfast. Located in a quiet residential neighborhood. *502 E. 24th Street; 307-778-7182.*

Rainsford Inn Bed & Breakfast. On the National Register of Historic Places, this downtown Victorian mansion has five large suites with private baths and whirlpool hot tubs; full breakfast. *219 E. 18th Street; 307-638-2337.*

the Ameses are by the famous sculptor Augustus Saint-Gaudens. Nobody cares. The noses of the Ameses have been shot off by hunters. *Sic transit gloria mundi.*

The second detour—to the north, a few miles west of the Sherman exit—leads to natural rock formations the Indians called the **Vedauwoo** ("VEE-dah-voo"), an appropriately weird name for a weird spectacle. Under the shade of the principal Vedauwoo is an extensive camping and picnic area, shady and picturesque (see page 55). The Vedauwoo sit atop a plateau of about 8,000 feet in altitude; to the north are Pole Mountain and its companions—all bare on the east side, forested on the west. Though these are pretty mild mountains, they're the first that a westbound traveler on Interstate 80 would see in quite some time, and they're likely a welcome change from endless plains.

This plateau ends at Sherman Hill, the high point on Interstate 80, where the descent to Laramie begins. At this summit of 8,640 feet, a towering black **bust of Lincoln,** by noted Wyoming sculptor Robert Russin, stands on a pedestal, commemorating the bygone Lincoln Highway (old Route 30). Sherman Hill was also the highest point on the first transcontinental railroad of 1868. The campground and visitor platform there are high, but totally viewless.

◆ HAPPY JACK ROAD   *map page 54, C/D-4*
A parallel route, Happy Jack Road, travels west in a more intimate and ingratiating way. Beautifully engineered and maintained for smooth sailing through unspoiled scenery, it's a typical specimen of Wyoming's secondary highways, the glory of the state's road system.

To reach Happy Jack Road from Interstate 80, take the Interstate 25 exit (toward Casper) to Missile Drive, one of the entrances to the Warren Air Force Base. The road curves around the south side of the base, near a new base housing development, and heads west out of Cheyenne. You'll be out on the range almost immediately; antelope pose on hills right outside of the city.

The scenery along this highway is wide open, all right: nothing here but cows and those antelope, once you get past the high fences that guard Warren Air Force Base to the north. For some 15 miles, the road grandly swoops and curves toward the mountains. At last the endless plains give way to something different. After a scattered bit of semi-suburbia, and then more range, the road curls up onto an open plateau, interrupted by copses of evergreens and the projections of odd rock formations.

Soon you pass through **Curt Gowdy State Park,** named after a beloved, late native sports broadcaster. The park is centered around a pretty reservoir in a valley, with campsites and a marina. Then Happy Jack Road crosses into the Pole Mountain area, one of the four distinct parts of **Medicine Bow National Forest.** This segment of Medicine Bow encompasses the scattered, modest peaks of the Sherman Mountains—Twin Mountain and Green Mountain on the east edge, Pole Mountain and others farther west—which sit atop the plateau of the Laramies.

The surrounding country, totally uninhabited, is fenced off in places for private cattle ranging and has some popular camping and picnic sites—Blair, Wallis, the Vedauwoo, Pole Mountain (with a small stream through it), and Tie City. (The

SOUTHEAST

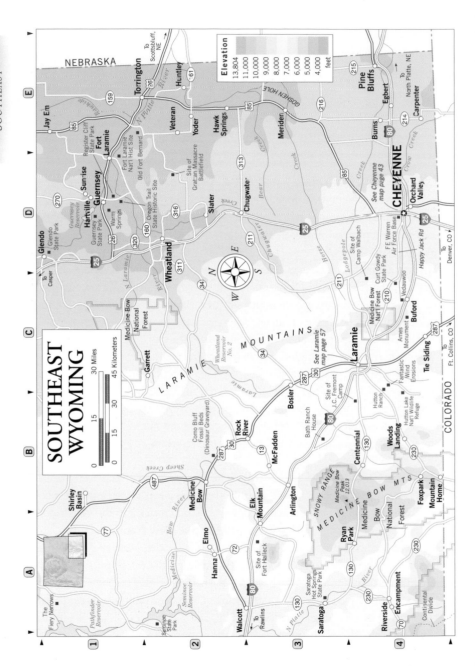

SOUTHEAST WYOMING

Elevation

13,804 · 11,000 · 10,000 · 9,000 · 8,000 · 7,000 · 6,000 · 5,000 · 4,000 feet

NEBRASKA

COLORADO

CHEYENNE

Laramie

Wheatland

Torrington

Fort Laramie

Guernsey

Glendo

Hartville

Sunrise

Jay Em

Veteran

Yoder

Hawk Springs

Meriden

Burns

Egbert

Carpenter

Pine Bluffs

Orchard Valley

Chugwate

Slater

Garrett

Rock River

McFadden

Medicine Bow

Elmo

Hanna

Elk Mountain

Arlington

Bosler

Centennial

Woods Landing

Walcott

Saratoga

Riverside

Encampment

Foxpark

Mountain Home

Ryan Park

Shirley Basin

Buford

Tie Siding

Vedauwoo

GOSHEN HOLE

LARAMIE MOUNTAINS

SNOWY RANGE

MEDICINE BOW MTS

Medicine Bow National Forest

Medicine Bow Peak 12,013

Continental Divide

Register Cliff State Park

Fort Laramie Nat'l Hist Site

Old Fort Bernard

Site of Grattan Massacre Battlefield

Oregon Trail State Historic Site

Warm Springs

Guernsey Reservoir

Guernsey State Park

Glendo State Park

Wheatland Reservoir No. 2

Como Bluff Fossil Beds (Dinosaur Graveyard)

Bath Ranch House

Site of Fort Halleck

Saratoga Hot Springs State Park

Site of J.C. Fremont Camp

Fantastic Wind Erosions

Hutton Ranch

Hutton Lake Nat'l Wildlife Refuge

Ames Monument

Site of Camp Walbach

Curt Gowdy State Park

F E Warren Air Force Base

Happy Jack Rd

See Cheyenne map page 43

See Laramie map page 57

The Fiery Narrows

Seminoe State Park

Pathfinder Reservoir

Seminoe Reservoir

To Casper

To Rawlins

To Scottsbluff, NE

To North Platte, NE

To Denver, CO

Ft. Collins, CO

To Denver, CO

N Platte River

Rawhide Creek

N Laramie River

Laramie River

Medicine Bow River

N Platte River

Horse Creek

Lodgepole Creek

Crow Creek

Bear Creek

Chugwater Creek

Sheep Creek

25 · 25 · 25 · 80 · 80 · 80 · 85 · 85 · 85 · 87 · 287 · 287 · 287 · 26 · 26 · 26 · 61 · 159 · 270 · 320 · 160 · 311 · 316 · 313 · 34 · 34 · 30 · 30 · 13 · 72 · 77 · 487 · 130 · 130 · 130 · 230 · 230 · 230 · 70 · 210 · 211 · 211 · 211 · 214 · 215 · 216

Scale: 0 · 15 · 30 Miles · 0 · 15 · 30 · 45 Kilometers

N · E · S · W

VEDAUWOO *map page 54, C-4*

Just before the Rocky Mountains fade into the great table of prairie that stretches uninterrupted all the way to the Appalachians, one extraordinary ridge of alpine territory makes its stand: Vedauwoo. Five minutes from Interstate 80, Vedauwoo ("VEE-dah-voo") merits only one humble freeway sign, but make no mistake: This is the kind of magnificent scenery that some neighboring states would steal a man's horse for.

Vedauwoo's famous rocks are some of the oldest exposed stones in the world. Battered by hot, high-altitude sun, hard-driving ice and rain, long winters of sub-zero temperatures, and winds that roar down from the Snowy Range or build speed across Nebraska's flats, these carved and whittled granite stacks poke up out of the golden grassland in unbelievable forms: tilted mushrooms and off-kilter pyramids, bizarre duckbill shapes and breadloaf monoliths. Thickly carpeted in lichens, the granite looks dull grey at a distance; brown, yellow, and pale green up close; and a gorgeous orange in late afternoon sunlight. Silvery-green fir trees and stands of rattling aspen soften the otherwise otherworldly landscape.

The Vedauwoo rise up like some bizarre, sculpted dreamscape.

Rock climbers cross the continent to sample the coarse granite. Vedauwoo is known for its cracks—actual splits in the stone, usually caused by freeze-thaw cycles. Climbers work the cracks by wedging fingers and toes inside, gaining momentary purchase while they slither another couple feet upward. Some cracks are wide enough to accept a whole body. Especially exhilarating or dangerous cracks get special names such as *Pretty Girls with Long Knives* and *Reading Raymond Chandler*. On any sunny afternoon, a fascinating hour can be spent sitting on a picnic blanket, watching climbers creep carefully up the dark fissures splitting the cliffs.

Hikers, mountain bikers, snowshoers, and trail skiers enjoy Vedauwoo's uncrowded backcountry, too. The wilderness stretches for miles up the Medicine Bow range, most of it empty of human traffic. Mind the weather while exploring, though: Vedauwoo looks like low country, but sits at 8,000 feet. There are hailstorms in July and snowstorms in June and September.

Vedauwoo's intrigue extends beyond its beauty. The name, which means "Earthborn Spirit" in the language of the Medicine Bow, alludes to a deeper mystery. Even practical Wyoming residents, not usually given to mystical exaggeration, say that strange things happen up at Vedauwoo. Shadows are darker. Coyotes are smarter and deer more watchful, the forests look empty but don't feel it, and the winds carry whispers.

A night alone at Vedauwoo may therefore be a bit much for the fainthearted. But for all who pass, a daytime visit is a taste of Wyoming not to be missed. Stretch some road out of your legs, or simply relax amid rocks so ancient, air so clean, space and quiet so vast.

— Mike Papciak, contributor to *Outside Magazine*

latter was once a camp for tie-hackers, lumbermen who cut railroad ties.) Shortly after Tie City, Happy Jack turns south and is devoured by Interstate 80.

Before the junction, though, two picturesque, gravel Forest Service roads connect Happy Jack to Interstate 80. One takes off before you get to the first outcropping of the Shermans and wanders eight slow but rewarding miles through open country, rangeland, and copses; it's interspersed all along the way with an amazing assortment of those Vedauwoo rock formations, making the pleasant meadows seem like an African veldt, with herds of stone hippos grazing. Eventually you reach the big Vedauwoo campground, just north of Interstate 80.

The other, even more scenic route, Blair-Wallis Road, takes off from Happy Jack beyond the first of the Sherman Mountains, and goes all the way up to Sherman Hill on Interstate 80, where Happy Jack ends. It has weird rock formations and more exciting wooded scenery than the parallel road from Happy Jack to the Vedauwoos.

As for Happy Jack, his true identity was Jack Hollingsworth, a woodhauler who had a ranch in the 1880s in the foothills beyond Cheyenne. He was always singing at his work, and the road past his adobe shack was much traveled, so he became a local character.

In the same decade, a short-lived gold boom took place in the area. A Professor Aughey announced a discovery he named the Carbonite Belle that would, he claimed, outshine the Comstock Lode. Eager Cheyenne businessmen prepared to invest $500,000, only to discover the professor had salted the area with specimens of ore.

■ LARAMIE   *map below; and page 54, C-4*

Laramie, with a population of around 27,000, is the second largest city of the southeast corner and the third largest in Wyoming. It lies west of the Laramie range, on the Laramie plains, and along the Laramie River. One may wonder who

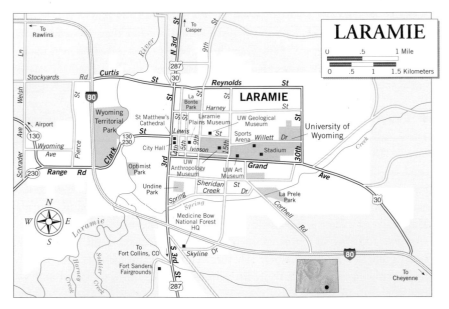

Laramie was, to be so thoroughly memorialized. In fact, nobody much. He was a French trapper, Jacques la Ramie (or Ramée), who was killed by Indians somewhere along this river in about 1820. His trapper friends must have loved him, because they named everything in sight after him. Later came Fort Laramie and the town and county of Laramie.

As the seat of the University of Wyoming, the first (1887) and for a long while only college in the state, Laramie is the educational and intellectual center of Wyoming. (There are now community colleges scattered about in Casper, Riverton, Rock Springs, Cheyenne, Torrington, Powell Jackson, and Sheridan.) Of necessity, the university's practical side gets the emphasis—animal husbandry, geology, engineering—but the humanities make a showing. The library is famous for its coverage of Wyoming writing and mining records and for a huge American Heritage Center (opened in 1993) with collections of things pertaining to the West, from paintings by Alfred Jacob Miller and Thomas Moran to Hopalong Cassidy's saddle.

When Old Main, a semi-Gothic Victorian mass of yellow stone, was built in 1887 out on the flats, it gave the effect of being the only collegiate edifice within 1,000 miles. Actually, nearby Colorado and Utah had gotten into the act, but Old Main was certainly one of a kind in Wyoming. Now it's flanked by a big bustling modern institution. This is not a campus full of Old World charm, but it does exude a certain progressive Western energy. There are about 11,000 students now.

Altogether, however, Laramie is quieter and prettier than most cities in Wyoming and, indeed, the West. Though on the flats, it is ringed by mountains, near and far, and the street trees have had time to grow tall. But its early history is just as active as Cheyenne's. It, too, suffered from the excesses of Hell-on-Wheels.

◆ EARLY SETTLEMENT

There had been some earlier settlement in this area along the Overland Trail during the 1860s. As at Cheyenne, a military post, Fort J. Buford (later Fort Sanders), had been set up to protect the wagon trains. The railroad and its passengers first arrived on May 9, 1868, and of course all hell broke loose. There was the same outburst of business and mayhem. Law and order were imposed in that first May, when a vigilante group lynched a desperado called The Kid. This was a mistake. The Kid's friends terrorized the town that summer, and in the fall, the vigilantes grew to a formidable 500. They raided outlaw strongholds, such as the Belle of the West dance hall. In the ensuing battle, five were killed and 15 wounded. Four outlaws who surrendered were hanged on as many telegraph poles. Many outlaws headed west with Hell-on-Wheels. A committee of the righteous took over in December. Albany County was created in 1868, with Laramie as its seat. Unfortunately, residual outlaws, under a mask of respectability, took over the reform committee. Things went to pot. Dakota Territory revoked the town's charter, dissolved the committee, and put the town under the jurisdiction of federal courts until 1874. By then, Wyoming was its own territory.

♦ RIGHTS ISSUES THEN AND NOW

Things quieted down and women emerged as a force impaneled on a state grand jury as early as 1870. This early fruit of the struggle for women's rights received worldwide attention. King William of Prussia cabled his congratulations to President Grant on such evidence of human progress, and a jingle made the rounds: "Baby, baby, don't get in a fury; your mamma's gone to sit on the jury."

On the other hand, Laramie was also the site of one of the state's saddest episodes. On October 7, 1998, police discovered Matthew Shepard, a gay UW student, tied to a fence in the frigid hills above town, pistol-whipped and barely alive. He died a few days later. While on trial, his two assailants tried to use the "gay-panic defense" to explain their attack. Shepard's murder—and Laramie—became a symbol for intolerance of all stripes. The community, state, and nation embarked on a long, painful discussion; at this writing, a federal hate crime bill known as the Matthew Shepard Act was under consideration in Congress.

♦ BILL NYE AND OTHERS

Wyoming's first famous writer, Bill Nye, was a prominent early Laramie citizen. Nye came to Wyoming in 1876, served in the Territorial Legislature, and became postmaster and a justice of the peace. He began his literary career at the fledgling *Sentinel,* then started his own *Boomerang* (named for his mule) in 1881. His writing style was widely copied all over the country, and by the time he finally left in 1885 he was famous. From 1881 till his death in 1896, he published a series of books including *Bill Nye and the Boomerang* (1881), *Forty Liars and Other Lies* (1882), and *Baled Hay* (1884). He belongs to the tradition of early Mark Twain, Josh Billings, and other poker-faced, tall-tale humorists of the period—the nation's first jokesters with a wholly American accent.

Since then, Laramie has continued to harbor the muse, but never with the same acclaim. As an undergraduate, Ted Olsen practiced his poetry and went on to earn a considerable reputation as a prize-winning poet. He returned to Laramie in the 1920s as the editor of the *Boomerang,* before moving on to the *New York Herald-Tribune.* Thurman Arnold, born in Laramie, became well known as the author of *The Folklore of Capitalism* (1937) and as a legal figure of prominence (assistant attorney general of the United States). Olga Moore, too, gained a respectable reputation as a novelist. Though none of these came close to the national fame of Nye, they and others from and in Laramie have kept the flag of Wyoming native literature flying.

◆ UNIVERSITY OF WYOMING

Laramie is still very much dominated by the **university campus,** which stretches along Grand Avenue from 30th to Ninth Streets. It has the usual collegiate effect of an oasis, particularly because it's surrounded by such dry, flat, open countryside. Almost all the buildings are built of the characteristic yellow stone of the area, which you see when you look east up the main streets toward the bluffs above town. The buildings are mostly early modern (1930–50), block-like constructions—handsome, solid, and by now looking pleasantly old-fashioned. There are huge, ornamental spruce trees, and lawns desperately kept green by sprinklers in summer—so you're sure to get wet on walks around campus at that time of year. **Old Main,** more than a century old, is preserved in a sort of garden-corner of the grounds, at Ivinson and Ninth, with the biggest trees and greenest lawns on campus, and even some flowers. Along the sides of the campus are fraternities (north) and sororities (south)—a pleasant promenade when the sun isn't too hot or the wind too cold, especially at sunset.

On the campus there are at least four noteworthy sights. You can find them on a compact map, available at the **Visitor Services Center**, 1408 Ivinson, near 15th Street. The **Anthropology Museum** is almost directly across the street, and the **Geological Museum** is buried back across campus in a row of grandiose buildings devoted to engineering, agriculture, and mining. Both museums are small, but choice. The anthropology museum covers the known human history of the state. One thing it makes clear is just how very recent the presence of the horse is in Wyoming's history. The Indians that so wonderfully adapted their lives to horsemanship did so only in relatively modern times—not long before the first appearances of French trapper-explorers, in the mid-18th century. In the thousands of years preceding, the native population wandered afoot, chipping spear points, driving bison over cliffs for food, and making pictographs and petroglyphs on high cliffs or rock recesses. The geological museum displays the more remote history of the state as evidenced by prehistoric rocks and animals, and is dominated by an immense and gloriously terrifying Wyoming dinosaur skeleton. *Anthropology Building; 307-766-5310. Geology Building; 307-766-4218.*

The **Centennial Complex** is a new six-story building that resembles a teepee and houses the **American Heritage Center,** a source of pride for the university. Over the years, all sorts of people have donated manuscripts, scrapbooks, photographs, and art pieces relating to the Old West, and now those gifts are suitably displayed. Besides an enormous reference collection of papers, notably mining archives, the center possesses one of the state's most significant collections of Western art, including nine paintings by Alfred Jacob Miller. His best-known piece, *The Rendezvous Near Green River,* documents the rendezvous of 1837, one of the annual fur trappers' rendezvous that took place in Wyoming in the 1830s and 1840s.

By contrast, the **University of Wyoming Art Museum**—also housed in the Centennial Complex—deliberately does not concentrate on Western art (which in this part of the country means cowboy art of the Far West). Though it does have plenty of examples of that among its 7,000 items, it prefers not to compete with the Whitney Gallery of Western Art in Cody. The museum ranges over the entire spectrum of Western art in its broader meaning, concentrating considerably on 20th-century American art. Its nine galleries always contain works from the permanent collection, plus changing exhibits throughout the year. *2111 Willett Drive; 307-766-6622.*

Anthropology, geology, history, and art will keep you busy and well-exercised as you peruse the various buildings from one end of the campus (paying homage to Old Main) to the other. Concerts and plays are performed in the Fine Arts Center.

◆ Laramie Town

The campus, like the capitol in Cheyenne, observes the usual odd Wyoming contradiction of ruggedness and sophistication. Here it's the contrast of the rough-hewn, native-stone, big academic structures, with the elegant Fine Arts Center and its exhibitions alongside the special treasures of the American Heritage Center and the Wyoming Territorial Park. In town, somewhat of the same contrast exists. As you proceed down Ivinson Street westward, from its beginning in the heart of the campus to its end on Third Street, you will pass some especially attractive residential blocks of greenery and nice-looking houses. At Sixth and Ivinson is the grand, turreted, late-Victorian **Ivinson Mansion,** with spacious grounds and a big coach

COTTAGE GROVE PUBLIC LIBRARY

house. Edward Ivinson was an Englishman, born in 1830 on St. Croix in the Virgin Islands, who made his way west and to Laramie. There he made his fortune, beginning with general merchandise and groceries, and spreading out in all directions, mostly in ties for the railroad. He flourished later as a banker and real estate operator. He arrived at the very beginnings of the town, in 1868, and died in 1928 at the age of 98. He and his English wife, Jane Wood, determinedly set the tone for Laramie's atmosphere of civility, which is still evident. He was involved in everything civic—treasurer of the university's first board of trustees, mayor of Laramie, a candidate for governor of the state in its second election of 1892 (unsuccessful—after all, he wasn't a cattleman).

Ivinson was also senior warden of Laramie's St. Matthew's Cathedral. It is surely due to him as much as anyone, and to his constant beneficence, that the Episcopal Church has had an oddly widespread and long-time preeminence (now much reduced) not only in Laramie, but all over Wyoming. In nearly every Wyoming town, you can count on finding three sacred edifices—the Catholic, the Latter-day Saints, and the Episcopalian churches—usually huddled together in the center of a shady older section of town. Lutheran, Methodist, Presbyterian, and, nowadays, more freewheeling sects flourish, too, but none more centrally, solidly, and traditionally than those first three.

The Ivinson house, saved from the wrecking ball at the last moment, as usual, is now a wonderfully all-embracing house museum, despite the misleading title of **Laramie Plains Museum.** The emphasis is on the Ivinsons and their devotion to good form and good taste, but it's not so much a preservation or even restoration of the original Ivinson glories, as it is a survey of all aspects of domestic life in the latter third of the 19th century in pioneer Wyoming. The house is full of old-fashioned oddities: quaint bathrooms, antique kitchen equipment, clothes, toys, handsome furniture, woodwork, lamps, even a nice shelf of books from the period, including quite a few Nye titles. It's also full of families from all over the United States taking the tour. *603 Ivinson Avenue; 307-742-4448.*

Down Ivinson Street from the Ivinson house is the Ivinson church—**St. Matthew's Cathedral**—a beautiful example of Anglo-American neo-Gothic, very exotic on this site, with a charming if anachronistic garden-close next to it and a handsome neo-Gothic office beyond. Inside, the church is a model of its kind. Two big chancel windows memorialize Mr. and Mrs. Ivinson. The side chapel and high altar are especially handsome.

(opposite) The Ivinson Mansion houses a rich collection from early Wyoming.

Unfortunately, the surroundings are less than romantic. This part of town has been left to decay—broken sidewalks, no trees, dreary vacant lots, inappropriate commercial buildings—as so many civic centers have. City Hall is across the street and one block up from the cathedral. The handsome church of St. Laurence O'Toole (one can't help but wonder who he was) is one block over. The Masonic Hall is a neighbor, and the big Albany County Courthouse fills a nearby block. Yet the impression is that of a depressed neighborhood.

On the west side of Laramie, **Wyoming Territorial Park** is housed within the 1872 territorial prison, a structure dedicated to "evil doers of all classes and kinds." It remained a prison until 1902, when the inmates were transferred to the new penitentiary in Rawlins. The old prison served as the university's experimental livestock farm for the next eight decades. Finally, in the early 1990s, the decrepit buildings were transformed (at a cost of $5 million) into a first-rate museum and Old West town. A wooden stockade surrounds the red sandstone prison and adjacent broom factory where prisoners were forced to work. The interior has been reconstructed using the original cells and period fixtures; modern additions include excellent short videos describing the prisoners' lives. The convicts who served time here—including Butch Cassidy—glare down from giant photos on the walls. The old horse barn contains the National U.S. Marshals' Museum downstairs, and a dinner theater upstairs. A short distance behind the prison lies a recreated frontier town, with costumed historical characters in the summer months.

College kids take their parents to **Cafe Jacques** at 216 Grand Avenue for a fancy meal. **Cavalryman Supper Club** is at 4425 S. Third Street. This old-fashioned club, one mile south of Laramie, is popular with locals who enjoy their prime rib, steak, and lobster straight and simple. **The Overland Restaurant,** at 100 Ivinson Avenue, is popular with locals and tourists alike; it has an impressive wine list and sophisticated dishes. Come for a brunch of yellowfin tuna with eggs, or a buffalo-chili omelet, and champagne by the glass.

■ CIRCLE TOUR: THE SNOWIES, SARATOGA, MEDICINE BOW

This tour starts and ends in Laramie and includes the first taste since the east of *real* mountain scenery: the 12,000-foot peaks of the Snowies. You climb above the timberline going over Snowy Range Pass at 10,847 feet and pass right alongside glacial lakes (Mirror Lake, Lake Marie, Silver Lake), canyons, and gorgeous vistas. (The pass, incidentally, is very easy driving, though it's closed by snow from October or November through May.) On the lower slopes grow forests of evergreen and aspen, full of game. Streams flow through them, full of fish. Picnic places line the route, and winter sports opportunities abound here.

◆ **CENTENNIAL**   *map page 54, B-4*
Wyoming State Highway 130 leaves Laramie and passes almost immediately through tawny rangeland, with the Snowies right ahead and other mountains to the south. Before the start of the pass on the east side lies Centennial, which once had a population of thousands and now has about 200 residents. Centennial is a picture-postcard of a small mining town. Its old buildings contain shops for tourists and a museum down in the old depot. Though the whole town is visible at a glance from the road, it's worth a stop. This area was the scene of short-lived booms, most of them in the 1870s and 1880s. A platinum mine operated as late as the 1920s, but today Centennial is known as an artist colony, with a tourism industry catering to summer visitors and winter skiers.

Centennial is also the eastern gateway to the part of **Medicine Bow National Forest** that encompasses the Medicine Bow Mountains, including the Snowies. The Medicine Bows were sacred to the Indians, who gathered here each year for powwows. The cedarwood in the area made such accurate bows, the Indians considered it "medicine"—something that gives control over natural or magical powers—hence the name.

◆ **THE SNOWIES**   *map page 54, A/B-3/4*
The Snowies are a striking example of the Wyoming geological phenomenon of "range upon range." Like the portion of the Laramies between Cheyenne and Laramie, this part of the Medicine Bow Mountains consists of a great, rather flat plateau, out of which stick almost autonomous super-ranges. The Snowies are, in fact, part of the Medicine Bows, but have a distinct character of their own.

The road from Snowy Range Pass comes down from these high mountains on the west side into the North Platte River Valley, fringed with mountains and containing bosky riverbanks down the middle. Handsome, rolling ranchland lies all about. The river is clear, rippling over stones and drifting through shallows before it takes off north through semidesert, then through mountains and dams to start its long curve eastward toward Nebraska, where it joins with the southern branch of the Platte and, ultimately, with the Missouri and Mississippi. Altogether a long, long way to go from its fresh beginnings, here in the Snowies.

(following pages) A pond near the Gap Lakes, in the Snowy Range.

SOUTHEAST

◆ **SARATOGA**   *map page 54, A-3*

Heading north, State Highway 130 takes you by magnificent ranches to Saratoga, a charming little spa and (across the river) village. Starting in 1878 as a trading post, it gradually became popular for its hot springs, particularly after a railroad was built south from the main line of the Union Pacific to serve nearby Encampment during the Sierra Madre mining boom. The springs were christened Saratoga in honor of the fashionable New York State spa and horse-racing center, and since the turn of the century Wyoming's Saratoga has been a mildly active summer resort. A renaissance of sorts is now underway in this quaint Western hamlet. It has a well-established and comfortable spa hotel, the **Saratoga Inn** (601 E. Pic-Pike Road; 307-326-5261), good eating and shopping in the tiny "city center," other nice tourist facilities, and fishing along the river. It's a delightfully remote stopover for anyone going to or from nearby central Colorado, or for those poking around the environs of the Medicine Bows and Sierra Madres. Don't miss a meal at the nicely reconstructed **Wolf Hotel,** in the town center (*101 E. Bridge Street; 307-326-5525*; see also page 335). Handsome summer houses surround the spa's golf course on the east side of the river.

Driving north through increasingly flat, open plains to Walcott, you cross Interstate 80 and continue on old Route 30 (U.S. Route 287). This highway, curving back to Laramie, is the last remains of the old Lincoln Highway in this corner of the state. It circles around the north end of the Medicine Bows along with the equally dispossessed Union Pacific. On the way east it passes the town of Hanna (built on coal and oil, of which there's quite a lot scattered about this northern part of Carbon County) and then through the vast, open valley of the Laramie Plains. To the south are the Medicine Bows, and to the north, the Shirley Mountains, the easternmost edge of the chain of central belt ranges that starts where the Wind Rivers end. Far to the north, and bending around to the south and east, are the Laramies. You are never out of sight of some of these encircling ranges, but they are often far, far away, with nothing in between but enormous, wide rangelands.

◆ **MEDICINE BOW**   *map page 54, B-2*

The town of Medicine Bow, 37 miles from Interstate 80, was once famous as the setting for the novel *The Virginian.* This is where Owen Wister himself got off the train and began the experiences that led to his writings at the turn of the century. His fictional hero, the Virginian, first appears in this town, and the climax of the story, the gun battle with the villain Trampas, took place here. In 1939 a stone

MEDICINE BOW AND OWEN WISTER

At the beginning of *The Virginian*, Owen Wister gives a graphic and unflattering description of Medicine Bow as it was in the 1880s. The "I" of the story, pretty obviously Wister himself, steps off the train as a rather haughty, very green dude, and meets the hero, the Virginian.

Enthralled with the first sight of his hero, he is less enthralled with Medicine Bow. "Town, as they called it, pleased me less. . . . But until our language stretches itself and takes in a word of closer fit, town will have to do. . . . I have seen and slept in many like it since. . . stark, dotted over a planet of treeless dust, like soiled packs of cards. . . . Houses, empty bottles, and garbage, they were forever of the same shapeless pattern.... They seemed to have been strewn here by the wind and to be waiting till the wind should come again and blow them away. Yet serenely above their forlornness swam a pure, quiet light such as the East never sees. . . . I took its dimensions, twenty-nine buildings in all—one coal chute, one water tank, the station, one store, two eating houses, one billiard hall, two tool-houses, one feed stable, and twelve others that for one reason and another I shall not name. . . . There they stood . . . amid a fringe of old tins while at their very doors began a world of crystal light."

Washing required "a trough. . . slippery with soapy water." A roller towel, dirty with use, was changed only at the beginning of the new day. But the pretty hotel keeper changed it especially for the Virginian. She evidently had her reward. And eating? "Canned stuff it was—corned beef. And one of my table companions said the truth about it. 'When I slung my teeth over that. . . I thought I was chewing a hammock.' We had strange coffee and condensed milk." Sleeping was no better, but the narrator managed a clean night on top of a store counter.

The standard of living at Medicine Bow has risen in modern times, but the town still has an air of forlornness and still sits in the middle of the shining plains as something of an intrusion. There are now lots of trees on the few streets, but no more commercial buildings than there were a century ago; just different ones. A fine modern school and a pretty small church seem the most substantial buildings visible except, ironically, all those memorials to Wister: the Virginian Hotel, the pyramid, the cabin moved from Jackson Hole, and the museum in the depot (a different depot from that of 1880) that celebrates Wister and *The Virginian*, among other things.

pyramid made of petrified wood was erected in memory of Wister, and there are other mementos. Some may have forgotten him, but Wyoming hasn't.

The most striking building in modern Medicine Bow is a big oblong of yellow stone, the **Virginian Hotel** (also see page 335), opened in 1911 on the expectation that the phenomenal success of the novel would bring it fame and fortune. Though the modern town of Medicine Bow is as derelict in its own way as the Wister town of the 1880s, the structure is in very good shape. Now a hotel museum on the National Register of Historic Places, the Virginian has bedrooms decorated in styles from 1880 to 1910. There is an Owen Wister Suite and, downstairs, an exceptionally cozy dining room and bar full of local characters. The scene is probably not unlike the Medicine Bow of 1880—except for us tourists and better food. *409 Lincoln Highway; 307-379-2377.*

Opposite, across the wide desolation of the almost deserted Lincoln Highway, is the former U.P. depot, built in 1913, now the **Medicine Bow Museum.** Next to it is the **Owen Wister log cabin,** moved from its original site on Wister's ranch in Jackson Hole, but not yet fixed up for visitors. Trains don't stop at the station anymore, but they still go by—endless freight cars of coal or cattle, with their nostalgic train whistles. There is something altogether odd and remote about this memorial enclave alongside the railroad and the empty highway, its traffic siphoned away by thundering Interstate 80. *Medicine Bow Museum; 307-379-2383.*

◆ COMO BLUFF *map page 54, B-2*

The other towns along the 57-mile trip to Laramie are equally marooned. Shortly beyond Medicine Bow is Como Bluff, not even a pretense of a town, but the site of one of earth's most famous treasure troves of dinosaur bones. This was the scene of the epic battle between two famous dinosaur experts Othniel C. Marsh (1831–99) and Edward Drinker Cope (1840–97)—representing the Peabody Museum of Yale, in New Haven, Connecticut, and the Academy of Sciences in Philadelphia, respectively. They were led to their discoveries by two local men named Reed and Carlin, who worked for the Union Pacific. These two stumbled upon a lone camp hut built entirely of huge dinosaur bones, and when the news percolated to the rival scientists, Reed became Marsh's man and Carlin became Cope's. The two scientists struggled for decades over bones from the local quarry, writing diatribes, wresting prize skeletons from one another more or less at gunpoint, blackening one another's reputations in the press, and sending their loot back to New Haven and Philadelphia. It was one of the classic scientific feuds of all time, but the battlefield is moribund now. There's little left of the quarry site itself, a mile or so north of the road, but the dinosaur-bone cabin is preserved alongside the road, inside a stone hut, as a paying tourist attraction.

◆ ROCK RIVER   *map page 54, B-2/3*

The town of **Rock River** (on Rock Creek), some 20 miles from Medicine Bow, sits in a pleasant riverside grove of trees. In 1865, Rock Creek was the scene of an Indian attack on an emigrant train of 75 wagons. Among the victims was the Fletcher family. The mother was killed; the father, wounded, escaped with three sons; and two daughters were taken prisoner. Mary was eventually sold to a white trader, but sister Lizzie became completely adapted to Indian ways and lived with the Arapahos for the rest of her life. Thirty-five years after the sisters were captured, Mary learned that her sister was living on the Wind River Reservation. Lizzie chose to stay with her husband, Broken Hand. The now vanished town of Rock Creek, then a railroad stop, was a lively place and a starting point for a stage route up to Junction City, Montana—a 400-mile trip. The railroad stop was abandoned around 1900 in favor of Rock River, and the stage was gone by then. Things have been pretty quiet since.

◆ BOSLER   *map page 54, B/C-3*

As for **Bosler,** it is now a sort of memorial, both sad and funny, to the decline of the Lincoln Highway. It consists of a huddle of derelict buildings leaning together in vacant despair, labeled with "Tourist Court," "Dancing," and other inscriptions indicative of roadside prosperity and whoopee. Nothing seems to remain of Bosler but these raffish mementos. The Medicine Bows, west, and the Laramies, east, loom in the distance over the great silent spaces. In about 20 miles, you're back in Laramie.

■ EAST CENTRAL: THE STAGECOACH CORRIDOR   *map page 54*

Due north from Cheyenne to the Black Hills, five smallish counties (including the southernmost part of Laramie County) exhibit similar general characteristics: plains broken by ridges and penetrated by green cottonwood valleys, the rivers nearly all flowing west to east. This region has no true mountain ranges in it, but the Laramies loom large to the west, and a fringe of the Black Hills reaches into the northeast corner. Otherwise, it's wide open.

On the other hand, except for a brief intrusion around Torrington, there's none of the endless cultivation and gridiron road systems of the true Midwest. The very names of the numberless creeks that cross the region are enough to establish its Far West character: Horse, Bear, Rawhide, Lance, Sage, Lightning, Thunder, Beaver, Lodgepole, and Dogie (an orphan calf, but used sarcastically for cattle generally, as in the song lyric, "Whoopie-ti-yi-yo, git along little dogies, you know that Wyoming will be your new home"). The larger rivers are already familiar—the North Platte and Laramie, plus the Cheyenne farther north, nowhere near the city of the same name.

Historically, this region is famous as a way to other places. It was the route of the stagecoaches from Cheyenne in the south to the Black Hills and Deadwood, South Dakota, in the north. The Oregon Trail crossed it, east to west, along the course of the North Platte. The Texas Trail, the cattle drive route from Texas to the Powder River, also went through the area. Emigrants started passing through as early as the 1840s and continued till the 1860s. The cattle drives peaked in the 1870s and 1880s, along with the gold-rush mania. After that, there were coal and oil booms. The whole area had been a prime hunting area for generations of horse-mounted Indians, and there is evidence of hunting and camping even before that by mysterious aborigines.

■ TOWARD GOSHEN HOLE *map page 54, E-3*

You leave Cheyenne for the north on Interstate 25, but once out of the city, you take U.S. Route 85 northeast, toward Goshen Hole and Torrington. Of all the routes so far suggested by this guide, the 30-mile stretch through Laramie County is no doubt the closest to being really dull. It's a rather splendid sort of dullness: great, rolling range country rich in grass and hay—the delight of ranchers and wheat growers. Just when you think enough is enough, the road turns north—and suddenly the landscape opens wide into the depression of **Goshen Hole,** a big basin named, as usual somewhat inaccurately, for an oddly named French trapper, Gosche. Goshen Hole is "real West": cottonwood river courses wriggling away and grim, broken tablelands all around. It's a grandly spacious (if not exactly inviting) landscape, and you can get a good view of it if you exit and head over to one of the state rest areas on the west side of the highway. Like so many Wyoming landscapes, it requires early morning hours, clouds, or—especially—late afternoon or sunset viewing, to bring it out.

◆ TORRINGTON *map page 54, E-1/2*

Beyond the Hole, the road continues straight up to Torrington, first penetrating a great, long, yellow wall of castle-tipped ridges, and then through a dull, flat, irrigated belt of green farmland. By now you're deep into Goshen County, which has more cropland than any other in Wyoming—which isn't saying very much. Beets, alfalfa, potatoes, and even fruit are grown, most notably along the fertile North Platte River. The low altitude (about 4,000 feet) helps this production. Torrington has been a center of Wyoming's considerable sugar beet industry for years, growing, storing, and processing the vegetable. The landscape of small surrounding villages connected by perpendicular roads seems an invasion of the agricultural Midwest and is altogether a contrast to anything covered so far. Torrington itself, with nearly 6,000 inhabitants, counts as one of the state's more prosperous and stable towns. But it's not Wild West.

At the crossroads of the Oregon Trail, the Cheyenne-to-Deadwood Stage Route, the Mormon Trail, and the Texas Cattle Trail, the **Homesteader's Museum** seems to sit atop history. It is housed in the old brick Union Pacific depot, built in 1926, the same year the Holly Sugar plant came to Torrington. Although the sugar plant still operates, the last train stopped at the depot in 1964. Today, the depot houses a small museum that focuses on the thousands of homesteaders who flocked to eastern Wyoming during the late 19th and early 20th centuries. Displays include artifacts from the 4A Ranch and an interior reconstruction of a local homestead, plus a marvelous collection of old black-and-white photos. Outside is an 1824 Concord stagecoach (considered the Rolls Royce of travel at that time), an old homestead cabin, and a windmill. *495 Main Street; 307-532-5612.*

■ THE GRATTAN MASSACRE

From Torrington, you're in a position to follow the emigrant route up the Platte River, a highway infused with Oregon Trail history and mementos—and with increasingly beautiful scenery. From 1841 until the 1860s, hundreds of thousands of emigrants made their way west along here. This was where the various widespread routes from the northeast concentrated to funnel all the traffic through to such western destinations as Oregon, Utah, Nevada, and California. Souvenirs of one kind or another are scattered all along the route. Just beyond Torrington, across the river, was a trading post, site of the so-called Rock Ranch battle of the early 1850s, in which Indians attacked a group of pioneers. This kind of not uncommon incident was made special by the fact that these particular emigrants had brought along their black slaves. Some of these were killed and buried under the floor of the post. Except for the presence of such part-black trapper-guides as Jim Beckwourth and Ed Rose, these were perhaps the first African Americans of record in Wyoming or the Rocky Mountains of the Northwest.

Farther west was the site of the Grattan battle of August 19, 1854—one of the most significant, if basically trivial, incidents of Indian conflict history. Some Mormons who were camped along the trail accused several Miniconjous, a subgroup of the Sioux, of butchering a cow belonging to them. A friendly chief, Brave Bear of the Brulés, came to Fort Laramie to straighten things out and agreed to pay for the cow. But a hot-headed young graduate of West Point, Lt. John Grattan, wanted action. He insisted that the malefactors be arrested and, against all advice, set out with 28 men and two howitzers to bring the culprits in. He marched into a village

(above) The famed Deadwood Coach used in Buffalo Bill's Wild West Show. Photo by Robert Weiglein. (Courtesy, Buffalo Bill Historical Center, Cody).
(opposite) Oregon Trail ruts in the sandstone hillsides near Guernsey.

of some 5,000 Oglalas, Brulés, and Miniconjous, and demanded to be given the killers. (Things were confused by the fact that Grattan's Indian interpreter seems to have been drunk.) The Indians refused to comply and made their own threats. Grattan lost his nerve and fired. He and all of his men died. Some of the Indians were killed, too, including Brave Bear, the peacemaker. The long war with the Sioux would continue until after Lt. Col. George A. Custer's death in 1876; and though the war was inevitable, it all really began with Grattan. Now there are peaceful farms along the river. Laramie Peak is faintly visible to the west.

■ FORT LARAMIE   *map page 54, D/E-1*

Twenty miles west of Torrington on U.S. Route 26, you come to Fort Laramie—yet another memorial to that unfortunate Frenchman. It began as a trading post of the Rocky Mountain Fur Company under Robert Campbell and William Sublette, and was originally called Fort William, after Sublette. In 1835, it was sold to a syndicate of trappers, who in turn sold it to the American Fur Company. American then rebuilt it and rechristened it Fort Laramie. The federal government finally purchased it in 1849. (This was about the earliest permanent settlement in

Fort Laramie, as painted by Alfred Jacob Miller in 1851.
(Collection of Gilcrease Museum, Tulsa)

Wyoming—founded decades before the cities of Cheyenne and Laramie.) By the 1840s, Fort Laramie was a major stop on the increasingly busy Oregon Trail. The Oglala Indians held rendezvous there when white-Indian relations were relatively peaceful. Later, when the situation was no longer peaceful, Fort Laramie was the permanent and prominent base of operations for U.S. troops.

A treaty with the Indians was signed at the fort as early as 1851, guaranteeing the Indians a subsidy for not harassing pioneer wagon trains. Other treaties were signed there in 1865, 1868, and 1876. But despite treaties, or because of them, things deteriorated steadily, climaxing in the vicious fighting of the late 1870s and Custer's death in Montana. The fort continued to be garrisoned until 1890. It then fell into disrepair and was sold at public auction. Today it is federal property, run by the National Park Service as a **National Historic Site.** *307-837-2221.*

The fort, three miles south of the town of Fort Laramie, is probably the most impressive display of past military might extant in Wyoming. Other such forts, notably Fort Bridger, have their beauties and interests, but Laramie has both more original buildings and more of the feeling of what it really must have been like when it was an active fort. The surrounding country, though beautiful, is very austere and particularly evocative of the days of emigrant trains and Indian attacks. Also, the magnitude of this military installation is immediately evident: there are almost a score of structures scattered about the wide, bleak area, giving you a sense of the importance of this oldest of Wyoming posts.

Starting at the old **commissary**, now the large visitor center and museum, a most rewarding tour leads along the row of buildings on the west side of the wide, empty, *hot* (in summer sun) **parade ground.** Here, in a line, are an **enlisted-men's bar** (where you can now get *cold* non-alcoholic drinks), **officers' houses, surgeons' quarters, a powder magazine,** and, most handsome and evocative, a lovingly restored bachelor officers' quarters nicknamed **Old Bedlam.** This is the original two-story verandaed building, rescued from ruin in 1938 and now restored. It dates from 1849 and as such is probably the oldest extant building in the state of Wyoming. It was at this building that Portugee Phillips appeared, nearly dead, on Christmas Eve, 1866, after his epic winter ride from beleaguered Fort Kearny. One of the parties that inspired the building's name was going on when Phillips staggered in. But that story belongs to the Powder River. (See page 144.)

(following pages) Elk Mountain looms over an abandoned homestead.

SOUTHEAST

■ OREGON TRAIL MONUMENTS   *map page 54, D-1*

Pleasantly situated on the North Platte River, the town of **Guernsey** was named after the original promoter of the nearby Hartville-Sunrise mines. The damming of the Platte above town has made several reservoirs that are popular recreational areas: the lower, smaller, more picturesque, mountain-ringed Guernsey Reservoir and, upstream, the larger, flatter Glendo. Small roads lead to areas for boating, fishing, swimming, and camping.

From the center of Guernsey, you can cross the river and follow marked gravel roads to two of the area's most curious relics of the great covered-wagon trek. One is **Register Cliff,** where (like the more famous Independence Rock farther west) emigrants carved their names when they camped, one day's journey (11 miles) beyond the safety of Fort Laramie. Set back from the river, the cliff is a high, white, sheer landmark, and is indeed covered with names. Unfortunately, the first part of it you come upon is covered with modern carvings (though some of these go back to the 1880s). Farther along, protected by a high fence, are the older signatures of Oregon Trail days, distinguished by their large size and regular design. The later vandalism diminishes the thrill, but the cliff is awesome nonetheless.

Somehow more mind-boggling are the **Oregon Trail ruts,** worn in stone by thousands of wagon wheels clanking west. Oregon Trail National Monument preserves several hundred yards of the sunken road. You climb a short hill on foot from the parking lot, and there is a deep, narrow gash in the white rock, made by those thousands and thousands of covered wagons, traveling hundreds and hundreds of miles west a century and a half ago. It's hard to explain why it's so moving, but many people testify to this emotion. The site is beautiful, too. If you can find your way to the top of the low summit, you'll get a restful view up the romantically tree-bowered river, and westward to the Laramies.

Register Rock, near Guernsey, records the names of hundreds of Oregon Trail emigrants, one of three such sights in Wyoming.

COTTAGE GROVE PUBLIC LIBRARY

NORTHEAST CORNER
BLACK HILLS & THUNDER BASIN

◆ **AREA OVERVIEW**

The Black Hills proper belong to South Dakota, but Wyoming possesses a somewhat separate western enclave that makes up Black Hills National Forest and includes the Bear Lodge Mountains and Devil's Tower. Around this forested and elevated core of hills, about 6,000 feet high, lie foothills, canyons, streams, and open range. The lowest point of the state lies at the junction of Oak Creek and the Belle Fourche River, near where Montana, South Dakota, and Wyoming meet: an altitude of only 3,125 feet. The atmosphere and vegetation here are reminiscent of eastern states, with the only proliferation of oak trees found in Wyoming, and ponderosa pines rather than lodgepole. Even the highest points are below 7,000 feet, which is level ground in much of the state. Warren Peak, at 6,656 feet, is the giant of this region, but by Wyoming's standards that's nothing; the surface of Yellowstone Lake is at 7,731 feet.

Weather: The weather is mild compared to the rest of Wyoming. January temperatures average 19 degrees F and July temperatures average 70 degrees. Lows below zero should be expected in the winter and highs in the 90s are common in summer.

Food & Lodging: There is ample camping and lodging throughout Crook County and Thunder Basin. Most of the food in the area can be found at diners, although Gillette has a number of fine restaurants.

■ HARTVILLE AND NORTHWARD   *map page 54, D-1; and page 91, C-5*

U.S. Route 26 goes west from Guernsey to be swallowed by Interstate 25; but back east, hardly more than a mile from Guernsey, **Wyoming State Highway 270** takes off north across the railroad tracks to Hartville and eventually on to Lusk. This road is another happy surprise, like Happy Jack Road: a nearly empty and masterfully graded, engineered, and paved road—through scenery of red gorges and green rangeland—that hardly anyone seems to know about.

Hartville is more or less a ghost town, but it was once the site of an important Indian village and is Wyoming's first town, incorporated in 1884. In 1889 a copper boom struck and faded, in that pattern so familiar all over the state. There followed an iron boom. Finally, Hartville settled down as a rail depot when Wyoming's second railroad—the Chicago, Burlington, and Quincy, now the Burlington Northern—came through on its way west. At nearby **Sunrise**, a massive open-pit iron mine flourished for many years, but no more. Hartville was the scene of a rather remarkable event in 1902: the defunct White Swede, assisted by friends, sat in on a poker game. The cards were propitious and the corpse won enough to pay for his own burial.

The town lies in a gully of great, red, tree-spotted ridges and seems to be pretty well decomposing. You see ruined cabins along the road as you go up through handsome wooded heights to a plateau ringed by forested ridges and punctuated by grassy buttes. A road shortly after Hartville goes west to Guernsey Reservoir; a second one 10 miles farther takes you to Glendo. Wyoming State Highway 270 continues smoothly on to Manville, where you turn east. After nine miles on U.S. Route 18/20, you're in Lusk.

■ SPANISH DIGGINGS   *map page 91, C-5*

An interesting sight you're not likely to see unless you take the trouble is called, incorrectly, the Spanish Diggings. Among the most curious remnants of prehistoric history in the United States, this is a series of hundreds of ancient stone quarries north of the Platte, west of Lusk. Early settlers believed the holes had been dug by Spaniards looking for gold, which is not the case. Rather, they were dug by the original inhabitants of Wyoming, who lived centuries before the present-day Plains Indians. They may have been ancestors of the Plains Indians, but they had a different culture—one based on the extensive use of stone tools and pottery. They were given to making pictographic (surface painting) or petroglyphic (incised) murals in caves or on high cliffs, which the Plains Indians did not do. These old quarries were worked for perhaps a good thousand years and produced material that was fashioned into artifacts that can be found as far away as the Ohio and Mississippi River valleys. The stone is identifiable as coming from Wyoming. It was Wyoming's first industry. The mysterious quarries now are mostly on private land and can't be seen just at pleasure, but ask in Fort Laramie for guided tours. *307-837-3052.*

■ LUSK   *map page 91, C-5*

With a population of about 1,300, Lusk owes its existence to the railroad (Chicago and Northwestern) and cattle shipping; its location at the junction of U.S. Routes 20 and 85 also helped establish it. Lusk is the county seat of Nio-brara, which has the smallest population (2,300 or so) of any county in the state. The cow population no doubt exceeds that of humans. Lusk is probably more remote than any other town of comparable size in the state (though there's a good deal of competition): it's about 70 miles west of Chadron, Nebraska; 60 miles east of Douglas; 80 miles south of Newcastle; and 70 miles north of Torrington. The town has a well-organized, self-reliant, sure-of-itself look. Lusk had a big moment in 1918, when a Buck Creek Dome oil strike suddenly boosted the population to 10,000. Things then settled down pretty quickly, but nearby Lance Creek is still an oil-spouting area.

Modern Lusk is a town where travelers can take refuge in spruce motels (notably the Covered Wagon) and restaurants. Annually in mid-July, a rather odd pageant celebrates one of the strangest stories that clings to the region. This particular legend concerns **Rawhide Butte**, that rugged height you see off to the west as you head north toward Lusk on Route 85. The butte gets its name from an emigrant traveling west, who swore he'd kill the first "Injun" he saw. The first he saw was an Indian maiden, and he shot her. She was suitably avenged when her relations caught him, skinned him alive, and stretched his skin to tan on top of Rawhide Butte—hence the name and the pageant. In fact, the road south and, particularly, north of Lusk is so full of old tales that a small book would be required to hold all of them. This was the preeminent stage route from Cheyenne to Deadwood in the Black Hills, and the fact that soldiers were stationed at the old Hat Creek Stage Station, about 20 miles north of Lusk, did not seem to prevent all sorts of devilment.

In 1876, some Black Hills freighters were attacked by 500 Indians, and rescued (Hollywood-style) by cavalry in the nick of time. Hat Creek was a favorite locale for holdups. Stuttering Brown, who had been sent by the stage owners to stop this kind of thing, died at the Hat Creek station after being shot by Persimmons Bill Chambers, who got his nickname from his birthplace in the unlikely (for a Western outlaw) state of South Carolina. Two men of the Tom Paris gang, operating along the road, were captured and taken to Cheyenne for trial. Court had just adjourned, so the criminals were taken right back toward Deadwood for another attempt. En route, a masked posse kidnapped them and strung them up on the nearest cottonwoods.

In August 1877, Boone May and a companion, guarding a passenger coach on a trip to Hat Creek, were attacked by road agents near Robbers Roost. May shot and killed one of the bandits, Frank Towle, whom he knew. When he got back to Cheyenne, he found that a reward of several thousand dollars had been posted for Towle, so he went back to the scene of the shooting, found Towle's corpse in the bushes, cut off his head, and returned to Cheyenne to collect his reward. But by that time, word had gotten around that Towle was no more. The reward offer had been withdrawn and May had made his return trip for nothing—and with a head on his hands.

Passengers on the new transcontinental railroad helped destroy the massive Plains bison herds with their track-side "hunting." (Courtesy, Kansas State Historical Society, Topeka)

Mrs. Thomas Durkin had no such difficulties. She took the stage to Deadwood right after the notorious murder of the entire Metz family, on the route in South Dakota, by that same Persimmons Chambers. Mrs. Durkin was carrying $10,000 in her handbag to finance her brother-in-law's new bank in Deadwood. Nobody stopped her.

The problem that faced Phatty Thompson could safely be called unique. In 1877, he decided that the dance hall girls in Deadwood were lonesome for pets. To fill that need, he gave the kids of Cheyenne 25 cents for each stray cat they brought him. Then he started north with a huge crate full of cats. En route, his wagon toppled over, the crate broke, and the cats got loose on the range. Somehow he got them back into the crate, took them to Deadwood, and sold them all to the girls for $10 to $20 a piece.

With so much colorful stagecoach history, it's not surprising that Lusk is home to the **Stagecoach Museum**. Climb up the steep, narrow stairs to find its reason for being: an old coach built by Abbott & Downing of Concord, New Hampshire, in the 1860s. Used for many years on the famed Cheyenne–Black Hills Stage and Express Line, the stagecoach is one of only two in the world; its sister is in the Smithsonian Institution. The difficult 300-mile stage route passed through Indian territory, over treacherous river crossings, and past hideouts of notorious road agents. Drivers made the trip in three days and three nights, and station stops lasted just long enough to change horses—usually less than three minutes. First-class fare from Cheyenne to Custer was $20; third class (which bought one a spot on the top of the coach) was half that. *322 South Main; 307-334-3444.*

The museum also houses a treasure chest broken open during the Canyon Springs stage robbery of 1879. (The chest once contained gold bullion from the Black Hills destined for Cheyenne.) Other attractions include an old buggy, a sulky, a dray, covered wagons, Indian artifacts, a photo collection from Niobrara County's one-room schoolhouses, and a 31-star U.S. flag from 1876. Ask for directions to the Hat Creek Stage Station, north of town.

■ NEWCASTLE   *map page 91, C 3*

Dozens of maudlin tales decorate the history of this especially lonely route, but by the time you get to Newcastle, in Weston County, the mountains and forests have encroached from the north and east, and you come to a very different and more amiable world. Newcastle is in the steep, forested foothills. It was established as a coal mining center and named nostalgically for the great English coal port, Newcastle upon Tyne. Nearby, the extinct mining town of Cambria was named for the ancient appellation of Wales.

Newcastle uncannily retains the atmosphere of a somewhat aged Appalachian mining center. The picturesque setting doesn't help the downtown area look any nicer, but there are pretty residential sections tucked away in the surrounding hills. It is properly looked upon as the southwestern gateway to the Black Hills. Try the local favorite, chicken-fried steak, at the 1917 landmark eatery, **Old Mill Inn**. *500 West Main Street; 307-746-2711.*

Upon leaving Newcastle, you are suddenly transported into another world: forest, mountains, deep valleys with rushing streams, fresher air, greener everything. First there's the dense ponderosa pine forest of the foothills. Eight miles north of town on U.S. 85 the road passes alongside a fantastic vision: the **Flying V Cambria Inn**. This huge Tudor castle, set in a valley (Salt Creek Canyon), was originally called the Casino and was built as a memorial to the discovery and development of anthracite coal at **Cambria.** The castle now functions as a summer pleasance, with a golf course and other amenities. A trail from it leads to the Cambrian ghost town. *23726 Highway 85; 307-746-2096.*

The hard coal mined at Cambria from the 1880s through the 1920s was the only such deposit being mined in the West. A polyglot population of Austrians, Italians, and Swedes survived in this atypically saloonless Wyoming town, where the owners forbade the sale of hard liquor (an Italian barkeep did manage to sell beer, however). The town and mines of Cambria closed down completely in 1928, and nothing is left of them in the canyons but debris.

By the time you reach Four Corners (with its combination store, cafe, and post office, and nothing more), you are on a high, rather bare plateau—a "hole" ringed by mountains. Most significant of these, to the west, is isolated and rugged Inyan Kara Mountain, intimately associated with Custer. The nearby South Dakota Black Hills lie to the east. Turning northwest toward Sundance on Wyoming State Highway 585, you cross the line into Crook County and into Wyoming's Black Hills.

(following pages) The Belle Fourche wends its way through the Black Hills near Hulett.

■ BLACK HILLS HISTORY

Sundance Mountain was the rendezvous place of the Sioux and their allies in summer, when they held their annual sun dance religious ceremonies, interspersed with berry-picking, dancing, and gossip. One particular ritual, however, was no laughing matter. It was meant to test a young brave's courage and endurance. Medicine men would gather the skin on the brave's back, run a knife through the fold, and thread a line of rawhide through the wound. In one version, the thong would be fastened to a high scaffold. The brave would then let himself fall from the scaffold, his weight supported only by the thong, and jerkily dance about until the rawhide tore through his flesh. The rest of the tribe would form a surrounding circle and dance and sing to help him keep up his courage. When he got through the ordeal the medicine men would cleanse the wound and lead him to a special teepee to rest and recover.

In contrast to this scene is the surprising story of another sort of encampment in the Bear Lodges, the local home for the Black Hills. In 1874, Lt. Colonel Custer and his cavalry were sent on a massive expedition to survey the Black Hills. The goal, ostensibly, was to determine the area's worth for its projected purchase from the Indians by the United States government. The less-publicized purpose was to find out if there was any gold there. At the time, Custer's was the largest and best-equipped expedition ever sent into the American Northwest. There were over 1,000 men involved—ten companies of the Seventh Cavalry; 100 Indian scouts, guides, and interpreters; 110 wagons, 1,000 cavalry horses, 300 beef cattle, and a military band. They camped first on Soldier Creek near Newcastle. They then proceeded up to Inyan Kara Mountain, that semi-isolated promontory just north of the Weston County line and west of what is now Wyoming State Highway 585. Custer climbed to the top and carved his name. Then he and his group camped on Spring Creek, a tributary of Sand Creek. The valley where they settled was a riot of wildflowers. Custer immediately named it Floral Valley, and a sort of flower festival took place. The soldiers festooned their hats and horses with wreaths of flowers, and the military band climbed up on a ledge and played "Gerry Owen," "The Mocking Bird," "The Blue Danube," and selections from *Il Trovatore*—surely one of the more fetchingly bizarre episodes in the history of the Wild West, but somehow in tune with at least the more amiable aspects of the Black Hills.

The mission was a (temporarily) secret and disastrous success. Horatio W. Ross, one of the two geologists on the expedition, made (or so it is supposed) the first

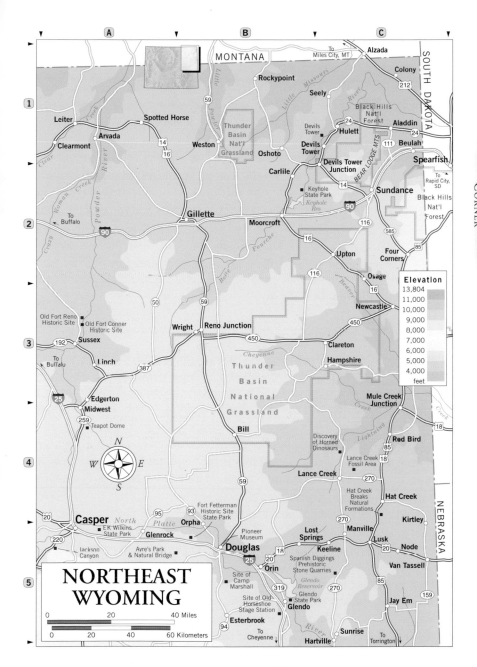

NORTHEAST WYOMING

A B C

MONTANA

To Miles City, MT · Alzada
Colony
212
Rockypoint
Seely
SOUTH DAKOTA

Leiter
Spotted Horse
Thunder Basin Nat'l Grassland
Arvada
Clearmont
Weston
Oshoto
Devils Tower
Hulett
Aladdin
Beulah
Spearfish
Carlile
Devils Tower Junction
To Rapid City, SD
Keyhole State Park
Keyhole Res.
Sundance
Black Hills Nat'l Forest

Gillette
Moorcroft
Upton
Four Corners

Osage
Newcastle

Elevation
13,804
11,000
10,000
9,000
8,000
7,000
6,000
5,000
4,000
feet

Old Fort Reno Historic Site
Old Fort Conner Historic Site
Sussex
Wright
Reno Junction
Clareton
Hampshire

To Buffalo
Linch
Thunder
Basin
National
Grassland
Mule Creek Junction

Edgerton
Midwest
Teapot Dome
Bill
Discovery of Horned Dinosaurs
Red Bird
Lance Creek Fossil Area

N W E S
Lance Creek
Hat Creek Breaks Natural Formations
Hat Creek

Casper North
Platte
Orpha
Fort Fetterman Historic Site State Park
E K Wilkins State Park
Glenrock
Jackson Canyon
Avre's Park & Natural Bridge
Douglas
Pioneer Museum
Lost Springs
Manville
Kirtley
Lusk
Node
Keeline
Orin
Spanish Diggings Prehistoric Stone Quarries
Van Tassell

**NORTHEAST
WYOMING**

0   20   40 Miles

0   20   40   60 Kilometers

Site of Camp Marshall
Glendo Reservoir
Glendo State Park
Glendo
Jay Em

Esterbrook
To Cheyenne
Sunrise
Hartville
To Torrington
NEBRASKA

authentic gold discovery in the Black Hills on July 30, 1874. When the news got back to Cheyenne, the rush was on.

This put the government in a difficult position. They had turned the area over to the Sioux in the treaty of 1868, which temporarily ended the ongoing war with the Sioux begun in the 1850s. Now, of course, they wanted it back. They decided to buy it back. They offered the Sioux either six million dollars cash, or rent of four hundred thousand dollars a year. The Sioux demanded six *hundred* million and a promise that the government would feed and clothe them for seven future generations. (After all, they had been there for seven past generations, so naturally the government should take care of the next seven.) Much to the surprise of the Sioux, the government decided to just *take* the Black Hills. They ordered the Sioux to evacuate by January 31, 1876. The Indians paid no particular attention; they went to winter quarters and ignored the injunction. Pretty soon the final phase of the war began, resulting in the ultimate victory of the whites. But only two years later, Custer would be mortally defeated by the Indians at Little Bighorn; no bands played at Little Bighorn, far to the west.

■ SUNDANCE   *map page 91, C-2*

Sundance lies in a valley between the Bear Lodges (northwest) and the Black Hills of South Dakota (east). With a population of about 1,160, Sundance is the only town of any prominence in Crook County. It's the county seat, and it lies in a delightful mountain-shaded valley with choice scenery and sights nearby. There are several cozy motels, and one nice-enough restaurant. Other than that, there's just a wide main street and a **historic museum** connected with the courthouse complex. Mementos of Harry Longabaugh (known as the Sundance Kid for his imprisonment in the local jail) are extensively displayed 307-283-3666. Otherwise, Sundance merely invites you to pass by.

A frontage road (old U.S. Route 14, kept paved for use by ranchers) heads east from town as a continuation of Sundance's main street. Though parallel to the interstate, it's prettier, and really part of the landscape. The town of **Beulah** (pop. 33) lies about 17 miles up the road. This tiny and picturesque town is the staging area for touring one of the most significant archeological sites of the region, maybe even the West: the Vore Buffalo Jump. For more than 300 years, Plains Indians stampeded bison over the rim of a bluff into a sinkhole, after which they harvested meat, skins and other raw materials from the dead animals. Scientists

(opposite) Glen "Gabby" Solberg enjoys a fall afternoon at the Aladdin store.

estimate that up to 20,000 bison were trapped here, making it a very effective means of hunting. In 1989, the family of Woodrow and Doris Vore donated this singular archaeological site to the University of Wyoming, and today visitors can watch as excavation and analysis continues. A museum in Sundance and interpretive programs help visitors understand the site. *Vore Buffalo Jump; outside of Beulah; 307-283-1192.*

Back at the junction of Route 14 and **Wyoming State Highway 111,** about 11 miles east of Sundance, begins one of Wyoming's best happy surprises. The trip up toward Aladdin (which lies east of the main road), and then westward on **Wyoming State Highway 24,** around the edge of the Bear Lodge Mountains, is one of the loveliest in the state. The scenery really deserves the word "unique," at least for Wyoming. On the east side of the mountains, where tributary creeks of the Belle Fourche (French for "Beautiful Fork") come down from darkly forested hills into sunny valleys, a pastoral world of meadows and glossy-leafed oak trees, farms, and small ranches exists—like some beautiful, tucked-away New England or Appalachian spot, only with an exotic Western accent. To the north are glimpses of vast, distant plains.

The highway circles around the mountains, sometimes through Black Hills National Forest. Some 45 miles from Sundance, you reach the hamlet of **Hulett** (pop. 408), a quaint place alongside the meek, meandering Belle Fourche River. Food and gas are available here for the first time since Sundance.

Finally comes Devils Tower, 10 miles south of Hulett. This is the one certified famous sight in Crook County. You get exciting, far views of it sticking above the forests all along the highway before Hulett.

■ DEVILS TOWER   *map page 91, B/C-1*

This startling monument, which rises 1,267 feet straight up over the valley of the now-tiny Belle Fourche, is the petrified core of a volcanic upsurge of lava, some 20 million years old. The volcano has melted away, but the core remains, a circular pylon of volcanic rock (phonolite) in long, vertical prisms. Like everything in the Black Hills, this formation was sacred to the Indians. They called the phenomenon Bear Lodge, or Mateo Tepee, which the whole surrounding mountain range is named for. Various rather charming legends give accounts of the tower's odd appearance. According to one, maidens were gathering flowers when they were

(opposite) An unusual apparition in the daytime, Devils Tower displays an even more distinct aura at night.

attacked by bears. They climbed up a rock, and the bears followed after. The gods made the rock grow higher and higher as the bears clawed their way up, causing striations in the stone. Eventually the bears fell off and were killed (a butte in South Dakota is supposed to be the corpse of one such bear). The girls braided ropes from their flowers and got down safely. A similar story tells of seven little maidens attacked by bears while playing. These maidens, too, got up on a rock. This one shot up into the sky. Once again, bears clawed the rock, broke their claws, and fell down. The children went soaring up into the sky and became the stars composing the constellation of the Pleiades, or Seven Sisters.

Devils Tower and the surrounding 1,347 acres was the country's first national monument, created by Theodore Roosevelt on September 24, 1906. It stands as a natural memorial to his pioneering efforts as a conservationist. More recently, the climax of the movie *Close Encounters of the Third Kind,* the Spielberg classic, was filmed at Devils Tower. Extraterrestrials and spaceship landings somehow seem appropriate for the tower.

Nowadays this spectacle is inundated by crowds on nice summer days. Tourists anxiously watch mountain climbers crawling up the impossible heights. The first ascent was on July 4, 1893, when two local ranchers gained the top with the help

(above) Sunset colors the face of stumplike Devils Tower.
(opposite) Devils Tower's massive columns dwarf two climbers.

of wooden pegs they had jammed into one long crack. Other notable incidents on the tower include a stunt perpetrated by George Hopkins, who in 1941 parachuted out of a plane and landed on the summit. His rope, however, was blown away and he was stranded for six days until a climbing team led by the famed Jack Durrance (for which one classic climbing route up the tower is named) rescued him. By now, ascending the more than 200 routes is an established science, and 5,000 visitors go up each year, on their own or carefully guided. Native Americans, who consider Devils Tower sacred, want the climbing stopped, and in 2006, an updated climbing management plan provided for continued voluntary closures in June and climber education programs. Several years ago there was also a push to rechristen the monument Mateo Tepee. After some heated public debate, the effort was abandoned. Roundabout the tower there are long, forested walks. Postcards and information are available in the building at the edge of the parking lot, but no food. The eerie quality of the place comes out best in the early morning, when the deer are about and there are fewer people, and in the evening, when the light enhances the always awe-inspiring shaft of this uncanny column.

■ BLACK HILLS EXIT *map page 91, B/C-2*

On the way to Moorcroft, you pass through **Keyhole State Park.** The park includes **13,000-acre Keyhole Reservoir,** another one of those many water parks of which Wyoming is so full and so proud. These offer the local citizens, particularly those living on dry plains, some refreshing summer recreation, but they are often not particularly scenic or secluded. The recently incorporated town of **Pine Haven** (pop. 235) is situated near the southern end of the reservoir and offers all the services needed to enjoy the waterhole and surrounding hills any time of year.

All through this corner of Wyoming there are various other side roads, vistas, and campsites. On the whole, Crook County makes for a sort of enchanted island of refreshment, surrounded by an ocean of barren plains, ranges, and badlands.

◆ MOORCROFT *map page 91, B-2*

Moorcroft was named by the English Miller brothers, owners of a big horse ranch nearby, after their ancestral estate at home, Moorcroft Acres. The town became a stockloading center after the first railroad came along. From Moorcroft on, you are quite definitely out on the plains of what is broadly designated the Powder River Basin (though at this point the river itself is a good 50 miles to the west). The direct route across the basin is Interstate 90 through Gillette.

◆ **UPTON**   *map page 91, C-2*

But if you want to linger a while in the Black Hills, then head east from Devils Tower on old U.S. Route 14 to the junction of Wyoming State Highway 116 (just west of Sundance and south of Interstate 90). This road passes west of Inyan Kara Mountain and near the area of Custer's Floral Valley. Handsome, open, rolling country with forested hills lies all about. Eventually you come to Upton, almost, but not quite, on the plains. The town is built on a long, lone, low, pine-crested ridge—the last gasp of the Black Hills and of such woodland greenery for a hundred miles south and west. Upton greets the traveler with the surprising sight of a town golf course, and then a sign proclaiming (more or less) that it's the best little ol' town in the world. That's debatable, but the town is nice enough.

From Upton, U.S. Route 16 heads northwest back up to Moorcroft and Interstate 90, passing through a section of the Thunder Basin Grasslands, which cover a large part of the plains to the south.

■ THUNDER BASIN OVERVIEW   *map page 91*

When you leave Moorcroft, you cross the border into Campbell County and onto the Great Plains. The drive from Cheyenne to Newcastle might give any traveler a sufficiently good taste of such plains, but on that route the plains are broken up by buttes and rivers, valleys, farmlands, towns, and views of distant mountains. This section of Wyoming, on the other hand, presents an unadulterated sweep of almost total emptiness.

From the Appalachians to the Wind Rivers, the North Pole to the Laramies, there's nothing to stop the wind. This slice of Wyoming remains pretty much the same as when the trappers, Indians, soldiers, emigrants, and still-resident cowboys and sheepherders first saw it (though oddly enough, it hasn't the special historical color of the lower eastern border). The only things really different from the past are the actual road you drive on, the few traces of oil and coal you come upon, and a secretive coal railroad (Burlington), which you don't see until you get to the town of Bill. Most tourists don't tour this part of Wyoming, for obvious reasons; but to experience the Thunder Basin is to grasp the vast emptiness so integral to Wyoming's character. After all, the name Wyoming is Algonquin for "bright and shining plains."

For the some 150 miles from the Montana border down to the Platte River, there's nothing except Gillette. For another sweep of 100 miles to the west, from Casper (on the Platte) to Shoshoni, you get more such plains, but these are always in sight of some sizable mountains (however distant), and there are quite a few little settlements along the way; in the vast area from Douglas north to Gillette, and way beyond, it's just space all the way.

To give an idea of the vastness of Wyoming's plains, imagine a straight, diagonal line of flight from Gillette to Rock Springs. It would pass over virtually nothing at all but uninhabited terrain and some mines and oil wells. It would cross only three major highways—Interstate 25 and U.S. Routes 26 and 287. The Sweetwater would be your biggest stream, the Antelope Hills or Green Mountains your only serious bumps. You would cross the Continental Divide twice on the line of flight over the Great Divide Basin. At last, you would pass over Interstate 80, thick with its trucks and travelers, and the metropolis (relatively speaking) of Rock Springs.

There's a question of just how much of this space can be profitably absorbed by the average traveler. It depends first of all on conditions. Steady rains or completely cloudy weather are most unfavorable. Terrific heat or cold are most unpleasant. But varied skies, especially earlier and later in the day, can be particularly glorious. Under the proper conditions, these empty, enormous stretches have an oceanic quality of purity and variety. In the broad, hot glare of noon, the landscape flattens out and loses all its color. By later afternoon, a miracle of transformation takes place, and by evening light, what seemed total desolation becomes a symphony of blues and browns and greens and magical distances; and toward the edges, remote peaks and pinnacles.

This aspect of the state presents what the chamber of commerce must recognize as a touristic problem of considerable dimension. To get from one group of pretty parts in the southeast and northeast to another in the northwest, you have to traverse this barren diagonal somewhere. You can avoid most of it, notably by a dash from the Black Hills to Buffalo via Interstate 90; but then you will certainly miss a big slice of native Wyoming: austere but, in its own way, beautiful.

■ GILLETTE   *map page 91, B-2*

Gillette is itself fairly austere, as well. It has only one economic reason for existence: coal. It's the center for strip-mining of low-sulphur coal, still useful for power plants. The area roundabout is full of huge gouges where the coal comes from. As far back as the early 1800s, trappers and explorers were puzzled and terrified, as were the Indians before them, by the pall of smoke that sometimes hung over the area from fires in subterranean coal seams. These fires, ignited by lightning, sometimes burned for years, opening sudden smoldering rifts into which unwary horsemen might ride to their deaths. No trees or natural greenery surround Gillette. It's too far from either the Black Hills or the Big Horns for mountain views. There's not even a sizable river.

Yet Gillette is a hive of activity and a source of wealth. Until recently, it was a boom town of oil and coal; it's still well-supported by that old standby, coal and now coalbed methane. Roundabout is a great stock-raising area. As a result of this prosperity, the school system is the envy of the state. It has its own planetarium, and culture is encouraged through symphony concerts, theater, and art exhibits.

There are, however, two Gillettes: the old town on the north side, along the railroad tracks, and the new town to the south, along Interstate 90. Old Gillette is a compact, rather snug city. You still see brown prairie at the end of most streets. The business section is neatly impressive, with big, modern bank buildings and planted trees, which are such a pleasing new touch in Wyoming cities. There are good stores and restaurants, and a general air of solid establishment. The residential section is one of close-packed small houses, thickly shaded by trees and bushes, as though to protect them against blizzards. There is a beautiful green cemetery next to a town park on the heights to the south, and on the high points of town are perched a few elegant houses with glimpses of the rangelands far beyond. The inevitable grid is distinguished by its patriotically named streets commemorating not presidents, but Wyoming's founding fathers, such as Carey, Kendrick, and Warren (whose memorial plaques adorn the capitol rotunda in Cheyenne). You still hear train whistles from the long coal trains that rumble through town.

New Gillette, the obvious result of the late boom, is a horrific phantasmagoria of modern synthetic culture: every syndicated fast-food joint in the United States, from McDonalds to Pizza Hut; big, bare shopping malls; massive, impersonal motels; and packed traffic going south toward Interstate 90. This is perhaps the most flagrant contrast between an urban Old West of a stable, indigenous sort and a New West of national standardization with nothing uniquely Wyoming about it whatsoever. There is also a residential "new part of town," with snappy, modern houses huddled together up on bare buttes—what might be called suburbia.

There are exceptions to "nowhere fare" in Gillette. **Bailey's Bar and Grill** is housed in a handsome brick building at 301 S. Gillette Avenue; great for chicken-fried steak or Mexican standards. For steak and seafood, journey to **Packard's Grill**

at 408 S. Douglas Highway. To see the state's largest dance club, and for steak and seafood, head to **Boot Hill Nightclub** at 910 N. Gurley Avenue.

■ ROUTES THROUGH THE PLAINS   *map page 91*

There are several different routes south from Gillette to the Platte River. Wyoming State Highway 59, discussed in the next section, takes you through the ultimate of Wyoming's wide, open spaces.

An alternate route, for those particularly interested in oil history and development, swings southwest from Highway 59 onto Wyoming State Highway 387, past the brand-new mining town of Wright, and through the oil fields of Edgerton and Midwest. From there, Wyoming State Highway 959 heads southwest past Teapot Dome to Interstate 25, and then to Casper. (That route will be discussed later in this chapter.)

An unadventurous route that bypasses Gillette takes Interstate 90 from Moorcroft to Buffalo, and then Interstate 25 down to Casper. The scenery along that route is gorgeous—the Big Horn Mountains, badlands, great rangelands, and the Laramies as you approach Casper—but of course you won't get a picture of Wyoming life.

A variant route leading north from Gillette on old U.S. Routes 14 and 16 also takes you through beautiful country, to a spectacular crossing of the Powder River in its canyon, and then either to Buffalo (Route 16) or Sheridan (Route 14) through increasingly picturesque landscapes.

All these different routes have their beauties and interests; but the emphasis here is on the more offbeat Wyoming State Highway 59, which is less traveled and gives you a real exposure to these impressive plains.

■ THUNDER BASIN NATIONAL GRASSLAND   *map page 91, B-3/4*

Just south of Gillette, Highway 59 cuts down from Interstate 90. You pass Reno Junction after 38 miles. After another 40 miles, you pass Bill. In 35 more miles, you're in Douglas. That's it. This route is pretty much a test of how the traveler feels about wide-open spaces. If you feel expanded and released and inclined to yell "Whoopee!" and "Don't fence me in!" this is certainly your place. If not, it's not.

What you see is something called the Thunder Basin National Grassland (a distant

(preceding pages) Some of the loveliest ranching country in Wyoming lies near the tiny Powder River Basin settlement of Recluse.

cousin of the national parks and forests). This enormous stretch (572,000,acres) of more than two million acres has been set aside by the government as a soil preservation and conservation experiment. During the 1930s, when dust bowls became a national menace, it became obvious that the well-meaning and open-hearted homestead program, instead of making for happy rural prosperity, was creating a wasteland. Soil that should not have been plowed, was. The idea behind the grasslands project was to try to restore nature's status quo. National grasslands are scattered about the Plains states, notably Nebraska and eastern Colorado, but Thunder Basin is by far the largest and longest-established. The Bureau of Land Management controls not only grazing in the basin, but also oil exploratory roads and even archaeological digs and access—anything that might permanently damage the rich, but fragile, ground cover. Many dust bowls, past and present, might have been prevented if this policy had been inaugurated sooner and in more places. 307-745-2300.

As you come down from Gillette, the country is at first all grass—grass not only on the flat places, but covering the buttes and ridges as well. Little oil pumps bob up and down. But the single most striking sight along the road is the big buffalo ranch some dozen miles south of town. Here, the green, hilly range near the roadside is populated by dozens of the great, black beasts of both sexes and all ages. Though they are really domestic stock, just like sheep or cattle, the setting here is so like a George Catlin painting that you expect at any moment to see Indians charging from around the grassy bumps. Antelope and, of course, cattle and horses, also hang about.

One of the only towns on Highway 59 is newcomer **Wright.** It's off to the west from Reno Junction, a sort of model company town attached to new coal excavations. But you don't see these from Highway 59. The town itself looks very new and spic-and-span. It's sort of a shock, sitting bare out in the middle of the enormous space and silence.

After Wright, the country flattens and grows less fertile and much emptier—sagebrush, rather than just grass. Far to the east is the dim, grim, tall castle of a coal mine establishment. Otherwise, all is earth and sky—and sheep. Eventually you cross one of the usually dry forks of the Cheyenne River, with its inevitable cottonwoods. Here a new Wyoming state rest area provides a pleasant, much-needed stopping place. Then you come to Bill.

Except for Reno Junction and Wright, **Bill** is the only dot on the map before Douglas. It's been on the map for years, but Bill's future is sadly uncertain. Bill is a small store and post office operated for years by an old-timer, sure enough named Bill. But Bill, the postmaster, eventually died, and Bill, the town, was put up for sale.

Patronized by local ranchers, passersby, and railroad men from the Burlington (which has been sneaking down parallel from Gillette and now appears alongside the road), Bill must serve a purpose vital enough to preserve it. After all, there's nothing closer than Wright or Douglas. It should still have some future.

By this time, the countryside has begun to degenerate visually. Like some interminable, not so interesting symphony, things begin to dawdle scenically (just before a finale with all the trumpets blasting): few or no hills, the close-by railroad impinging on the sense of isolation and freedom, not even much in the way of far vistas. And then the road crosses the tracks and turns away west. Suddenly, you get a first glimpse of blue Laramie Peak over the undulating rangelands; then (about 10 miles north of Douglas), one of those jaw-dropping visions that highlight travel in Wyoming: from a rising sweep of the road, the whole panorama of the Laramies is strung out before you, southeast to northwest. After the long preparation of the grasslands, it's dramatic and exciting beyond expression.

■ DOUGLAS   *map page 91, B-5*

When you reach Douglas, with a population of about 5,300, you are no longer on the plains, but in the Platte River Valley. Here, that great emigrant trail comes around the foot of the Laramie Mountains, following the water and trees. You're now back in civilization, so to speak. Douglas is a relaxed, pleasant town with nice, comfortable residential areas, big houses shaded by big trees, and an old-fashioned business section that's somewhat disorganized by railroad sidings.

A big collection of old train cars sits outside the town's historic depot. Down along the river are the fairgrounds, where the famous annual Wyoming State Fair is held in August. After the immense bareness of the plains, Douglas seems a very welcome refreshment. Douglas is famous (or perhaps infamous) for its jackalope, the largest in the state. Jackalopes are supposedly the offspring of the antelope and the jackrabbit, both denizens of the plains to the north. In the old days, dudes were fooled into thinking they were real animals.

◆ DOUGLAS SIGHTS

The people of Douglas point with pride to their spacious **Pioneer Museum,** located just inside the fairgrounds. Here you will find the rifle of Nate Champion, a suspected rustler murdered in the Johnson County War; an army trumpet and bullets from the Custer massacre site; and saddles that once belonged to outlaw Tom Horn and to Governor Joseph Carey. Check out the special "running irons" used by rustlers to alter cattle brands, and the bison-fur mittens worn by Portugee Phillips on his famous ride from Fort Phil Kearny.

Back rooms house a gorgeous old Wurlitzer jukebox, various fossils, and several wagons and carriages, including an army escort wagon from the 1880s. The extraordinary collection of Indian artifacts includes a Sioux wooden flute, beaded moccasins, an Indian bow from the Wagon Box fight, hundreds of arrowheads and other implements from the Spanish Diggings site southwest of Lusk, and even a stone war club from the Black Hills. Before you exit this fine museum, drop a penny in the slot of the old-fashioned scales to check your weight. *400 W. Center; 307-358-9288.*

Signs mark the exits off Interstate 25 to **Ayre's Natural Bridge,** a handsome rock arch in the mountains. There is a wealth of natural beauty and possible excursions up in the Laramies. Hiking and riding trails abound, but it's wise to check out road conditions and directions locally. *307-358-3532.*

Fort Fetterman, well worth a visit, is named in honor of one of the unfortunate victims of the Powder River Indian wars (see page 149). The fort, in operation from 1867 to 1882, can be reached via a good minor road, Wyoming State Highway 93. It's hard to explain the odd impact of the fort. Unlike Fort Laramie, there is really nothing left that's original. One restored old building houses a nice, small museum that explains the fort's history with exhibits and a 15-minute video. However, the site itself does conjure historical meditations.

At the time Fort Fetterman was activated, it was the only military post in the vast region west of Fort Laramie and directly south of the Powder River forts, which were closed in 1867. The high, bare promontory on which the fort sits—with mountains behind, the big, green Platte winding below, and the great tan plains endlessly north—is somehow the perfect setting for the epic tales of those days. Soldiers, Indians, emigrants, and cowboys inevitably people the scene in one's imagination. It's as evocative as Fort Laramie, and the setting is more beautiful. *Seven miles northwest of Douglas on Highway 93; 307-358-2864.*

■ GLENROCK   *map page 91, A-5*

Wyoming State Highway 93 continues across the river and northwest through the rangelands, with mountain views emerging behind. Joining State Highway 95, it returns to the river at Glenrock. From there on you're in oil country. Casper is 30 miles west. You can keep on Wyoming State Highway 20 (and 26) from Glenrock to see a mixture of refineries and pleasant river valley ranches, or (more efficient) go up

Interstate 25, which zips along through surprisingly bare rangeland. In any case, when you get to the outskirts of Casper you had better get onto the interstate to avoid the traffic.

Not to be missed in Glenrock is the **Hotel Higgins** (also see page 335). This hotel, built on the Oregon Trail in 1916, has been beautifully restored as a bed-and-breakfast with two suites and four rooms, all with private baths. Interesting antiques are everywhere, from the sewing machine sink in the lobby ladies room to the glamorous lampshades in the Highlander Bar. It houses the **Paisley Shawl**, a gourmet restaurant that attracts people from throughout central Wyoming. *416 W. Birch Street; 800-458-0144 or 307-436-9212.*

■ THE OIL ROAD TO CASPER   *map page 91, A-4*

A better preparation for the oil-town character of Casper might be the alternate route (Wyoming State Highway 387 at Reno Junction) from Gillette that goes right through Midwest and the Salt Creek oil fields, where Casper's first oil spouted a hundred years ago. The scenery around **Midwest** is dramatic—sharp buttes thrusting up towers over gulches and badlands. One of these buttes south of Midwest is the notorious **Teapot Dome** (which doesn't look anything like a teapot; also see page 117, next chapter).

Midwest itself is a striking example of the impact of industrialism. Coming out of the empty range, you suddenly enter a valley of rumpled pink and white badlands, completely covered in every direction by oil pumps and electric lines and century-old evidence of use and abuse. It's quite a shock. Just as shocking is the by-now antique and terribly shabby shack-town of Midwest, huddled slightly to the north of the fields in struggling greenery, with some of its bungalows boarded up. It's a fascinating place, but certainly not pretty. The whole history of Casper is intimately involved with the goings-on here.

(opposite) Black-tailed prairie dogs, a threatened species, are concentrated in northeast Wyoming.

NORTH-CENTRAL
PLAINS & BIGHORN BASIN

◆ **HIGHLIGHTS**

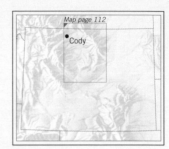

Map page 112

Cody

◆ **AREA OVERVIEW**

Casper is the off-and-on biggest city in Wyoming. Casper's fortunes were once based on oil, and oil isn't what it used to be, as any Texan will tell you. Today, older towns like Laramie and Cheyenne have developed a sort of staid, settled, tree-shaded character that's almost mellow. Nobody would say the same of Casper.

Beyond Casper, you're in the Wild West. There are cowboy towns here, badlands, and plenty of history. For part of the way, the route follows the old Oregon Trail, still rutted by the wheels of the covered wagons that carried hundreds of thousands of emigrants westward before the arrival of the transcontinental railroad in 1869. As mountains go, the Laramies, Snowies, and Black Hills of eastern Wyoming don't begin to compare with the Big Horns in this part of the country. Wyoming has its share of desolate highways cutting through the arid, the flat, and the uninteresting, but they lead straight on to some of the most awe-inspiring panoramas in the state.

Weather: Average temperatures are in the mid to upper 80s from May through September and summer rain is rare. Wind is a fact of life and can howl in the winter. Thunderstorms occur on hot days and release short cloudbursts in the midafternoon.

Food & Lodging: There is a full range of lodging options in Casper, Riverton, Thermopolis, Worland, Meeteetse, and Ten Sleep. The few other small towns have hotels that can prove most welcoming. Campsites are easily found throughout the Bighorn Basin.

■ History of the North Platte Area

From the 1840s on, emigrants on the Oregon Trail came along the North Platte River and traveled west through the future site of the city of Casper on their way to the Sweetwater and to South Pass. For two decades, the site of Casper, where many crossed the river, was crawling with emigrants. A Mormon ferry crossed the North Platte as early as 1847, and in 1859 troops were stationed there to protect travelers. That same year, a rickety bridge that succeeded the ferry was replaced by a fancy new one costing $60,000. A military post was finally established at the bridgehead in 1863.

On July 26, 1865, 3,000 Indians on the warpath after the Sand Creek Massacre in Colorado assembled in the hills above the North Platte River. Sergeant Amos T. Custard, heading a party of army wagons coming from the Sweetwater toward the Platte, was ambushed by Indians 17 miles upriver at Willow Springs. Twenty-one-year-old Lieutenant Caspar W. Collins, who had just reported to the post at the bridge the night before, was ordered to lead a party of 25 men to rescue Custard.

Collins crossed the new bridge and followed a road northwest, where he was attacked by a force of some 600 charging Cheyennes and 1,800 Sioux. He was, shall we say, outnumbered. The fighting was hard. In attempting to rescue a fallen soldier, Collins tried to lift the wounded man to his saddle, and his horse ran away, straight into Indian forces. Collins's body was found the next day, mutilated almost beyond recognition. All of Custard's party was killed, but only four of the Collins party. The following autumn, Maj. General Pope declared the army post at the Platte River bridge to be "hereafter known as Fort Caspar"—not Fort Collins, as might be expected. That name had already been given to the fort (now city) in Colorado, in honor of Caspar's father. The one in Wyoming is still called Fort Caspar, but unfortunately for Caspar's memory, the names of the town and the mountain behind it are, for some obscure reason, spelled *Casper*, not *Caspar*. No one knows why. One explanation is that some ignorant mail clerk made the mistake on all the mailings. In any case, Caspar is the fort, and Casper the city.

Fort Caspar is nicely reconstructed, with a big and prestigious **historical museum.** It's on the far southwest side of town, on a bend of the Platte, and is easily reached by the wonderful Wyoming State Highway 258, which encircles the whole city. (This road, incidentally, is itself really worth the drive, since you get a panoramic view of the city to the north and a splendid view of Casper Mountain to the south.) The restoration and museum are well worth the detour, but the park

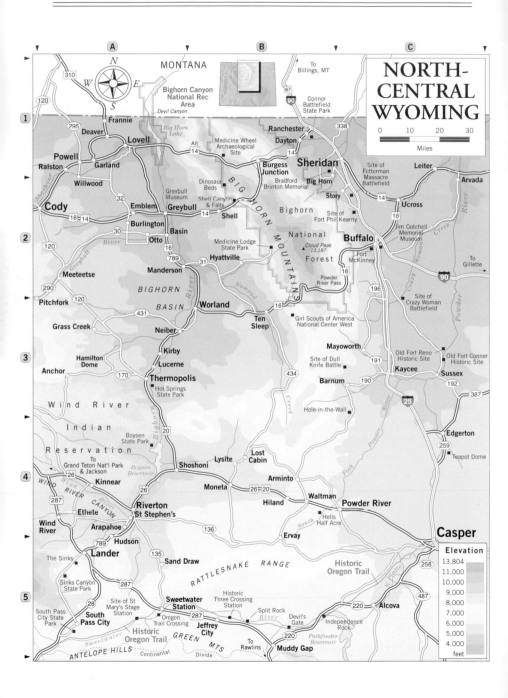

NORTH-CENTRAL WYOMING

0   10   20   30

Miles

Elevation

13,804	
11,000	
10,000	
9,000	
8,000	
7,000	
6,000	
5,000	
4,000	
feet	

in which they stand is a disappointment. Instead of a nice, big, city park full of cottonwoods, it's a skimpy area surrounded by commerce on all sides, unworthy of both the fort and the city. Too bad. This should by rights be Casper's crown jewel. *4001 Fort Caspar Road; 307-235-8462.*

■ CASPER   *map page 112, C-5*

The first ranch house in the Casper vicinity was built in 1876 on the CY Ranch of Judge Joseph M. Carey, patriarch of one of the state's most famous families, who trailed his 12,000 head of cattle up from Austin. (Carey later became a U.S. senator and governor of Wyoming.) The nearby Goose Egg Ranch was founded by the Searight brothers, who arrived from Texas with 27,000 head of cattle. In 1877 they built a large stone ranch house that was used by Owen Wister in *The Virginian* as the setting for that Saturday night dance where all the babies were deliberately mixed up by prankish cowboys. (The babies had been lined up on the floor during the course of the dance; when the parents got home, miles away, the resulting mix-up took quite a while to straighten out.) All this, less than two decades after Lt. Caspar Collins lost his life.

The usual rough stuff went on during Casper's founding. It became a cattle shipping center (Chicago & Northern) after 1885, when Judge Carey of the CY designated part of his ranch the site for a new town and railroad station. By the time the first passenger coach pulled in on June 15, nearly 100 people already lived there. The town was plotted, lots were sold for about $250 each, lumber for construction was carted down from the forests on Casper Mountain, and the city was ready to go.

By 1889, there were eight saloons along Main Street, and the town was incorporated. Although there was a town ordinance prohibiting the discharge of firearms on the streets, within a year the mayor himself had beaten his man to the draw in a duel on Main Street while passersby ducked for cover. It was also unlawful for any woman to "use any vile, profane, or indecent language, or to act in a boisterous or lewd manner, or to smoke any cigar, cigarette, or pipe on Casper's streets, or to frequent the barroom of any saloon between 7 A.M. and 10 P.M." This, of course, didn't interfere with business at all, 10 P.M. to 7 A.M. being the real shank of the evening. As usual, the public school and the Congregational Church were starting up at this same time. Virtue and vice grew side by side.

Natrona County was authorized in 1886, but, "owing to financial inability," didn't function till 1890. There was a fight with the neighboring settlement of Bessemer, which intended to quickly surpass Casper and snatch away the honor of county seat. Casper won. Bessemer just faded away.

◆ MODERN CASPER

Nowadays, Casper (pop. 51,000) itself has no interest in being Old Western. It's the Chicago, let's say, of Wyoming, and just wants to get ahead. It's brisk, clean, busy, and full of fine new buildings; it has nice new residential sections up the slopes south of town, and is altogether a place of many advantages. There are all sorts of driving, hiking, riding, and camping options up in the mountains, as well as plenty of wide-open rangeland to the north. Water recreation and wildlife areas are found not far away to the west, on the beautiful Alcova, Pathfinder, and Seminoe reservoirs (see below).

People once came to Casper to strike it rich. Now they stay because they count their riches differently. The low stress of a 20-minute commute, the joy of a blue-ribbon trout stream on the edge of town, and a ski area within sight mean much to the young families and many retirees choosing to live here. As a belt buckle sold in the state proclaims, "Wyoming is what America was." That doesn't mean the Wild West. It means the sweet life before the late-20th-century woes of big cities and crumbling communities. In Casper, walk Eleventh Street in the "tree area" crossing Center, Beech, and Lincoln, to recall how beautiful a small town with mature trees and varied, charming homes can be. Visit the **Nicolaysen Art Museum and Discovery Center** (400 E. Collins Drive; 307-235-5247), imaginatively designed in the kind of old brick industrial building that was once demolished for "progress." Or marvel at the Casper-based Wyoming Symphony Orchestra, which is considered one of the country's best small-city orchestras and made up almost entirely of local musicians. 307-266-1478.

For some reason, two of Casper's best restaurants are Italian, and **Bosco's** (847 E. A Street) is the more intimate one, featuring unusual dishes, "Heart Smart" cooking, and killer hot-fudge sundaes.

Cottage Cafe (116 S. Lincoln Street) has tasty, eclectic, light breakfasts, lunches, and dinners in a charming cottage.

The **Goose Egg Inn** (5 miles southwest of Casper on U.S. 220; 307-473-8838) is a jeans-and-boots place popular with local ranchers. Beef is the thing to order in this cozy atmosphere. The inn is next to a bald-eagle winter nesting area.

La Costa (1600 E. 2nd Street; 307-235-6599), a wonderfully authentic Mexican restaurant, is well worth a visit.

■ CENTRAL PLAINS *map page 112, B-5*

When you finally leave Casper and its rather extensive fringe of development, you're back in the Wild West with a vengeance. Through Natrona County and into the eastern part of Fremont County lies another great swath of plains stretching east to west, unlike the north-south-running plains between Gillette and Douglas. There is a distinct physical difference between these two areas. Whereas the eastern plains are uninterrupted prairie, the terrain west of Casper is broken and surrounded by all sorts of mountains, buttes, ridges, and badlands, and carved by river valleys, notably that of the Sweetwater. You're in sight of mountains most of the time as you pass through. Right in the middle of the region is the rugged, bare, forbidding, and no-doubt aptly named **Rattlesnake Range.** Along the southern edge of the plains are the curious short ranges of the central belt. To the north, the Owl Creeks and the very end of the Big Horn Mountains cut these plains off from the Bighorn Basin.

So this second, weltering installment of the plains has a good deal more to offer visually than the plains farther east. Furthermore, the trip west from Casper along the Platte and Sweetwater Rivers is not only beautiful, but chock-full of historic interest. This route follows the Oregon Trail, practically retracing the still-evident path of the covered wagons, until the trail branches west toward South Pass. History follows you all the way.

Shortly after leaving Casper, heading west on Wyoming State Highway 220 and following the North Platte River, you pass the site of Bessemer, which once challenged Casper's bid for county seat. One might expect to find ruins of some great steel mill here, but such a thing never existed. The historical marker that once pointed the place out seems to have vanished. The town was founded in 1888 as a grandiose real estate development that was to be the "Queen City of the West"— 49 city blocks were planned for a future capital of Wyoming—but by 1891 it was abandoned. Casper was never seriously threatened.

Thirty miles beyond Casper, you come to an area of spectacular dams on the Platte, creating Alcova, Pathfinder, and Seminoe Reservoirs. Though miles of beautiful riverside wilderness were submerged and destroyed, the resultant lakes are also very beautiful and provide campsites, a game refuge, and recreation areas. A road detours southward from State Highway 220 to small Alcova, west to large Pathfinder, then back to the main highway. It gives you wonderful views of bare but fascinating, subtly colored open spaces and of oddly shaped mountain masses.

THE TEAPOT DOME SCANDAL

In 1895, the Pennsylvania Oil and Gas Company erected Wyoming's first refinery, in Casper. Crude oil had to be hauled by wagon from the fields, 20 miles away, which delayed prosperity until pipelines were finally built in 1916. The antics of Wyoming's previous booms were repeated once again. (Most of the speculative trading took place in the lobby of the Midwest Hotel, then the Hemming.) Land grabbers and claim jumpers forced legitimate companies to hire line-riders to protect their leases. The Midwest Oil Company grew in ten years from a tiny local corporation to a $50-million outfit, before being swallowed by the bigger-yet giant Standard Oil.

Casper's population jetted up to 30,000 in 1925, with 2,000 more outside city limits. The value of lots and land skyrocketed. Luxurious hotels and office buildings sprang up. A million dollars was spent on a new high school. Casper aimed to supplant both Denver as the metropolis of the Far West and Cheyenne as the capital of Wyoming. But in the later 1920s the boom ended, and the depression of the 1930s completed the debacle. In that decade, the population decreased by half, to about 16,000.

Under the Harding Administration in the early 1920s, Casper made headlines, along with Standard Oil and the Teapot Dome. The dome was an old stagecoach landmark that may once have actually resembled some sort of teapot. (Erosion, however, has been at work.) By 1910, oil fields surrounded it. President Taft closed the area around the dome to private exploitation and made it a naval oil reserve. Early in his administration, Harding transferred the dome from the Navy to the Department of the Interior, where his great and good friend Albert B. Fall was secretary. Fall leased it secretly, without competitive bids, to his great and good friend Harry Sinclair, whose local operation was the Mammoth Crude Oil Company.

One of the first wells Sinclair drilled there proved to be the largest gusher in state history, producing 25,000 barrels a day. Between 1922 and 1927, Mammoth drilled 87 wells there. Oil gushed, but scandal leaked out. In early 1929, the Supreme Court invalidated the lease and restored control to the Navy. Sinclair was imprisoned for three months and fined a mere $500, after which he went back to pumping oil. Fall, however, got a three-year sentence and was fined $300,000. He was the first U.S. cabinet officer to land in jail. It was one of the major scandals of the Harding administration, and the name "Teapot Dome" was known throughout the country.

(opposite) Floor hand James Lock works an oil-drilling rig in central Wyoming.

This whole area, in fact, especially from Casper to Muddy Gap, is the quintessence of Wyoming's characteristic plains-and-mountain scenery. Grim under the glare of noon or leaden skies, it blossoms miraculously under other more gracious lighting effects and viewing times. If you find the landscape dour, barren, forbidding, or boring, hurry on north. If you can respond to the constant enticement of the varied distant ranges, the enormous open spaces, a meandering river valley, moving patterns of shade and sun, subtle color variations, the buildup of storm clouds, and the effects of early-morning and late-afternoon light, then you're properly initiated into the special beauties of Wyoming.

■ INDEPENDENCE ROCK *map page 112, B/C-5*

Thirteen miles beyond Alcova lies **Independence Rock**, the most striking and famous milestone on the Oregon Trail. Having crossed Poison Spider Creek and bypassed the Rattlesnake Range on their way west, the emigrants stopped with relief on the wide, watered meadows that surround the rock. Rounded, pink, and isolated, it juts out of the flat valley like a miniature version of Australia's Ayers Rock. The naked hump has been described by geologists as "one of the most significant erosion remnants in the West." What makes it even more significant is its long history as a beacon and campsite along the trail.

Summer thunderstorms frequent the skies of central Wyoming.

CATTLE KATE

Wyoming, despite its atmosphere of aggressive masculinity, has also shown an aggressively feminist side. The Equality State commissioned the country's first female justice of the peace, Esther Hobart Morris, and elected the first female state governor, Nellie Tayloe Ross. These worthy ladies have been joined in Wyoming history by some others perhaps not as worthy, but who are still prime examples of independent women, among them Calamity Jane and Cattle Kate.

Calamity Jane's Indian fighting and her love affair with Wild Bill Hickok during the Black Hills gold rush play a prominent part in Western legend. Unfortunately, in the harsh light of modern revisionism, it's become evident that none of her self-made story is backed by stern fact. She seems to have made the whole thing up, including her famous affair with Hickok.

Cattle Kate is less famous, more unsavory, and perhaps more authentic. Her real name was Ella Watson. She and her supposed husband Jim Averill were involved in a store and saloon business in the now vanished "town" of Bothwell, 10 miles east of Independence Rock. Averill accepted cash from thirsty cowboys in his bar. Kate, who had a homestead nearby, accepted donations of stray calves onto which she put her brand. Soon, her brand was on a sizable bunch of the neighbors' cattle, and in their irritation these neighbors suggested that the Averills leave the area. When they refused, the neighbors strung both of them up from a tree. Needless to say, nothing was done about this except to cut the pair down and bury them near the former saloon. Cattle Kate thus has the distinction of being among Wyoming's firsts: the first woman lynched in the state.

It may have been seen and even named by the returning Astorian, Robert Stuart, on Independence Day in 1812. It is mentioned as Independence Rock in a diary of 1837. Father Pierre Jean De Smet in 1840 referred to it as the "famous Rock Independence, registry of the desert." Lt. John C. Frémont, in 1842, described the rock's inscriptions: "Everywhere within six or eight feet of the ground and in some places 60 to 80 feet above, the rock was inscribed with the names of travelers. I engraved on this rock of the far west a large cross covered with black rubber . . . to resist wind and rain." (This particular souvenir was destroyed by a gunpowder blast during Fourth of July celebrations in 1847. The fact that

Frémont left this "Catholic symbol" on the rock was used against him in his unsuccessful presidential campaign in 1856, when he ran as the first Republican candidate; one thing that has not changed is politics.) Brigham Young passed the rock in 1847. A bronze plaque honors Narcissa Prentiss Whitman, wife of the missionary Marcus, and her companion Eliza Hart Spalding, the first white women to cross the continent. Another tablet commemorates Wyoming's first Masonic meeting, held (by some agile Masons) on top of the rock on July 4, 1862. Almost all of the some 50,000 names once inscribed on the rock are now obliterated, which slightly diminishes the impact of the historic site. Alongside, there are still dim traces of the wagon tracks, and if you walk along the bottom of the rock, heading south from the plaque area through nettles and flowers, you can discover on your own a few faint old inscriptions; but Register Cliff near Guernsey is far better preserved, if generally less impressive.

All along this reach of highway, the road plays hide and seek with the Sweetwater River, which so succored and guided the travelers on their way to South Pass. Odd protrusions of the central belt mountains, a series of disjunct and curiously contrasting elevations, also accompany the road to the south. East to west, they are the **Shirley Mountains,** the **Seminoes,** the **Ferris Mountains,** the **Green Mountains,** and the **Antelope Hills.** To the north emerges a separate range—the **Stoneys,** or **Granites**—very appropriately named since they look like immense piles of gray stones (not unlike the Vedauwoo).

■ DEVIL'S GATE   *map page 112, B-5*

About five miles from Independence Rock you pass **Devil's Gate,** an odd, short canyon cut through the tail end of the Stoneys. It has no *visible* geological reason for existence. The Sweetwater runs through it, but any ordinary river wouldn't have taken the trouble. Despite its sinister name, it really doesn't amount to much. But it *is* strange. Eighteen-year-old Caroline Todd, traveling west with her emigrant family, fell into the chasm and was buried under a tombstone inscribed:

Here lies the body of Caroline Todd
Whose soul has lately gone to God.
Ere redemption was too late
She was redeemed at Devils Gate..

(opposite) A few names remain of the Oregon Trail emigrants who camped at Independence Rock.

Which is one way of looking at it. Equally horrendous was the fate of Captain Howard Martin's company of 576 English immigrants, a short distance west at Martin's Cove, in 1856. They were part of a group of a thousand Mormon converts who left England for Utah and found when they arrived in America that the Mormons could not afford to provide wagons and oxen to transport them from the end of the railroad in Iowa. They were forced to pull *handcarts* holding their belongings for the remaining thousand miles. They started across the continent in two groups, soon losing the few stock they had to marauding Indians, but managed to get to the Sweetwater, where they made two separate camps a few weeks apart, in October and November, 1856. They were both marooned there by blizzards. The group that camped at Martin's Cove suffered most. More than a hundred people died and were buried in a single trench. The survivors were eventually rescued by fellow Mormons from Salt Lake. The Mormon Church opened an excellent visitor center near Devil's Gate in 1997, complete with handcarts that you can pull along the old trail. 307-382-2953.

■ BEYOND MUDDY GAP *map page 112, B-5*

Muddy Gap Pass marks the end of Wyoming State Highway 220 and the junction with U.S. Route 287, which comes from the south through the desolate eastern edge of the Great Divide Basin. At this point, the Oregon Trail turned north and west to follow the Sweetwater. Historical markers at turnouts tell about the trail and its events and curiosities. To the south, the belt mountains, with their curious shapes and sizes, continue. The Ferris Mountains are tall, steep, sharply serrated, and only moderately timbered. The Green Mountains are softly rounded and heavily green with timber, as their name indicates. Still farther west are the bare, brown, castellated Antelope Hills, and then the south end of the huge Wind Rivers.

West of Muddy Gap, **Split Rock** is a bare, oddly shaped pink butte, conspicuously split into two sections. Like Independence Rock, it was easily visible to emigrants along the Oregon Trail and lent its name to a pony express station.

The scenery becomes less and less compelling as you head northwest on U.S. Route 287. The Green Mountains subside, the Stoneys peel away northward, the landscape becomes sagebrush flats, and though the Sweetwater runs alongside, it, too, veers away from the road. There is only one bit of habitation along this part of the Sweetwater Valley: **Jeffrey City,** a modern uranium camp that once boomed with a population of some 2,000. Now it's derelict and mostly deserted. The paved roads, once lined with white trailers, are now lined with weeds. A sign on a big store along the highway reads "Jeffrey City Grocery"; somebody has painted a big "?" afterward. The grocery is shut tight. However, on a bluff farther along is a bit of suburbia on a circular drive, so something must still go on in the area.

Once more, just as in the approach to Douglas, things begin to seem pretty desolate. Then, about ten miles beyond Jeffrey City, the road rises and the Wind Rivers emerge. From now on, they grow closer and closer, more and more majestic. Tantalizingly, they appear beyond the final crossing of the Sweetwater, where the river and the Oregon Trail veer off toward South Pass; but the real surprise occurs ten miles beyond the Sweetwater crossing. At the top of a long descent into the enormous valley of negligible Beaver Creek, there's a big truck pull-off. It's marked by the conventional sign warning of a steep downgrade, but there's no indication whatsoever of the fact that this is one of the most magnificent viewpoints in the whole state of Wyoming. Stopping here, you look across the deep, wide, rough valley, and behold the entire epic panorama of the white-capped Wind Rivers.

■ WIND RIVER BASIN   *map page 112, A-3/4*

As you approach Lander, the land gradually becomes greener and the mountains closer, while the peaks become hidden by foothills. You are entering the south fringes of the Wind River Basin. To complete this tour of Wyoming's central plains, you should turn north at Lander on State Highway 789, toward Riverton, Shoshoni, and the Bighorn Basin. (Lander and the Wind River Indian Reservation are discussed in the "WEST-CENTRAL" chapter.)

The 46-mile drive from Lander to Shoshoni on State Highway 789 is, unfortunately, pretty homely. When you drive it in the opposite direction, you face the Wind Rivers in their majesty all along; going north, you don't. At first there's rural scenery with oil in it, then the debauch of hideous, crowded commercialism on the strip outside of Riverton, then rather bland farmlands and bare buttes to Shoshoni. From Boysen Reservoir and Shoshoni itself, things improve.

Riverton (pop. 10,000) aims to be stylish but seems to have taken Gillette as its model; the city is fast becoming one long strip mall. Once a farming center with big grain elevators all around, Riverton has begun to think of itself as a little Casper. There are fancy new residential areas and shops, but the changeover is far from complete. The annual fair remains the big event of the year.

As for Riverton's strip, it may be bleak, but it does contain motels such as the nice, old-fashioned **Hi-Lo Motel** (414 N. Federal Street; 307-856-9223). There's the stylish **Ol' Wyoming Motel** (203 E. Main Street; 307-856-0555), housed in a wonderful 1906 building with a wide-ranging menu including duck, lobster, and prime rib. The **Airport Cafe,** at the Riverton Airport, is the best local breakfast place. There are even a couple of espresso joints in town.

From Riverton you may continue on north to Shoshoni and the Wind River Canyon.

■ CASPER TO SHOSHONI VIA ROUTE 20/26   *map page 112, B/C-4*

An alternate route from Casper to Shoshoni, more direct but much less interesting, is U.S. Route 20/26. One of the state's more desolate highways, it follows the Bridger Trail, marked out by Jim Bridger in hopes of redirecting traffic from the fatal Bozeman Trail through the Powder River Basin, farther east. (Unfortunately, it didn't work.) The route passes through 100 miles of semidesert—rough, dry buttes and gullies and enormous, wide-open distances. The Bridger Trail then turned north into the Bighorn Basin, through the mountains, and on to Virginia City, Montana.

The modern highway goes straight to Shoshoni, passing through quite a few tiny dots on the map. You get glimpses of mountains the whole way—far and faint, but there. Side roads lead off to energy sites, notably the defunct Gas Hills uranium development. Some 45 miles from Casper, near the town of Waltman, is a curious little wonder called **Hell's Half Acre,** a smallish, Grand Canyon-type of hole in the desert, full of fantastic eroded pink pinnacles. Used as an alien landscape in the 1997 movie *Starship Troopers,* it should be called Hell's Half Mile, for it's a lot more than a half acre. Don't expect a guided tour—the development at its entrance is boarded up—but the view is spectacular, well worth the stop, and free. It's the only such sight on the highway.

■ BIGHORN BASIN OVERVIEW   *map page 112*

The historical approach to the Big Horn Mountains—the way most pioneers, fur trappers, and settlers approached them—was from the east, either from the Yellowstone River in Montana, or from the Black Hills, or up from the North Platte. This is still the usual approach for tourists from the east—it's quick to zip west along Interstate 90 or north along Interstate 25—but it's not really the preferred route.

A better way is the back door, from the south, through the Wind River Canyon to Thermopolis, which you might otherwise miss. This route takes you east across the beautiful plateau of the Big Horn Mountains. (If you continue following the suggested route, you will later cross the basin again, heading west toward the northern Absarokas.)

Entering the Bighorn Basin from this back door, the traveler enters the area of Wyoming's most massive scenic splendor.

A basin is a "hole" in Western parlance; that is, a valley more or less completely surrounded by mountains. The particular mountains in this case are the Owl Creeks, to the south of the Bighorn Basin; the Big Horn Mountains, to the east; vague ranges like the Pryors, north; and the Absarokas, west.

The Bighorn Basin is a great *big* hole, with a good deal of varied topography and character inside it, and so spacious that from the middle of it, the mountains are more or less invisible. The basin slopes down towards the north into a desert depression well below 4,000 feet. That's pretty low for Wyoming. Quite a bit of the basin is badlands, but some is irrigated farmland. To the south and west, below Cody, it's big, open cattle country. The area contains lots of towns, especially for Wyoming: Thermopolis, Worland, Ten Sleep, Basin, Greybull, Lovell, Powell, Cody, and Meeteetse. Yet it is still full of empty spaces. Some parts of the basin are more interesting to look at than others. Much of it is a paleontologist's dream, chock-full of bones and fossils. It's oil rich, too.

The Bighorn Basin was the bastion of the Crow Indians after the Sioux drove them out of the Powder River area. The Crow and Sioux were historically enemies. Lots of horse stealing and fighting and counting of coups went on over the decades before the white men came. There is evidence that those mysterious tribes of prehistoric times lived here, as well. (Who were they? What happened to them? Were they direct ancestors of the Plains tribes, or not?) Later on, trappers explored the basin, and cattlemen came to stay. There were no significant Indian-white conflicts, as there were in the Powder River area, but later on, the sheep and cattle wars culminated here.

The Bighorn Basin presents a special problem to travelers. There's really no logical or sensible way to view it. Neither a trip up the middle nor a circle round the perimeter makes sense, so a rather peculiar zigzagging route is suggested, which in the end will give a taste of the varied beauties and curiosities of the basin without subjecting the visitor to the less pleasant parts. (For, to tell the truth, the center of the valley, from Thermopolis north to Lovell, is about as dreary as Wyoming gets: gray-brown semi-desert without even distant mountain scenery.)

(following pages) Log cabin near the town of Shell.

NORTH-CENTRAL

■ WIND RIVER CANYON   *map page 112, A-3/4*

There's no grander introduction to the basin than the **Wind River Canyon.** It's one of the great sights of the West. The preparation for it begins right beyond Shoshoni with the Owl Creeks, which seem inconspicuous when seen from a distance. Suddenly, though, they begin to loom in a grim, broken, desert-brown grandeur. Meanwhile, alongside is the blindingly blue (on a bright day) **Boysen Reservoir,** totally artificial in this badland setting, but a wonderful contrast. Just as you come to the mountains, some great, pointed, dark red rocks thrust upward. Marinas and a bare, new picnic ground are situated alongside the lake. Then comes the dam, and you are in the canyon.

Thousand-foot-high cliffs and pinnacles and castles close in. The Wind River rushes green to the left, with a little railroad running on the other side of it. Geological information signs point to the rocks, which you daren't look at if you're driving; and the whole is such a violent contrast to anything you'd have seen in southeast Wyoming, you might think you're in the deserts of Utah.

This awe-inspiring traverse from Shoshoni to Thermopolis is only 32 miles long, but it's worth the trip. When you emerge at the north end, the by-now big river alongside is called the Bighorn, *not* the Wind River, and you come almost immediately to Thermopolis and its hot springs. The town is rather new, even by Wyoming standards, but the springs have been known and used for ages. The Indian legend is that the strong, continuous wind that blows down the canyon wafted a feather, which led the first Indians to the springs, hence the name Wind River. For decades, the waters were believed to confer perpetual youth and to assist courtship. Great Chief Washakie of the Shoshones had his private bathhouse here, and the springs were once part of the Wind River Reservation.

The explanation of how one river got two names is that Lewis and Clark named it the Bighorn, while the Crow Indians called it the Wind River, and early explorers somehow concluded that they were two separate waterways. So the two names stuck in the two regions, and now it's too late to change the situation.

■ THERMOPOLIS   *map page 112, A-3*

With a population of about 3,250, Thermopolis is unique among Wyoming towns in having a classical name. The West doesn't go in much for such names (unlike New York State with its Syracuse, Utica, and Ithaca), and this particular name is part of the confused history of the place. There was originally a rough, tough, little cow town to the north called Andersonville, founded in 1890. There, outlaws from the Hole-in-the-Wall gang to the southeast used to drop in, and on one occasion tried to take over the town during an election. A gun battle cleared them out. Later, in 1894, a first version of Thermopolis was founded in anticipation of the hoped-for opening of the hot springs (then part of the Wind River Reservation) to white settlers. This opening finally occurred in 1897, when a treaty with the Indians removed the springs from their jurisdiction. Andersonville and Thermopolis packed up and moved together to the new site, where they remain to this day. Dr. Julius A. Schuelke is credited with naming the town Thermopolis, "city of hot springs" in Greek. It quickly became the spa town it is now. It also became the county seat when Hot Springs County was created in 1911.

Town and springs are now quite separate. The town is a rather pleasant, ramshackle, and random place that has spread all up and down the surrounding hills in an accidentally picturesque fashion. It boasts of having more than 300 sunny days a year, and the town's many bright gardens seem to prove it. A grand boulevard of a main street was first laid out with a grass median (in something of the style of New York City's Park Avenue), but the grass plots are now parking lots, and many of the older stone buildings along it have fallen into disrepair. The area has seen some improvements and restoration in recent years, with some of the older buildings

The hot springs at Thermopolis.

having earned themselves notice on the National Register of Historic Places. U.S. Route 20 passes through with a continual growling of trucks and cars. On the east side of U.S. Route 20 is a good restaurant, Pumpernick's, at 512 Broadway; 307-864-5151. But, alas, there are no actual springs in the "city of hot springs."

In town stands the **Hot Springs County Museum and Cultural Center,** which calls itself "one of the best small museums in the country." It lives up to this billing with an impressive collection of old photos, wagons, Indian artifacts, and displays that re-create features of frontier life, such as a newspaper shop, a dentist's office (take a look at those frightening tools!), a blacksmith shop, and a general store. The cherrywood bar from the Hole-in-the-Wall Saloon, a Thermopolis landmark demolished in the 1970s, is particularly popular; here members of the famous outlaw gang (see page 162) tipped their glasses with sympathetic locals. Look for the outlaws' photos on the wall. Downstairs, you will find an elk hide painted by Chief Washakie of the Shoshones. Across the street stands a 1920 schoolhouse. Nearby is a petroleum building, a circa-1920s poverty flats cottage, an agricultural building with period farm equipment and a sheepherder's wagon, and an old Burlington Northern caboose. *700 Broadway; 307-864-5183.*

Also in Thermopolis is the **Wyoming Dinosaur Center**—or at least its museum, containing displays of various ancient, terrifying lizards. The center's dig sites, to which visitors are shuttled on guided bus tours in summer, is 2.5 miles away on the banks of the Bighorn River. The center has a variety of programs for kids and adults, including chances to actually help with the excavation of fossil quarries. *110 Carter Ranch Road; 800-455-3466.*

On Sixth Street is the **Old West Wax Museum**, containing wax figures of important Western figures of yore and displays of Western memorabilia, especially early maps and old newspapers. On the lower level is the **Dancing Bear Folk Center**, with a museum dedicated to the teddy bear and displays and demonstrations on spinning, quilting, weaving, and other needle crafts. *119 South Sixth Street, on Highway 20; 307-864-9396.*

◆ HOT SPRINGS STATE PARK *map page 112, A-3*
The springs, and **Hot Springs State Park,** are just north of town and across the river. The park is indeed an impressive place, a combination German spa and large county fairground. The springs themselves are pretty impressive, too—and peculiar.

A single hot, bubbling, green pool of water emerges from the very foot of a towering, deep red mesa and spreads out and over in large terraces toward the river.

These by-now tepid waters slip over a long, high, gray cliff made of mineral deposits and drip directly into the Bighorn River. Around the southern edge of the thermal springs—the largest of their kind in America and perhaps the world, spewing out four million gallons of hot water a day—is a line of public and privately run bathing establishments in which you can soak or swim. There's a capacious outdoor pool, and water slides for kids alongside the red cliffs, to the east. In the middle of the complex is a perpetual fountain, under a cupola and surrounded by watered lawns—a nice place to cool off. There are flower beds, full of roses in season, and it is indeed very German, as though in memorial to Dr. Schuelke. Farther back in the pleasant park are various buildings, including a Holiday Inn. During the summer, all of Wyoming is at the springs, splashing and sunbathing, and the dream of the good Herr Doctor seems thoroughly realized. During the first full weekend in August, the park hosts the annual **Gifting of the Waters pageant**, re-enacting the 1896 ceremony in which Wind River Reservation Indians passed the site over to the U.S. government. The pageant includes craft demonstrations, an arts fair, native dancing and food. *307-864-2176.*

After you leave the town and springs, you enter the Bighorn Basin itself, either by driving west from Main Street onto beautiful, lonely Wyoming State Highway 120 toward Cody, or north on the less beautiful and much less lonely Route 20.

■ THERMOPOLIS TO WORLAND   *map page 112, A-3*

Route 20 between Thermopolis and Worland gives you a taste of the long river valley that bisects the basin. The road goes along bare benches on the west side of the valley; in the greenery just below lie little villages such as Lucerne and Kirby. There was an oil boom in the Grass Creek Field, to the west, in 1917–18, and there's still plenty of oil out there.

The basin's first permanent settlements, mostly cattle ranches, were in this southern area. As early as 1871, J.D. Woodruff built the first house in the valley. The nearby Embar (M—) Ranch ran 50,000 head, and there are still plenty of cattle here. Down along the river, alfalfa grows in Lucerne, and there was once coal at Gebo and Kirby. Across the river, farther along, is **Tie-Down Hill,** where once lived Tie-Down Brown, so named for his skill in tying down and branding other people's calves. In 1880, his partner killed him with an axe, and for a good many years his ghost rode up and down the hill looking for revenge. All this is skirted nowadays by the big, not pleasant, truck-laden route north to Worland.

Worland, with a population of about 5,250, is situated in the midst of irrigated farmlands. A 20th-century town with lawns and trees in its residential area, Worland is the county seat of Washakie (named for the great chief). Like Torrington, Worland grew up with the sugar beet refinery and the railroad from 1906 onward. The surrounding rangeland—often so denuded in the Bighorn Basin that it resembles badlands—lies beyond the reach of irrigation. The Big Horns rise to the east, the Owl Creeks to the south, and the Absarokas very dim and far to the west.

■ MEETEETSE DETOUR   *map page 112, A-3*

The direct way east to Buffalo over the mountains would be to proceed from Worland to Ten Sleep on U.S. Route 16. But this would prevent you from seeing anything else of interest in the lower Bighorn Basin itself. So instead, turn west at Neiber, nine miles below Worland, onto **Wyoming State Highway 431.** This empty road begins tamely, heading up a flat, open creekbed, with low, drab ridges north and south, framing scanty green ranch pastures. As you glide smoothly over this excellent highway, the scenery gradually grows more grand. The ridges alongside push up into crags. The blue Absarokas ahead loom larger. Halfway along, due north, is a gulf of superb **badlands**—pink, white, red, buff, blue, gray—in all sorts of jumbled towers, palaces, temples, and ruins. These badlands accompany you off and on almost until you swing back into Hot Springs County, where you soon run into State Highway 120 swerving up from Thermopolis. Turn left, back towards Thermopolis, to visit the **Legend Rock Petroglyph site**, where 283 pictures date back 5,700 years (pick up directions at Hot Springs State Park). Or turn right to proceed to Meeteetse. From here, the scenery becomes still more exalted, with high, mountainous, cedar-spotted ridges and near-glimpses of the great Absarokas. The road crosses into Park County, with an immediate increase in scenic beauty, and descends into the Greybull Valley to Meeteetse ("ma-TEET-see"). The elevation here is 6,795 feet—a 2,700-foot increase from Worland, which accounts for some of the exhilaration of this trip.

◆ MEETEETSE   *map page 112, A-2*

Meeteetse, with fewer than 400 people, is a cow town, and still has an Old West atmosphere, despite the presence of the automobile. Its old buildings are scattered about a crossroads (State Highway 290 leads west to Pitchfork). There are three points of historical interest—the **Meeteetse Bank Museum** (1033 Park Avenue; 307-868-2423), located in an old, pink stone bank building built in 1901; and the

Meeteetse Museum and **Charles J. Belden Museum** (1947 State Street; 307-868-2423), which has a great collection of cowboy photos.

◆ PITCHFORK   *map page 112, A-2*
Pitchfork was and is the site of the Pitchfork Ranch of Charlie Belden, famous photographer of cowboy life in the 1920s and 1930s. Its previous owner was Otto Franc, whose real, full name was Count Otto Franc von Lichtenstein. A great cattle rancher and a notable big-game hunter, he settled here in 1878. One of the oddest incidents of his career was his involvement with famous outlaw Butch Cassidy. Cassidy, then called George Cassidy (his real name was George Leroy Parker), was arrested for the possession of horses stolen from Franc. After a dubious series of mistrials, he was found guilty and served a jail sentence from 1894 to 1896. The prosecutor who convicted him was Bill Simpson, progenitor of a notable Wyoming family, including a governor (Milward) and a senator (Alan). Butch never forgave Franc, and claimed he took seriously to a life of crime after his jail term. The rights and wrongs of the case are as confused as most Wyoming incidents, but there's no doubt about Cassidy's success in his later profession.

Franc lived in high style on the Pitchfork, and the style became even higher when the Belden-Phelps regime—the next and permanent owners—took over in 1901. In 1918, a great, gabled, frame and stone ranch house was built, which is still headquarters for some Belden descendants. The 100,000-acre spread still operates as a ranch and is a model of conservation. Charlie Belden's pictures of cowboy life have never been surpassed in beauty and authentic treatment of the subject matter. Specimens of his work are found in the museum at Cody and, indeed, all over the state.

From Meeteetse, State Highway 120 proceeds north for 31 beautiful miles to Cody, with increasingly spectacular views of the Absarokas; but our route heads east on Wyoming State Highway 30, some six miles beyond Meeteetse and down the rich, green Greybull River Valley. This is some of the most typical of Western scenery: a lush valley of huge cottonwoods and vivid pastures, flanked on both sides by the grim, bare cliffs of often fantastically carved red badlands. As long as you're in Park County, for about 20 miles, the views are good. But in Big Horn County, to the east, the river valley gradually widens, and you lose sight of the Absarokas and the cliffs alongside. The delta of the Greybull assumes the scruffy look characteristic of the central Bighorn Basin. The little town of **Otto** might seem to recall the romantic past, being named after Otto Franc von Lichtenstein; sadly, though, there is nothing noble or romantic about the place.

◆ BASIN   *map page 112, A-2*

The town of Basin is at the junction with U.S. Route 20, which comes up from Worland. Basin won the honor of being county seat of Big Horn County by a close vote in 1896: Basin, 481 votes, Otto, 420, and far-off Cody trailing with only 243. Basin was also later the scene of the famous court trials of the sheep and cattle wars. It still possesses its fine courthouse, but, unfortunately, little else. By now commerce has been sucked away by bigger, newer Greybull, eight miles north.

■ GREYBULL AREA   *map page 112, A-2*

Greybull is an up-and-coming city of about 1,800 people, with bentonite processing plants, brisk stores, and tidy gardens around the houses. The charming **Greybull Museum** has a collection of large and small ammonites—the whorled fossil shells of the modern squid's ancestor. In town are pleasant motels, as well as good restaurants. *325 Greybull Avenue; 307-765-2444.*

◆ GREYBULL WEST TO CODY   *map page 112, A-2*

After winding through town, the highway heads straight west for 54 miles to Cody. For the first 20 miles, the scenery is flat, irrigated farmland with no mountain views. After a non-place called Emblem, the farmland ends. Now you're in perfectly flat sagebrush range. But very gradually, hills begin to close about, and the Absarokas loom more and more majestically. You cross the border into Park County, and sure enough the scenery becomes park-like. Once again, you experience that characteristic Wyoming feature of vast plains heading for vast mountains. The odd ram's-horn peak of Heart Mountain is silhouetted to the northwest, and before you know it you're in Cody. (See page 140 for the essay "Lonely Heart Mountain.")

◆ GREYBULL EAST TO SHELL   *map page 112, A/B-2*

East of Greybull, the tiny town of **Shell** is a pleasant place with cabins and gardens. Above Shell, the road traverses the Bighorn Basin; red monuments stand roundabout, notably a striking deep, scarlet plinth to the south that looks like a cathedral tower. East, the road ascends precipitously toward brightly colored cliff walls. Shell Creek crashes down a splendid waterfall through the frighteningly narrow, deep, rocky Shell Canyon. A fine visitor center alongside the road provides a view of all these things and tells you more than you probably want to know about the geology, flora, and fauna of the place. (Restrooms, but no food.)

■ THE MEDICINE WHEEL *map page 112, B-1*

Nobody who's close should fail to visit Medicine Wheel National Historic Landmark. But no use trying if there's snow on the ground in June or September. You see snowbanks on the hillside not far above the road, even in July and August.

The Medicine Wheel is a prehistoric construction dating back 1,000 to 7,000 years—a remnant of the same horseless culture that produced the petroglyphs of Medicine Lodge to the southeast (see page 140). From the rock-pile hub in the center of a big stone circle, 28 spokes radiate outward like the spokes of a wagon wheel. The hub and spokes are thought to have been used to calculate astronomical phenomena such as various star paths and the sunrise on the summer solstice. Its significance was religious, similar to that attributed to the English Stonehenge. Though this is the most famous and accessible of such constructions, it is by no means unique. Other wheels are scattered about the West, always on such bare heights. But who built them, and exactly what purpose they served, is not known.

The Medicine Wheel is surrounded by an odd, outwardly flanged wire fence, on which Native Americans tie cloth bundles, mementos, bells, and fetishes.

Though the Wheel has no direct historical connection with the modern Plains Indians, they have adopted this as a sacred place. You'll need to walk the final one-and-a-half miles into the Wheel, though exceptions are made for those with disabilities. Native American interpreters are at the site in the summer. The whole setting and remarkable survival of this prehistoric site, like the descent into the valley below, is awesome.

Strips of cloth left in Native American ceremonies add to the mystique of the Medicine Wheel archaeological sites.

Cattle rancher and former Washakie County state representative John Rankine.

■ BIGHORN BASIN RANGELAND HISTORY   *map page 112, B-2/3*

The Bighorn Basin near Ten Sleep is famous, or infamous, in Wyoming, as the place where the long, bitter sheep and cattle wars came to a climax at the turn of the century. This was one of those unnecessary confrontations that could have been solved by some common sense. It began in the greedy, unregulated atmosphere of the post–Civil War period, when sheep owners simply ignored the prior claims of cattlemen to the ranges. They penetrated the Powder River Basin and then moved into the Bighorn Basin. In the process, they ruined the range for cattle and thus threatened to ruin the cattle ranchers. Instead of trying to settle the matter by persuasion, arbitration, or law, cattlemen, in typically high-handed fashion, just slaughtered the sheep. They shot them, poisoned them, drove them over rimrock precipices, and still failed to stop the inexorable advance. The war reached a violent climax near the Bighorn Basin town of Ten Sleep. In 1903 some herders were shot by masked men, and their sheep slaughtered. During the next six years, the violence continued, and 11 herds of sheep valued at $100,000 were

(opposite) The late sheepherder John Abyta prepares for a day among his 1,600 sheep in the Big Horn Mountains.

dynamited, rimrocked, and attacked by dogs. The sheep men didn't retaliate against the violence; they just went on obstinately letting their animals overgraze. In the fall of 1908, a lamb shipment valued at $2 million was shipped from the Bighorn Basin.

In the spring of 1909, Joe Allemand and a partner brought 5,000 sheep into the basin. On April 3, 20 masked men killed the pair and another herder on Spring Creek and cremated the bodies in their own wagons. This brought the feud to a head. The National Woolgrowers Association offered a bounty of $20,000 for the arrest and prosecution of the Ten Sleep raiders. A grand jury investigation was launched, and jurors, sheriffs, and witnesses were threatened. One witness committed suicide. Finally, seven men were arrested in May. When conviction became certain, influential friends of the cattlemen intervened. A deal was arranged so that the accused could plead guilty to lesser crimes than murder, and receive lesser jail sentences of three to six years. Justice perhaps was not exactly served, but the result was efficacious. Everyone calmed down. Deadlines were now determined by law, and boundaries were fixed beyond which sheep could not graze. Entire counties, like Teton, were thus set off-limits, and though sheep men and cattlemen would never be friends, at least no one got shot. Why didn't anyone think of that 20 years sooner?

Nowadays, most ranges are fenced, or under government control, to prevent overgrazing. Big owners run both sheep and cattle. But cattlemen and cowhands still despise woollies and think of sheepherders as mysterious "furriners" (many of them being Basques) who go crazy listening to that bleating and can't ride a horse worth a damn.

■ MEDICINE LODGE STATE PARK   *map page 112, B-2*

Our route through the Bighorn Basin turns south to Manderson, a tiny post office in a grove of big trees, where Wyoming State Highway 31 takes off for Hyattville. This is the site of Medicine Lodge State Park, an absolutely obligatory detour.

The scenery becomes progressively more striking as you go up Nowood Creek (which supports plenty of cottonwoods) and turn east into the foothills of the great, hulking Big Horns. The state park lies, rather inconspicuously, up Paintrock Creek (aptly named for the intensely red cliffs that wedge into the intensely green ranch valley), and then up Medicine Lodge Creek and beyond,

(opposite) Ed Shaffer, foreman of the HD Ranch,
near Hamilton Dome.

LONELY HEART MOUNTAIN

The dogs dug down through five inches of new snow until they reached dirt and lay in their cone-beds with their backs to the wind. McKay brought the horses in and saddled one of them. He had decided to open the pasture gates to let the cattle, who cannot paw through snow to eat, drift in. "Open gates, cut wire, do whatever you have to during a blizzard or the cattle will walk into a draw and suffocate there," his father had always warned him.

As he rode, Heart Mountain disappeared from sight. The cloud that took it did so quickly, like a hunger, McKay thought. Now the peak broke the skin of the cloud. Nothing about it resembled a heart. It was, instead, a broken horn or a Cubist beast, as McKay's mother had once remarked. Behind it the Beartooth Mountains veered north. Forty million years ago Heart Mountain broke off from the Rockies and skidded twenty-five miles on a detachment fault to its present site. There was no other limestone in the area like it and at its base was one of the most fertile hayfields on the ranch.

As McKay rode under the limestone tusk he looked up. A half moon hooked its side. So that's how love works, he thought and chuckled out loud. He reduced his mother's geology lesson to a list of words: detachment, skidding, breast, horn, heart. As he said the words a bank of snow clouds took over every mountain west of the ranch and McKay kicked his horse into a lope. When he reached the first gate, the cattle were already waiting.

—Gretel Ehrlich, *Wyoming Stories,* 1986

through a small gate leading to a shady campground. Across the creek is one of the wonders of Wyoming—a wide, smooth, pink cliff, covered with yards of petroglyphs (incised designs) and some pictographs (painted designs). Prehistoric tribes camped along this same cliff and stream. At least 60 cultural levels have been excavated, covering some 10,000 years of occupation. Summer shade, solar heat from the cliff in winter, and nearby water and quartzite for arrowheads all made this a continually attractive place. It still is. A stone canopy along the clifftop has helped preserve the images, which are mostly circular designs with decorations inside and protuberances outside. Some are recognizably animal, some human. This is the most beautiful, easily seen, and imaginatively compelling cliff decoration in the state. The setting alone makes it worth a visit: a lushly treed ranch with the beautiful, clear creek running through it. So far the prehistoric designs seem to have escaped vandalism, although a pair of cowboys 80 years ago did their best. With black paint, "Jinks Burgess" and "Speed Martin" immortalized (or damned) themselves for posterity on "8/10/16"—almost prehistoric by Wyoming standards. 307-469-2234.

At this point, it's best to return to the junction of the marked road up Nowood Creek to Ten Sleep. Turning south, you drive through wild, craggy, turreted rangeland, once a battleground of the sheep and cattle wars, where both sheep and cattle now range in peace. After some 20 miles you reach Ten Sleep.

■ TEN SLEEP   *map page 112, B-3*

With about 300 people, Ten Sleep was given its odd name by the Indians. It was ten sleeps (overnight camps) away from somewhere for the Crows, but no one seems absolutely sure from *where*. The Crows are now settled on their reservation in Montana.

The Crows occupied the Bighorn Basin before the first whites arrived. John Colter, one of the first mountain men to pass through, had brushes with other tribes, notably the Blackfeet, but the Crows welcomed him. Ed Rose and other trappers followed Colter. The basin was officially explored in 1859–1860 by the Raynolds-Maynadier expedition, accompanied by the famous scientist Ferdinand V. Hayden, later the true begetter of Yellowstone National Park. The Raynolds-Maynadier expedition had difficulties getting through the Wind River Canyon and even lost its wagons, but the group made the first scientific report on the region.

When John Bozeman proposed a trail up through the Powder River Basin to gain access to gold in Montana, trapper-guide Jim Bridger warned him of the Indian conflicts his route would (and did) start. Bridger instead suggested breaking a trail through the Bighorn Basin, passing by the more amiable Crows. Bridger and Bozeman had a sort of race to determine which route was quicker. Unfortunately, Bozeman reached Virginia City first. From then on it was bloodshed all the way along the Powder River; but not on the Bridger Trail through the Bighorn Basin.

The first cattle in the basin were trailed in from Oregon, of all places, in 1879. By 1883, the entire basin was stocked, largely by English, Scottish, and German

(Otto Franc, for instance) owners. Then came sheep, irrigation, homesteads, oil and coal, railroads, and sugar beets, with Mexican, Russian, and Japanese field hands: all the general influx of modern times—but somehow, except for the Ten Sleep murders, with less conflict and tension than on the plains.

Points of interest near Ten Sleep include the **Castle Gardens Scenic Area,** with impressive sandstone rock formations, located west off U.S. Highway 16, the **Ten Sleep Preserve,** a 10,000-acre Nature Conservancy preserve 10 miles east of town with rare and threatened wildflowers, wildlife, Indian sites, and pictographs, and a 12-mile stretch of **Canyon Creek,** which passes through a deep canyon carved into the southwestern flanks of the Big Horn Mountains. 307-366-2671.

■ THE BIG HORN MOUNTAINS   *map page 112, B-2*

U.S. Route 16 takes you away from Ten Sleep and into the mountains through spectacular **Ten Sleep Canyon,** rather like the Wind River Canyon in its towering yellow castles, but more open and smiling. High over the canyon on a pinnacle to the south is the **Leigh Creek Monument.** This marks a point where an English gentleman, Gilbert Leigh, who had settled near Ten Sleep and liked to wander about the mountains hunting game, fell to his death in 1884 from a 600-foot-high precipice. Buzzards led searchers to his body.

The road goes from bare, brown rangelands along Nowood Creek, up into the green forests and pastures of the Bighorn National Forest, which surrounds Cloud Peak—at 13,165 feet, the tallest in the Big Horns. Wide views begin to emerge as the road wriggles over the Powder River Pass (9,666 feet) and across the wide, forested plateau. The eastern descent is particularly engaging, with great grass-and-flower meadows and views north to snow-capped peaks. All along the route are campsites. There are also two pleasant guest ranches beside the road—**South Fork Mountain Lodge and Outfitters,** 307-267-2609, by a rushing stream, and the **Pines Lodge,** 307-684-9291 or 307-351-1010. Both have cabins and meals. The trees begin to thin out as you make the long descent to Buffalo. Sometime before you get to Buffalo itself, you'll know you are definitely back on the plains. (See page 337 for Guest Ranches in the Big Horn Mountains.)

(opposite) The Redbank Creek area south of Ten Sleep has terrain typical of the Bighorn Basin region.

POWDER RIVER BASIN

◆ **AREA OVERVIEW**

The history of the Powder River Basin gives travelers a real understanding of what they're seeing, especially east of the Big Horns and in the basin. The empty, barren landscape eastward from the Big Horn Mountains is the crucible in which the spirit of the state was distilled: it holds the essence of Wyoming's very dramatic past.

Buffalo to the south and Sheridan to the north are the civic centers of the Powder River Basin. Buffalo is the smaller of the two (about 3,900 people), and is more distinctly a cow town, being on the plains. Sheridan feels more like a real city with an old-fashioned city center that resembles Cheyenne's. Historically, these two towns represented the two factions of the Johnson County War. The Northern Wyoming Farmers and Stock Growers' Association was based in Buffalo, while Sheridan was dominated by the big cattle owners.

Weather: The weather here is mild most of the year. The average temperature in July is a comfy 70 degrees F, 27 in January, and Buffalo enjoys more than 250 sunny days a year, with a growing season of about 115 days. That said, snow and winter conditions can be expected even into late summer in the high passes over the Big Horn Mountains; check conditions and weather forecasts before embarking.

Food & Lodging: There are good campgrounds throughout Bighorn National Forest, but not many to the south and east in Powder River County. The same goes for food and lodging, with little to chose from south of Buffalo. There are plenty of places, however, between Buffalo and Sheridan, and west of Sheridan to Greybull.

POWDER RIVER BASIN

■ Mythic History of the Powder River

The history of the Powder River Basin from the Civil War and beyond was one of constant action. It was Wyoming's ultimate Indian-soldier-cowboy country, and its blood-soaked and epic history, full of heroics and horror, gives it a special glamour that no other part of the state, and few places in the Union, can match.

As a result, Powder River has become a symbol and a battle cry—quite literally, for soldiers from Wyoming in World War I would cry "Powder River, let 'er buck!" when charging into battle. If there is one section of the state that has inspired that bucking horse on the license plate, it's the Powder River watershed.

◆ Sioux and Their Hunting Grounds

When the Sioux arrived from the east and drove the Crows into the Bighorn Basin, they crossed the area from the Big Horns east to the Black Hills. The Black Hills in general remained a sacred place for the Sioux, while the plains between the two ranges, centered on the Powder River, were their chief hunting and camping grounds.

The difficulty between the Plains Indians and Americans of European descent stemmed from their differing approaches to the concept of property rights. To the white Americans, personal property was something sacred; bounded by borders or walls, it was a man's most precious possession. Land could be inherited by descendants and was to be fought for, tooth and nail. And agriculture, not nomadic hunting, was the essential basis of possession.

To the Indians, this idea of possession was totally alien. Land didn't belong to any person. The right of the tribe to hunt and camp across a huge, comfortable area "belonged" to the tribe strong and numerous and brave enough to hold it against other tribes. The Sioux thought of themselves as the bravest tribe around, and so they had the "right" to drive the Crows out of the Powder River. The Sioux were unable to comprehend that people "owned" ranches or that the United States government "possessed" all their hunting grounds.

On the other hand, white Americans tended to view the Sioux as either rebellious subjects or national enemies. The only possible way the Indians and the white men could ever live together was for the whites to adopt the Indian way of life, as the trappers often did; or for the Indians to be converted into property owners, as the reservation system has tried to do; or to just turn the whole of the American Northwest over to the tribes, and not settle there. Well-meaning whites tried to convert the Indians to "civilization." Ill-meaning ones tried to exterminate them. Neither policy worked. The government vacillated between the two extremes.

It was a while before this inevitable conflict of customs and ideas really became a problem along the Powder River. The fur traders had little effect; as often as not, they were converted to the Indian way of life. But the trading posts, though few and far between, and the army posts that followed them, such as Fort Laramie on the North Platte, did affect Indian culture. Indians brought furs to the posts and bartered for trinkets, tools, guns, and, fatally, whiskey. The encounter was usually disastrous. The so-called "ration Indians" who hung about the forts waiting for handouts were a sad lot.

Trappers did not really affect the Sioux, since the trappers worked in the mountains farther west. The early emigrants went through on the Platte, farther south. The hordes of travelers going by stage from Cheyenne to Deadwood, South Dakota, through the sacred Black Hills, or to Virginia City, Montana, through Sioux hunting grounds on the Powder River, are what brought about the final war.

◆ THE BOZEMAN TRAIL

Powder River Indian conflicts began with the Bozeman Trail. John Bozeman, a trapper and contemporary of Jim Bridger, determined in 1863 to lay out a trail along the eastern foothills of the Big Horns. It was to be an easy, if roundabout, way to western Montana and its gold strikes. The trail, which followed somewhat along the present route of Interstates 25 and 90, would cut right through the hitherto secluded Sioux heartland. The Sioux resented this. Bridger, the savvy trapper who knew what would happen, tried to persuade Bozeman to put the route up through the Bighorn Basin and the grounds of the more amenable Crows. Bozeman and his partner, John Jacobs, wouldn't listen. The Sioux, as expected, reacted belligerently. They were already on the warpath; the Sand Creek Massacre had been enough, and this road was the final provocation.

The Sand Creek Massacre of 1864 took place in Colorado, following conflicts with some renegade Cheyenne and Arapaho bands. Reverend John M. Chivington was sent with his regiment to chastise them. He mistook a camp of peaceful Cheyennes and Arapahos for the camp of his "malefactors," and attacked. The Indians were asleep in their teepees. Chivington set on them without warning and killed every man, woman, and child he could find—over 100 in all. However, a number of Indians did survive and escaped to alert the entire Indian population of the area, gathering recruits on the way to stir up their allies, the Sioux.

They marched from Colorado to the Black Hills, and then around to the winter quarters of the Sioux on the Powder River—400 miles, in December and January,

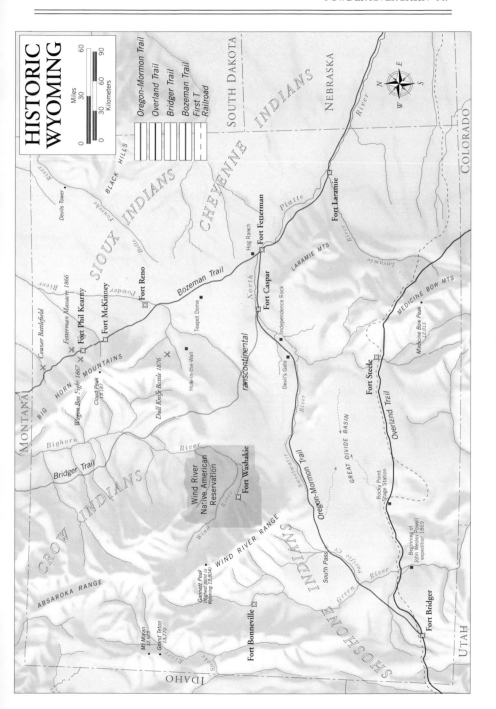

HISTORIC WYOMING

Miles
Kilometers

Oregon-Mormon Trail
Overland Trail
Bridger Trail
Bozeman Trail
First T
Railroad

SOUTH DAKOTA

NEBRASKA

COLORADO

BLACK HILLS

SIOUX INDIANS

CHEYENNE INDIANS

Devils Tower

Powder River

Fetterman Massacre 1866

Connor Battlefield

Fort Phil Kearny

Fort Reno

Fort McKinney

Wagon Box Fight 1867

Cloud Peak
13,167

BIG HORN MOUNTAINS

Dull Knife Battle 1876

Hole-in-the-Wall

Teapot Dome

Bozeman Trail

Hog Ranch

Fort Fetterman

Fort Caspar

North Platte River

Independence Rock

Devil's Gate

Fort Laramie

Platte River

LARAMIE MTS

Laramie River

MEDICINE BOW MTS

Medicine Bow Peak
12,013

transContinental

Fort Steele

Overland Trail

Sweetwater River

GREAT DIVIDE BASIN

Rocky Point
Stage Station

MONTANA

Bighorn River

Bridger Trail

CROW INDIANS

ABSAROKA RANGE

Wind River Native American Reservation

Fort Washakie

Wind River

WIND RIVER RANGE

Gannett Peak
(highest point in
Wyoming 13,804)

South Pass

Oregon-Mormon Trail

Pacific Cr

Green River

Beginning of
John Wesley Powell
expedition 1869

SHOSHONE INDIANS

Mt Moran
12,605

Grand Teton
13,770

Snake River

Fort Bonneville

IDAHO

Fort Bridger

UTAH

with women, children, old folks, and all their stock. Their progress stirred the tribes to the north into a frenzy of revenge. En route, the moving cavalcade killed more whites than Chivington had killed Indians. When they reached the lodges of the Powder River Sioux, the whole Wyoming plains Indian confederacy was on the warpath: Sioux, Cheyennes, Arapahos, Oglalas, Brulés—most of them previously friendly Indians. They devastated the whole area of the Oregon Trail through Wyoming, burned stage stations and wagon trains, and scalped and massacred anyone they found along their way. (This was part of the force that killed Lt. Caspar Collins. See page 111.) The telegraph lines were cut and the stage route closed for a hundred miles. For a time, the mail to California had to be sent via Nicaragua by way of the old sea route. The military, totally surprised, just holed up in their lonely forts. This began the final stage of the Indian wars that raged intermittently from 1864 to 1877. The provocations of Sand Creek and the Bozeman Trail destroyed any possibility of peace. As the Indians were outraged by Sand Creek, so the U.S. Army was outraged by the slaughter of whites along the Oregon Trail that followed as a consequence. Even so, before 1865 not one white man had been killed along the Powder. Things certainly changed.

◆ 1865: BUNGLING CONNOR EXPEDITION
General P. S. Connor, a veteran of earlier Indian conflicts, was sent in the spring of 1865 to build a strong fort and make a demonstration of U.S. Army presence on the Powder, in the heart of Sioux country. He was then supposed to move up along the Big Horn Mountains and meet up with two other units coming from the north and west. The combined forces were supposed to be 5,000 strong, and the Sioux were to be "taught a lesson." However, no one seemed to know exactly what lesson they were to be taught. The war, in fact, just sort of evolved on its own. In Washington, politicians were besieged by voters pressing from both sides. Some voters, mostly Westerners, were for exterminating Indians. Others, mostly Easterners, were for placating and cherishing them and, above all, converting them to Christianity. Congress spent the years backing and filling, switching from side to side.

In this case, the vacillation took the form of bungling the Connor expedition. Connor got off from Fort Laramie much too late, in midsummer, with only a third of the troops he was supposed to have. He got to the Powder and built his fort, as ordered, and then marched farther north to meet the other two forces, led by Colonels Cole and Walker. The three never met, Cole and Walker having gotten lost in the Powder River badlands. Connor continued to march up along the Big Horns, attacking a camp of Cheyennes and Arapahos under Old David and Black Bear on the Tongue River. They captured 1,000 horses and killed 65 Indians, with the loss of eight soldiers, but the main forces of the Sioux weren't touched, and the whole point of Connor's expedition was frustrated. The Sioux learned no lessons, except perhaps that the army was incompetent.

Connor was recalled in disgrace. His fort was later moved closer to the river and renamed Fort Reno. Altogether, the early episodes of the war were a fiasco. Except for Connor's Tongue River skirmish, no real fighting occurred.

A month later, Indians attacked an expedition led by Col. James Sawyer and besieged his troops for 13 days in a camp six miles west of the site of Connor's Tongue River assault. Still, there were few casualties, and Sawyer's men were rescued by Connor's cavalry.

◆ 1866: FORT PHIL KEARNY

After Connor left and his fort was moved, Colonel Carrington relieved Connor's inexperienced volunteer troops at the fort with 700 seasoned regulars and moved north to build two more forts: Fort Phil Kearny, 40 miles north of Fort Reno, and Fort C. F. Smith, in Montana. Fort Phil Kearny was a particular affront to the Sioux. It was built to protect the hated Bozeman Trail and was located in country the Sioux regarded as the center of their home grounds. Of all the Wyoming forts, it had the most sanguinary history. Finished on October 31, 1866, Kearny was a strong, well-built affair on a poor site: a low bench in an unprotected valley, not close enough to water, and far from wood. Already, 10 men had been killed during construction. During the first six months of the fort's existence, 154 more were killed. The Sioux could put up, reluctantly, with troops situated only as far north as Fort Reno, but Fort Phil Kearny was definitely going too far. Ironically, travel on the Bozeman Trail was by this time practically nonexistent.

In December of 1866, just after Fort Phil Kearny was finished, and just north of it, the Fetterman Massacre took place. Three officers and 76 privates, under Col. W. J. Fetterman, were killed by Sioux under Red Cloud, the leader of the war against the invaders of Sioux country. Fetterman was an eager hothead, chafing for action. He'd been distinguished for his bravery in the Civil War and wanted more of the same kind of glory.

A train carrying wood to the fort started from the Big Horns on the morning of December 21. A cavalry scout alerted the fort that the party had been attacked. A company of 76 men under sensible Captain James Powell was assigned to relieve the woodcutters, but the rash Fetterman pleaded to go instead. Carrington injudiciously gave in, choosing the wrong man. Fetterman was given strict orders not to pursue the Indians for any distance. Fetterman disobeyed that order. Having dispersed the marauders attacking the wagons, he allowed himself to be lured into an ambush. There were some 2,000 Indians hidden in wait for the soldiers, and though few had guns, the entire Fetterman party was massacred with hatchets, clubs, arrows, and spears. The only signs of Indian casualties were 10 dead Indian ponies and some 50 pools of blood on the ground. (Indians tended to quickly remove their dead from the battlefield.) At the time, the Sioux claimed that only 10 were killed, but later the Cheyennes admitted that 50 or 60 had died. Fetterman and one of his officers shot one another rather than face torture and mutilation. Red Cloud had directed the ambush. His outstanding warrior, Crazy Horse, had done most of the damage.

The fort itself was saved from attack by a blizzard. That night of the 21st, the temperature dropped to 30° F below zero, and the snow drifted so high that Carrington's men shoveled all night so the Indians wouldn't be able to sneak over the high drifts into the fort. In fact, the Indians had no intention of trying this; they preferred fighting in good weather. Carrington called for volunteers to ride some 230 miles down to Fort Laramie for help. A civilian scout called John Portugee Phillips volunteered. No one thought it would be possible to get through. In one of the most extraordinary feats in the history of Wyoming, Portugee Phillips, taking Colonel Carrington's own Arabian thoroughbred and a sack of oats and some hardtack biscuits, traveled through the blizzard for three days and two nights till he reached Horseshoe Creek, near the present town of Glendo. He telegraphed Fort Laramie, then rode on. The telegraph message was never delivered. Phillips' hands, knees, and feet were frostbitten. He reached the fort on Christmas Eve. The younger officers were giving a party in their quarters, "Old Bedlam." Phillips staggered into the merriment, told his story, and collapsed. His horse was dying outside. Fort Phil Kearny was relieved and saved. Phillips was rewarded with a purse of $300; but the Sioux, one year later, attacked his ranch, killed his cattle, and ruined him. (Carrington married the widow of one of the three officers killed in the massacre, but like Connor, he was relieved in disgrace and sent to Fort Caspar.)

This diorama accurately depicts the Wagon Box Fight. (Jim Gatchell Museum, Buffalo)

◆ 1867–1868: RED CLOUD AND CRAZY HORSE STRIKE

The following summer, Captain Powell, whom Fetterman had replaced before the massacre, had his revenge at the Wagon Box Fight. Fort Phil Kearny was by now better prepared for attack, but Red Cloud renewed his harassment in the spring. Once again there was trouble with a wood detail. This time it was Captain Powell and his men who were chopping wood in the Big Horn foothills, some five miles from the fort. Twelve men under a sergeant's command cut wood; 13 others and a sergeant stood guard. Captain Powell took no chances. He made a rough temporary fort by unloading the boxes from his wood wagons to form a corral, then piling sacks of grain on top. Across openings between the boxes he dragged the wagon carriages. He had plenty of provisions and ammunition. On August 2, Red Cloud, Crazy Horse, and at least 1,500 Sioux warriors struck. They first stampeded the wood party's horses, then chased the woodchoppers out of the timber. Four woodchoppers were killed immediately; the rest made it to the makeshift fort. Thirty-two men were inside the fort, including two civilian scouts. The Sioux came roaring down on horseback. Powell held his fire until the Indians were almost at the fort. The soldiers were fighting for the first time with new Springfield-Allin breech-loading rifles, with their deadly continuous fire, and the Indians were forced to retreat. They tried again, this time creeping up through tall grass. Again they were turned back. None of the defenders had even been wounded. The next charge was on foot, in such close-packed ranks that the Indians almost overwhelmed the fort; but again the charge was broken, and after a last desperate horseback attack, the Sioux were finally routed. As they removed their dead and wounded from the field in the dusk, the relief from Fort Phil Kearny arrived. In the end, seven of the defenders died, including the four woodchoppers, and three were wounded.

It was a devastating defeat for the Sioux. A force of 1,500 of their best warriors had been routed. Another battle up in Montana—the so-called Hay Field Fight, near Fort Smith on the day before Wagon Box—had been equally disastrous for the Sioux. Red Cloud's reputation as a warrior was permanently tarnished.

The Sioux retired, licking their wounds—some 180 warriors were killed at Wagon Box. Things quieted down. And then the government seemed to change its mind. The whole Powder River Basin, along with the Black Hills, was given back to the Sioux. A deadline was established after which no white man was to use the Bozeman Trail, and soldiers were now to be stationed only to enforce the deadline. In a way, Red Cloud had lost the battle but won the war.

In August of 1868, the garrison evacuated Fort Phil Kearny. Red Cloud and his warriors watched them go, then charged down to the fort. The soldiers could see a huge column of black smoke rising from the fort when they looked back.

◆ AFTERMATH OF INDIAN WARS

This was only the first chapter of the war with the Sioux. Between 1868 and 1874, instead of fighting the Sioux, the government supported them. Red Cloud toured the East Coast as a Chautauqua lecturer. In 1870, he addressed a great multitude at the Cooper Union in New York, making a splendid impression. He was dignified, sincere, and full of common sense. Red Cloud never led his people to war again. He ended up on the Pine Ridge reservation in South Dakota, an unhappy man.

Then, in 1874, Custer was sent with his magnificent expedition to evaluate the Black Hills. There was gold in those hills, and the land suddenly became very valuable indeed. Gold seekers were pouring in willy-nilly, and the attempt to keep it sacred to the Sioux was hopeless. The government had already given the Sioux six million dollars between 1868 and 1874 for support. The Sioux were now offered six million more by the government for repossession of the Black Hills. Refusing the offer, the Sioux instead demanded six *hundred* million plus support for seven generations. Government officials lost their patience: a peace conference at White River, Nebraska, broke up, and the war resumed. The "wild bands" of Sioux— those not already on reservations—were peremptorily ordered to surrender and relocate to reservations by January 1, 1876. Or else.

None of them paid the slightest attention. On March 1, the army under General Crook (after whom the northeast county of Wyoming is named) marched with

1,000 men from the new Fort Fetterman, on the North Platte, to enforce the law. Once more, the Sioux were to be taught a lesson. The expedition was not a success. There was a skirmish with Crazy Horse, now leader of the Sioux on the Tongue River, where Connor had won his small victory in 1865. Then Crook, with his soldiers freezing and his supplies low, marched back to Fort Fetterman.

Sitting Bull—Tatanka Yotanka—succeeded Red Cloud as leader of the Sioux forces. But by 1876 the center of action had moved up to Montana, and it was there that the disastrous last Indian victory at Little Bighorn took place, about 40 miles north of the Wyoming border.

Red Cloud. (Courtesy, Library of Congress)

The ironics were compounded. The army victory at Wagon Box was followed by the total capitulation of the government to the Sioux. The Indian victory at Little Bighorn was followed by a determined war of attrition that permanently defeated the Sioux, and drove them forever off their hunting grounds to the reservations in the Dakotas. But this last phase of the war is not really a part of Powder River history.

Military sites of the Powder River Basin Indian wars are preserved as historical monuments. **Fort Phil Kearny** (528 Wagon Box Road; 307-684-7629), 17 miles north of Buffalo, has a visitor center and museum. A monument marks the Fetterman Massacre site, a few miles up on the highway's other side. About 22 miles above Buffalo, near the small town of Story, is the site of the Wagon Box Fight. Connor surprised the Cheyenne and Arapaho camp on the Tongue River 11 miles north of Sheridan on U.S. Route 14, where it starts west over the Big Horns.

POWDER RIVER
BASIN

◆ Cattle Drives of the 1870s

As soon as the curtain fell on the drama of the Indian wars, it rose on that of the cattle boom and, later, the Johnson County War.

Without government prohibition and Indian attack, the grasslands of the great basin between the Black Hills, the Big Horns, the Montana state line, and the North Platte became wide-open for cattlemen. This opening was quickly filled, beginning in the 1870s, by cattle driven up from Texas along Wyoming's eastern border. Once they had come up only for summer pasture, but now they came to stay, and in the decade from 1877 to 1887 Wyoming witnessed its most spectacular and colorful boom-and-bust extravaganza. All through the area, but particularly along the strip at the base of the Big Horns, from south of Buffalo to north of Sheridan, a feudal cattle barony came into being almost overnight. In its swagger, arrogance, extravagance, and initially wild financial success, this barony set a permanent seal on the state in general and the area in particular. This golden age of cattle and the cowboy only lasted a decade, but its effect on the psychology of Wyoming has lasted a century. That bucking horse on the license plate remains a symbol a hundred years later.

The swagger and pride of the horseman is an ancient tradition in European culture, reaching its climax with the knights of the Middle Ages. The mystique was transferred to America by the Spanish conquistadors, blossomed in Texas after the Civil War, and struck Wyoming in full force in the late 1870s. The fact that the Plains Indians had also been the most dashing of horsemen fortified the mystique. The U.S. cavalry that had fought them had its panache, too, with its exploits from the Civil War, and even before that there was the Southern cavalier tradition. So when the cowboy culture struck the Powder River, the country was prepared.

♦ CATTLE RANCHING AND THE OPEN RANGE

Unlike, say, coal mining, where bosses and owners are not likely to work underground, owners of cattle ranches were usually working horsemen themselves. Many of them were old cowhands or soldiers. Others were Britishers with country fox-hunting backgrounds, or German hussars.

Although the setup of the ranch—with its hierarchy of owner, foremen, and hired hands—was semifeudal, the system was anything but rigid. It was democratized by the common bond of a universal admiration for good horsemanship, and any good hand could become a foreman or even an owner. Many owners had once been foremen and cowhands. Of course, many owners were absentee money grabbers, many foremen were hard-nosed and dishonest, and many hands were lazy. But the legend that endures does not tell that story. The mystique of the cowboy-horseman, like the older mystique of the woodsman-trapper, was and remains a central symbol of Far West glamour. In this place and time—the Powder River of the 1870s and 1880s—the legend crystallized. Wyoming citizens will never be made to believe the validity of claims from other Far Western states: The cowboy was really born on the Powder River, and that is that.

Today, most of Wyoming's economy isn't based on cattle, and except for this one brief period, it probably never really has been. Sheep raising, farming, mining (especially coal), oil, and now tourism have, especially during the 20th century, competed with the cattle business for land, political power, and money. But one of the few things you can do with those wide, open spaces is run stock on them. Cattle can't be run without cowhands, and cowhands can't operate without horses. So the cow, the cow horse, and the cowboy remain part of the economy of the state. Those involved in the business have a prestige to which no other group in the state can really aspire.

The towns of Buffalo and Sheridan owe their origins to the cattle boom. In this vicinity, cattle ranches, some of them pretty grandiose, sprang up in those first, flush days. Even before the Indian wars were over, cattle began arriving from Texas. By 1871, over 40,000 longhorns had invaded the state, and this was just the beginning. The southeast and central areas along the North Platte and the Sweetwater got cattle first. The north, of course, was closed; it belonged officially to the Sioux by the treaty of 1868. Even up in the Bighorn Basin, cattle were being run before the boom began on the Powder.

(opposite) Powder River roundup, framed by Army post photographer L. A. Huffman. (Montana Historical Society)

Many cattle ranches throughout the West, but particularly along the Big Horns, were under Anglo-Scottish ownership. Of the 20 big Wyoming cattle companies operating by 1884, half were controlled by Scottish or English owners, with a combined capitalization of over $20 million returning dividends of 10 to 20 percent. In the British Isles, this constituted an investment bonanza.

The secret of this bonanza, while it lasted, was the open range. You didn't have to own your feeding grounds; around your ranch, for miles and miles, stretched grazing land, all tax-free. Though some ranches were themselves enormous—ten or twenty thousand acres—the surrounding seas of unowned grass seemed unlimited.

The large scale and seemingly unlimited possibilities of these endeavors is represented by the Powder River Cattle Company of the English Frewen brothers, Moreton and Richard. Their brand was 76. By 1885, they ran 66,000 cattle on the Powder as far north as Connor's Tongue River and as far south as Fall's Teapot Dome. Their operations extended west into the Hole-in-the-Wall area—so named by the Frewens after a famous old tavern in London—with line camps all along the Middle and South forks of the Powder River. Log ranch houses resembled royal hunting lodges; one, in fact, was nicknamed Castle Frewen. The brothers threw hunting parties in the fall and house parties in the summer; private stages brought the guests in relays up from the nearest railroad station, 250 miles to the south. They used the same stages to import hothouse flowers from Denver, so that lady guests could wear corsages to dinner. Only a few years earlier, Indians had camped on the site of the ranch houses. Not so long before, Portugee Phillips had made his winter ride across the Powder River to Fort Laramie.

Most of the great spreads, including that of the Frewens, collapsed in the great blizzard of 1887–88. But things had already started to go wrong. The boom, like all booms, brought overexpansion; the ranges, even the seemingly unbounded ones of the Powder River, began to be overcrowded and overgrazed. Owners tended to be overconfident, lax, and, in increasing numbers, absentee. They spent perhaps too much time at the Cheyenne Club, in Cheyenne—drinking "rare wines," playing Boston, and contemplating the famous bullet-ridden copy of Paul Potter's picture of a bull—instead of riding the ranges. (Potter's copy of a famous Dutch painting hung in the Cheyenne Club, where a drunken member had plugged it full of holes.) Foremen got greedy and dishonest, and padded the inventory figures while surreptitiously subtracting items for themselves.

Then came the terrible winter of 1887–88. The summer of '87 had been abnormally dry, and feed was scarce. Cattle were already thin. The snow began falling heavily in October, and never melted. December was a month of blizzards. In January came a fatal chinook, a warm wind that melted the top layer of snow, which then froze when the temperature dropped again. Cattle could make it through snow, but not a coating of ice. The temperature plummeted to 40–50° F below zero. Cattle drifted into the beleaguered towns to die in the snow-clogged streets. Herds of thousands were reduced to hundreds. By spring, many cattle barons on the Powder were ruined, and the days of the unlimited open range and corsages from Denver were done.

■ OUTLAWS

◆ NATE AND NICK

One of the exasperating complications of the desperate (but also a bit humorous) Johnson County War was that the bad guys were heavily involved on the front lines of both sides. On the Buffalo side were those martyrs Nate and Nick. Not much is known about them, but they were rumored to have been part of the so-called Red Sash Gang in Texas, whose members wore red sashes to dances. Nate Champion was said to have been run out of Colorado for rustling, Nick Ray to have killed two men in Texas. Heroes they may have been, but they were also, no doubt, gunmen and thieves.

◆ ARAPAHO BROWN

Another hero in Buffalo was the unsavory Arapaho Brown. He was a huge, bearded, gangling Tennessee hillbilly who settled on a Powder River ranch, where he was rumored to have murdered his partner and the partner's family and then appropriated the ranch. Eventually, he was murdered by two inexpert young robbers in an extremely bloody fashion. Despite his popularity, he was generally considered a dangerous character.

◆ TOM HORN

Tom Horn was neither bearded nor gangling, and he was nobody's hero. He was the epitome of the calm, suave, deadly marksman who killed for hire: a successful businessman. Nobody could ever catch him or trace his crimes. He was officially a stock inspector, had served as a scout in the army, and was a champion rodeo roper. He was hired to terrify opponents of the WSGA. No one ever knew for sure if he had committed any crimes. His secrets went with him to the grave. He was finally caught in such a stupidly awkward fashion that everyone felt there must

POWDER RIVER BASIN

Johnson County War

The bonanza was over and the open range increasingly restricted by private or government ownership and control, but cattle was still king along the Powder. The last lurid phase of trouble around the Big Horns was, in fact, centered on cows; it was a battle between the remaining big-time cattlemen and a new generation of small-business cattlemen. This also involved a new breed of bad men, gunmen, and outlaws who became involved in the cattlemen's quarrel. Then there was the intrusion of homesteading farmers (called "grangers") onto the cattle range, and the slow advance of sheep. All this kept things bloodily busy in the 1880s and 1890s.

Since the big owners couldn't continue to control the range, especially after so many of them had gone bankrupt, a new breed of cattlemen, usually former cowboys who had amassed small herds of their own (though they were not always beyond suspicion of having "borrowed" calves from the big herds), began to compete on the market and on the range. Big owners' accusations of rustling and small owners' accusations of coercion finally became so pointed that the situation evolved into a real (if somewhat comic-opera) battle known as the Johnson County War, or the TA War (after a ranch where some of the action was centered.)

Backing the big owners was the absolutist Wyoming Stock Growers' Association (WSGA), based in Cheyenne—at the Cheyenne Club. The conflict was precipitated by the WSGA's series of high-handed actions, the most suspicious and drastic of which were the unsolved murders of various small ranchers—dry-gulched (i.e., murdered in canyons), shot in ambushes, or besieged in their cabins. No one knew exactly who the murderers were. Everyone claimed innocence. But everyone knew it was the big ranchers and their hired gunmen trying to terrorize the small ranchers.

The issue that actually started the war was a legal dispute. The all-powerful WSGA had always told the cattlemen of the state when to hold their roundups and when to drive their cattle to shipping points. This was all a salutary way of preventing confusion, disorder, and unbridled, competitive, cutthroat tactics. The Johnson County cattlemen, however, considered it dictatorship, and they founded their own Northern Wyoming Farmers and Stock Growers' Association. They defied the big ranchers and the WSGA by saying they'd hold their roundups whenever they damn well pleased. The WSGA (being the official state association) then instructed shipping inspectors to seize and sell all "blacklisted" stock and turn the money over to the association. This had always been a way to control rustlers and those ranchers who let rustlers use them as a respectable facade for selling stolen goods. In this case, the state association claimed that the Johnson County ranchers were rustlers or false fronts for rustlers, and some of them probably were. But in the spring of 1892, the small ranchers were going to hold their blacklisted roundup no matter what.

On April 6, a train arrived in the Cheyenne rail yards two days after the annual meeting of the WSGA. That night, the train pulled out, the blinds of the coach cars were drawn, and all telegraph lines north of Douglas were cut. Hidden on the train were a score of expert Texas gunmen with their horses, saddles, and ammunition, as well as a complete camp outfit and three wagons, on freight cars behind. At Cheyenne, an equal number of Wyoming men joined the group on the train; most of these joiners were foremen or owners of big Powder River outfits, including the TA ranch. The total holdings of the ranchers represented was estimated at some 100,000 head of cattle, 5,000 horses, and 86,000 acres of land. The object of this expedition was obviously to break up by force the "illegal" northern association's roundup.

Two young strangers joined the expedition for the fun of it: an Englishman, Henry Wallace, and a Philadelphian, Dr. Charles Penrose. The latter offered to act as surgeon for the party.

The group got off the train at Casper and headed for Buffalo. They never got there. There was a list of supposed rustlers, who were to be executed en route. Some of these in fact *were* rustlers and bad men, notably Nate Champion and his partner, Nick Ray. This pair had become involved with the Johnson County rebels and were looked upon in the north as heroes, making them thoroughly unpopular with the other side. "The Invaders," as the mysterious group coming up from Cheyenne got to be known, first visited a run-down cabin on the KC Ranch (now memorialized by the town of Kaycee, off Interstate 25). The Invaders laid siege to the cabin, hoping to flush out Champion and Ray. Two innocent trappers were also in the cabin, having just dropped in for the night; upon leaving the cabin to wash in the creek, they were captured and held prisoner.

The two outlaws, Champion and Ray, were besieged. Ray, obviously not quite aware of what was going on, went out to fetch water from the well and was wounded. Though dying, he managed to get back to the cabin. From dawn to dusk Champion fought a single-handed battle, and, remarkably, kept a diary while doing so. (The journal was found in the cabin afterward.) Eventually the Invaders fired on the cabin, forced Champion out, and shot him. On his chest they pinned a note saying "Cattle thieves beware." This, of course, made Champion more than a hero: it made him a sort of patron saint and martyr. His death was celebrated in a ballad, the words edited from the entries in the diary, but made to rhyme. The introductory words went as follows:

> I t was a little blood-stained book which a bullet had torn in twain.
> It told the fate of Nick and Nate, which is known to all of you.
> He had the nerve to write it down while bullets fell like rain.
> At your request I'll do my best to read these lines again.

. . . and at the end:

> The light is out, the curtains drawn, the last sad act is played.
> You know the fate that met poor Nate and of the run he made.
> But now across the Big Divide and at the Home Ranch door
> I know he'll meet and warmly greet the boys that went before.

This bit of strong-arm justice en route cost the Invaders the success of the entire enterprise. A neighboring rancher had seen the siege from a bluff and rode to Buffalo in a hurry to alert the town. By nightfall, 200 armed Johnson County men were riding down-country to stop the invasion. A bloodbath was in the making.

The Invaders had gotten separated from their supply wagons on the way to the KC. They heard the Johnson vigilantes were coming, and they galloped to the friendly TA Ranch, 30 miles north. They managed to get there in time to fortify it. They were now the besieged ones.

Meanwhile, the news reached Cheyenne. On orders from the capital, down from Fort McKinney (a new fort several miles west of Buffalo) rode three U.S. cavalry troops, who arrived just as the Buffalo besiegers were about to plant dynamite bombs and end the siege by blowing up the TA. In the end, casualties were light. Besides Nate and Nick, one Texan was killed by the accidental discharge of his own gun, and three others were wounded, two by Nate at the KC. This was the exciting, if almost ludicrous, end to what might have been a very serious affair.

The Invaders surrendered, with relief, to the soldiers and were taken to Cheyenne for trial—where, naturally, they were very popular. Waiting to be tried, they were housed in jail at night and were free to roam the streets by day. When they were released on bail, the Texans were told to be sure and report back to Wyoming for the trial. They promptly went home and were never heard of again. The case was dismissed in January, with the excuse that Johnson County had refused to pay the cost of prosecution. Wyoming justice, as always, had been served without too much quibbling about rights and wrongs, legality and illegality. The main thing was that nobody was shooting anybody anymore.

As for poor, young Dr. Penrose, he escaped and took refuge in Douglas, a center of rabid small-cattleman sentiment. He was about to be lynched as an Invader when the new governor, Amos W. Barber (a doctor and fellow graduate of the University of Pennsylvania Medical School) sent a marshal to arrest (and rescue) Penrose. Barber sat Penrose on the cowcatcher of a train headed eastward and told him not to get off till he crossed the Nebraska line. Penrose didn't dare come back to Wyoming for 20 years.

Tom Horn was hired as an enforcer by the Wyoming Stock Growers' Association to intimidate their opponents during the Johnson County War. Here he awaits his execution in the Laramie County jail. (Courtesy, American Heritage Center, University of Wyoming)

have been some mistake. He shot a 14-year-old boy—who was going out to the ranch corral—in place of the boy's father. How could such a master as Tom be so careless? He made a confession, and his hanging in Cheyenne in 1903 was the sensation of the year. Speculation was, and still is, rife. How could such a canny fellow be caught red-handed doing such a foolish thing? Was his confession genuine? Was he framed by the cattle association because he knew too much? Had he been promised that he'd be rescued at the last minute if he confessed? Or perhaps he really was rescued and a dummy was used in his place. Whatever the truth, Tom Horn remains a dark, legendary figure, half-admired still, as he was when alive. He probably did make that one fatal mistake and probably was hanged. But he remains a legend, due in part to his character and his bad-guy good looks—cool, collected, canny, mustached—and in part to his somewhat sinister name.

◆ Butch Cassidy

Another of Wyoming's favorite bad men is Butch Cassidy. Butch was everything that Arapaho Brown and Tom Horn weren't: charming, humorous, handsome in a cocky, easygoing, devil-may-care, Irish way. Like Horn and most professionals, he practiced his trade all over the West (there's hardly a town in Wyoming that doesn't boast of a visit by Butch), but he was particularly identified with the Powder River and the Black Hills. He had a prosaic real name: George Leroy Parker.

Incredibly, Cassidy was never known to have killed or even injured anyone on purpose. He was a crack shot, however. He wore his sombrero cocked over his red hair, and his blue eyes sparkled with mischief and humor. The Robin Hood legend suited him in particular, but was earned also by the gang he was particularly associated with—the famous "Hole-in-the-Wall gang," or the "Wild Bunch," as they liked to call themselves.

◆ Hole in the Wall Gang ("Wild Bunch")

The Hole-in-the-Wall was (and is), as its name indicates, a "hole"—a valley enclosed by hills, like Jackson Hole. This particular one is located southwest of Kaycee in a far corner of Johnson County. Its reputation as a hideout has given people the impression that it's some deeply secluded canyon, surrounded by cliffs and entered through a secret passage. And it is, in fact, entered by way of a gorge running between red cliffs. But inside, it is a wide, open range, bordered with fairly low hills, except for a long, red cliff to the east: not much of a mysterious, secret hiding place. Its reputation as a gang hideout may have been exaggerated, but the gang that adopted its name was certainly famous enough.

Leader Harvey Logan and partner Butch Cassidy first made a name for themselves in Wyoming with the 1897 Belle Fourche robbery in the Black Hills. Joining Cassidy were Logan's other lieutenants, such as "Big Nose" George Parrott, Harry Longabaugh (also known as the Sundance Kid), and numerous others. They operated all over the West and forged liaisons with other famous gangs. They had other hideouts, too, such as one southwest of Baggs on the Colorado border. Some of these men, Logan included, were deadly. Logan is presumed to have killed at least nine men. He was, like Tom Horn, the calm, civil sort.

They stole from the rich (banks and trains) and not from the poor (small ranchers), and so they became local idols. Banks and railroads got what they deserved. Eventually, though, Cassidy was caught. He stood trial in Wyoming but was released on the condition that he never again operate in the state. Wyoming's gain was Montana's loss. He went right across the border and robbed a bank there to pay for his Wyoming trial.

The Wild Bunch: Harry Longabaugh (Sundance Kid), Bill Carver, Ben Kilpatrick, Harvey Logan (Kid Curry), and George Parker (Butch Cassidy). (Courtesy, Buffalo Bill Historical Center, Cody)

◆ "Big Nose" George Parrott

The most notorious and most elusive outlaw in his time was "Big Nose" George Parrott (1841–1882). A prolific robber who preyed on stagecoaches and trains, Big Nose also was the biggest cattle rustler in Wyoming's Powder River region. By all accounts, Parrott was a braggart, drunkard, womanizer, and friend-betrayer who had a multitude of aliases. A ballad penned by Jean Osborne describes him thus: "This George, he robbed the U.P. train / And double-crossed his pals / Then freely spent his stolen loot / A-boozin' with the gals."

The outlaw was apprehended for the 1880 holdup of a Union Pacific train and the murder of two deputy sheriffs, and was sentenced to hang on April 3, 1882, in Rawlins. According to one account, he broke out of jail but was immediately captured by a mob that resolved to hang him. Big Nose had a rope put around his neck, but when he jumped, the rope broke. While some of the mob said another rope should be secured, others felt it wasn't worth the effort and shot Big Nose to death as he lay on the ground.

"Big Nose" George Parrott (Courtesy, Carbon County Museum, Rawlins)

A different account of his demise can be found in *Bloodletters and Badmen*, by Jay Robert Nash (who refers to Parrott as George Curry, not one of his aliases but a name that has stuck to him nonetheless). After participating in several bank and train robberies, Parrott rode back to the Hole-in-the-Wall and began rustling cattle. Caught red-handed by the sheriff of Vernal, Utah, while changing a brand, Parrott leaped on his horse and galloped off. The sheriff gave chase for 10 miles, and finally downed the outlaw with a "lucky shot." *Casper Star-Tribune* reporter Bill Bragg, though, believes Big Nose botched a train job near Medicine Bow, after which he and his gang were trailed by a couple of lawmen near Elk Mountain. "Both lawmen were killed and Big Nose fled to Montana," Bragg writes.

"One of the members of the gang was caught and a mad mob took him from the law at Carbon and lynched him. Later Big Nose was captured, and when he passed through Carbon, the same gang waylaid Carbon County Sheriff Rankin and tried to lynch Big Nose, too. But, even though they used the same telegraph pole, they didn't get the job done, and relented. So, Big Nose got to go to Rawlins where he was jailed." Yet another mob seized him from the jail and tried to lynch him. They failed in their first attempt but finally succeeded on March 22, 1881.

Dr. John E. Osborne (who would later serve as governor and senator of Wyoming) performed an autopsy and, for reasons best known to himself, the good doctor sawed off the top half of Parrott's skull and presented it to his assistant, Dr. Lilliam Heath (first female M.D. in Wyoming), who used it for many years as a doorstop. Osborne then stripped the hide from Parrott's chest, tanned it, and stitched either a tobacco pouch and a pair of slippers, or a medicine bag and a covering for his favorite pair of shoes. He pickled the rest in a whiskey barrel.

♦ INTRUDERS: GRANGERS AND SHEEP MEN

More disruptive to the 19th-century cattle kingdom than mere outlaws was the intrusion on the range of homesteaders ("grangers") and sheep men. The sheep men and their sheep crept slowly west toward Bighorn Basin despite sometimes murderous opposition by cattlemen. Grangers were a different problem. Cattlemen claimed that the sheep poisoned the range for cattle and overgrazed it, but at least the range remained range, however contaminated or denuded. Homesteading farmers plowed it up and destroyed it for good. They preempted water, and introduced a way of life opposed to that of the horsemen of the plains (like the earlier conflict between nomadic Indians and white settlers).

In some respects, the presence of the grangers was salutary. They brought a spirit of neighborly communal life to a countryside where it had not existed before. Green fields, snug ranches, churches, and schools flourished in places where farming was appropriate and successful. But unfortunately, not all the homesteaders on the plains settled where they should have, such as in potentially rich river valleys. This was especially true of dry farmers. Some settled on dry, high places and broke soil fit only for grazing—soil which the wind then blew away in dust storms. By the 1930s, deserted ruins of farmhouses all over the eastern counties testified to this disaster. (This is what the creation of national grasslands was intended to cure and prevent.)

A certain amount of zoning and control—and cooperation—has improved the situation today. New dams and reservoirs, which provide irrigation for farmers downstream, mean less rangeland for cattle and sheep; and all those dams have changed the character of Wyoming. This intrusion of the Midwest—as represented by eastern border towns like Torrington—into the Far West, does not please those who prefer the latter to the former.

■ TOWN OF BUFFALO   *map page 112, C-2*

Buffalo (about 3,900 people) is distinctly a cow town, as it has been from its beginnings in 1879. Though right at the foot of the Big Horns, it's more a plains than a mountain town. From Buffalo south to Casper, the plains dominate all the way, with cattle as far down as Kaycee. This open and desolate stretch is full of stories of grim events—not only the killing of Nate Champion at Kaycee, but earlier tales as well.

Farmers in Bighorn Basin irrigated cropland in 1920.
(Courtesy, Homesteader Museum, Powell)

POWDER RIVER
BASIN

Two prospectors stumbled into Fort Reno, southeast of Buffalo, in 1865, claiming that they and their companions had found a fabulously rich gold lode on the south fork of Crazy Woman Creek. They had built a cabin there, extracting $7,000 worth of gold in a week, before Indians attacked and killed all but these two survivors. A new party was thrown together and started back to the site. . . and was never heard from again. The cabin and mine had disappeared for good. Another version of the story has one survivor leading the second party back to the mine, when he goes crazy. The Lost Cabin story survives in many versions and variations. No one else has ever found gold on Crazy Woman Creek.

In 1861, four misguided missionaries built a log mission near Kaycee, hoping to convert the Crows. They didn't. In the first place, the Crows were no longer there, having been chased up into the Bighorn Basin by the Sioux. One of the missionaries deserted and one was killed. The two survivors gave up and headed east, and the Sioux, thoroughly unconverted, burnt the mission. No traces of the mission remain.

Buffalo was the nearest drinking place for the Hole-in-the-Wall gang and entertained such folk heroes as Butch Cassidy, "Big Nose" Parrott, and the Sundance Kid.

Buffalo nowadays remains one of the most distinctive Wyoming towns. It has the immense good fortune of a crooked main street, derived from a crooked ford across crooked Clear Creek in midtown. This was built up early on with stalwart brick and stone buildings, many of them hotels, so that the street couldn't be widened or straightened without total disaster. The result is a town center that looks like a town center instead of a collection of wayside tourist traps on a superhighway. It's a town where you can wander up and down the business street with amusement and pleasure, and rest on the seats of a memorial platform-bridge that straddles the creek which tumbles through the middle of the city.

A Historic Buffalo movement is making an effort to save the town's picturesqueness. It has already preserved or restored nearly two dozen old buildings in its downtown, with several on the National Register of Historic Places, including 90–94 South Main, built in 1892 and featuring decorative ironwork on the top edge; 84–89 South Main, with its second-story cast-iron facade, constructed in 1895; and 10–30 North Main, the famed Occidental Hotel, where Owen Wister's Virginian "got his man."

Buffalo's focal point is a splendid Victorian brick courthouse on a hill right in the center of the intersection where Main and Hart Streets meet. Behind the courthouse is the **Jim Gatchell Memorial Museum of the West,** comprising the main brick building with permanent installations and an old Carnegie Library building with temporary exhibits. *100 Fort Street; 307-684-9331.*

Strangely enough, the name "Buffalo" does not derive, as one expects, from the once-local beast, but from faraway Buffalo, New York. Too bad.

All the old hotels are closed, though the buildings and the signs on their facades remain. Motels abound on the outskirts, of course. One of the nicest in the state is the **Z-Bar Motel** (626 Fort Street; 307-684-5535), which has small log cabins and a big green lawn with spruces and a few apple trees, scarce in Wyoming. Another splendid motel on the strip is the **Super 8** (655 E. Hart Street; 800-800-8000 or 307-684-2531), distinguished by the Spillman Carousel, imported from Ocean City, New Jersey, with fiberglass reproductions of original wood carvings by Buffalo wood sculptor Bill Jennings. Several of the horses depict famous steeds from Wyoming history including Steamboat, Little Soldier —ridden by a Crow scout in the Battle of Little Bighorn—and Comanche, ridden by the sole survivor of General Custer's command at Little Bighorn. The carousel frame dates back to 1925. Today, it revolves to the accompaniment of many turn-of-the-century tunes and present-day squealing kids, and is altogether a rare delight, especially out here. There's also the Cloud Peak Ferris Wheel, built in 1936 by the Eli Bridge Company of Jacksonville, Illinois, for the Utah State Fair. Riders get a grand view of the Big Horn Mountains and the Cloud Peak Wilderness Area from the top of the wheel. The variety store next door is an enjoyable place to browse. Other accommodations include the **Pines Lodge** (U.S. 16, 14 miles west of Buffalo; 307-351-1010), which has pleasant cabins, a restaurant, and a lounge. The cute **Mansion House Inn** (313 N. Main Street; 307-684-2218) is right in town. **South Fork Inn** (U.S. 16, 16 miles west of Buffalo; 307-267-2609) has cabins and inn-rooms set on a rushing stream.

■ JOHNSON COUNTY CIRCLE TOUR *map page 112, C-2/3*

If you want to get a sense of Buffalo's status as the one and only civic center of Johnson County and to see what Johnson County is really like, this mildly adventurous circle tour is strongly advised.

From the main street, take Wyoming State Highway 196 south out of town, and almost immediately you are on the range. One of those finely paved Wyoming highways with nobody else on it, Highway 196 passes through grasslands and by the gates of big cattle spreads. The Big Horns run right alongside, to

POWDER RIVER BASIN

the west. Slowly, the country gets wilder and sparser. After 45 miles, you reach **Kaycee**, famous in song and story, where Nate Champion met his end. There's not much here now: the Hoofprints-of-the-Past Museum (307-738-2381) has some interesting exhibits, and every July brings the Sheepherder Rodeo and Dog Trials. But the stream the town is built on soon becomes the Powder River itself. More adventurous trips west to Hole-in-the-Wall country can start from here. Also in the region are petrified trees and prehistoric Indian art in a secluded cave.

JIM GATCHELL MEMORIAL MUSEUM OF THE WEST

The country around Buffalo absolutely overflows with history. The "Bloody Bozeman" Trail ran nearby, creating countless conflicts between Indians and the invading settlers and soldiers. The infamous Johnson County War was also fought not far away, and the Powder River drainage was a favorite haunt of Butch Cassidy's Hole-in-the-Wall gang.

During the first half of the century, Theodore James Gatchell, a friend of local Indians as well as whites, collected or was given thousands of historic items. Originally displayed in his drugstore, they are now the core of a collection that includes more than 10,000 artifacts, making Buffalo's county museum a real treat. It houses dioramas and displays of items found at the Wagon Box Fight, the TA Ranch siege (Johnson County War), and the Fetterman Massacre. You'll find guns, bayonets, bones, old clay pipes, and even jasper arrowheads taken from a soldier killed by Indians at Fort Fetterman. Most touching is the flattened horn of Bugler Adolph Metzger. His body was the only one the Indians did not mutilate after the massacre; instead they covered him in a buffalo robe out of respect for his valor.

Scattered around one room are some other surprises: a pair of Cheyenne medicine rattles used in the Dance of Victory after Custer's defeat at Little Bighorn, an arrowhead that belonged to Red Cloud, a cartridge belt made by famed mountain man Jim Bridger, and outlaw Tom Horn's spurs and a bridle, braided while he was awaiting execution in Laramie. Ask the folks at the museum to point out a rifle probably used by the cavalry at Little Bighorn and a shell that was fired from Custer's handgun.

— Don Pitcher

POWDER RIVER BASIN

Next, take Wyoming State Highway 192 due east, along the Powder River. After about 20 miles through more and more naked, rugged country, with the pleasant, cottonwood-dotted Powder to the right, the highway makes a sharp turn south to cross the river. At this point (marked Sussex on the map, though there's not the slightest trace of Sussex), a smaller road turns off to the north. This isn't marked until you get right up to it. It leads in the direction of the site of Fort Reno. Even if you could find the fort site, there is, in fact, nothing there. Beyond, the unnamed road soars north along the course of the Powder, but high above it. After a short distance, another road plainly labeled "Bozeman Trail" turns away inland and to the left. But the road you want to take proceeds north, to open up an incomparable vista of the rough and rugged Powder River country: precipitous benches over which the road wanders; deep, craggy draws; the river meandering far below; and steep ridges and far-stretching ranges to the east, across the river. If ever the mystique of Powder River can be made visible, it's along this perfectly feasible but seemingly reckless route. Eventually the road curves westward toward the mountains, and you have yet another of those wonderful Wyoming plains-and-

Dirt roads reach miles to ranches in the Barnum area.
(opposite) Many roads in the Powder River Basin are built from crushed clinker, a red rock created when coal is burned underground.

POWDER RIVER BASIN

mountain encounters. At this point, for no observable reason (perhaps someone bribed the highway department), the road becomes paved. More ranches are visible, horses and cows are more frequently seen. The Big Horns loom larger, and as an anticlimax you run perforce into Interstate 25 and traffic and road signs and modern times. But the surrounding landscape remains empty as ever.

■ NORTH OF BUFFALO *map page 112, C-2*

Heading north to Sheridan on Interstate 90, you pass **Lake De Smet,** a big, blue gem set in a frame of treeless, brownish-pink buttes. Locals come to enjoy the great fishing, boating, waterskiing, and swimming. You can exit from the Interstate and drive up to a Father De Smet memorial, but it's not really worth it. However, the lake is beautiful in its way, and it's one of the few historically peaceful sites in this whole region. Father Pierre Jean De Smet, the first Catholic missionary in this part of the Rockies, discovered the lake and no doubt preached to the Indians. Local lore includes various silly stories of water monsters and Indian maidens (always "maidens," never just "girls"). It is most curious that there should be a natural lake here at all; there's not another for hundreds of miles east and south. Back roads lead northeast to Route 14 and Ucross, home to a great art gallery, Big Red, on the site of an old stagecoach stop.

Soon, there's an exit labeled Piney Creek, and, seemingly as an afterthought, **Fort Phil Kearny** (also see page 153 and map page 112, C-2). A back road, Highway 193, takes you through pastoral country to a cutoff that leads left to the splendidly scenic site of the fort. It's a small plateau that would certainly seem ideal for a fort, except that it is almost entirely ringed by bare heights, behind which Indians could creep up unobserved. No original buildings stand (the Indians took care of that when the fort was abandoned), but there is a small yet informative historical museum with photos of all those army folk—Fetterman, Carrington, Powell—and their ladies, notably the Mmes. Carrington I and II. All of this gives you a vivid impression of the fort and its inmates.

An even windier, bush-lined country road, also well-marked, leads by ranch gates and through groves to the site of the Wagon Box Fight. One is indeed astonished at how far the soldiers had to go to get their wood, and how far from the forested foothills the Wagon Box site itself is. There's a big monument to the soldiers who died in that battle, but nothing at all in honor of Powell, to whom all the credit should be given. The famous failures—Caspar Collins, Fetterman,

Crook, Custer—are amply honored by things named after them. Not Powell, the only sensible, victorious one of the whole lot! Such are the rewards of virtue.

Another bushy road leads on north to the tree-hidden town of Story and meets Wyoming State Highway 193 again at Banner. This in turn dumps you onto U.S. Route 87/Interstate 90, where you turn south to get to the **Fetterman Monument.** The monument lies east of the road on a high hill, looking down over the scene of the battle. There's not much else to see. Turning north again towards Sheridan, you will soon come to Wyoming State Highway 335, which goes west toward the mountains and the town of **Big Horn.**

◆ BIG HORN   *map page 112, B/C-1*

Big Horn (pop. 198) looks more like an Old West cow town than just about any other town you're liable to see: two false-front, flourishing bars and a few other assorted old buildings. Along the road to it are beautiful, tucked-away ranches and houses. One extraordinary specimen of local ranch glory—yet typical in its grandiosity—is the nearby **Bradford Brinton Memorial** (239 Brinton Road; 307-672-3173). The estate looks as though it had been flown in from Manchester, Vermont, and dropped intact on Little Goose Creek. It lies in a beautiful, shady grove, but instead of giant elms there are giant cottonwoods, and the stone walls are made of round river cobblestones. Established by the Moncrieffe family in 1892 during the Johnson County War, the original ranch was bought and enlarged by Brinton in 1923. Its ranch brand is Quarter-Circle A. The house is a white clapboard, neo-Colonial mansion, like so many in New England, filled with handsome East Coast furniture, but also with many Western touches—pictures, statues, books, and Indian objects. Artwork in the permanent collection includes masterpieces by Remington and Boren. Brinton himself was from neither East nor West, but was a gentleman of means from Chicago. He devoted his life to cattle and collecting. What doesn't fit in the beautiful house overflows into a spacious gallery behind the parking lot, where permanent collections and rotating exhibits of Western art are housed. Especially if you've just come from the rough, tough banks of the Powder River and the blood-soaked grounds of Fort Phil Kearny, it's all hard to believe. Big Horn is also home to the **Bozeman Trail Museum**, housed in an old blacksmith shop that served travelers on the famous trail north.

Not far from the Quarter-Circle A is Wallop family ranch, where Queen Elizabeth II stayed when she visited. The Wallops were kin of the Moncrieffes, and both clans were established here by younger sons of British titled families. One of these sons, after the death of his elder brothers, found himself heir to the title. He returned to England to sit in the House of Lords, but refused to give up his Wyoming citizenship until forced to do so by law. More recently, Malcolm Wallop served three terms in the U.S. Senate, retiring in January 1995.

Off Wyoming State Highway 335, west of the Brinton Memorial, is the well-marked **Spahn's Big Horn Mountain Bed & Breakfast**, a stylish log home built by the owner. Unknown to most tourists, it has spectacular views of the plains below, and a host—Ron Spahn, a geologist and former Yellowstone Park Ranger—whose knowledge of the country, both plains and mountains, is encyclopedic. Horseback riding and guided tours including wildlife-viewing trips are available. *307-674-8150.*

Up the Red Grade Road west of the Brinton Memorial and Spahn's, you head into the mountains, climbing abruptly from the bare plains to the forested heights of the Big Horn plateau. The road is poorly graded, but you can make it with caution, in low gear. At the top, you emerge onto a broad, smooth Forest Service road that wanders about the lush mountain scenery of the Big Horns, through open meadows thick with wildflowers and deep woods of fir and pine, past small blue lakes, with striking views southwest to the Big Horns' highest mountains, Cloud

The historic Sheridan Inn, the "House of 69 Gables," was completed in 1893.

Peak and Black Tooth Mountain. With luck, you might also catch sight of moose, elk, and deer. All it takes is the grit to get up here.

■ SHERIDAN   *map page 112, C-1*

Finally you get to Sheridan (pop. 16,500), which seems overwhelmingly urban. In fact, it's one of the few places in the whole state—the others being Cheyenne, Laramie, and Casper—that feels like a real city. Even the larger Rock Springs and Green River don't have the same sense of cosmopolitanism. The entire length of Main Street is lined with stone or brick two- and three-story buildings, mostly from the early 1900s, occupied by businesses—a real old-fashioned city center that resembles Cheyenne's, but is more extensive and well-preserved. Though the usual commercial strip extends out towards Interstate 90, eastward, no one can doubt where the life of the town is—so totally different from Gillette, where all the action takes place out in Pizza Hut–land, near the Interstate.

Though the cattle business still dominates the town in fact and in spirit— weekly local ranch rodeos in the summer and annual public cattle drives in early July are part of the area's activities—other industries add to the economy. Coal has long been important here. There used to be mines to the south along the mountains, and some mines still exist to the east; but no one has ever thought of Sheridan as a coal town like Gillette. Coal brought an Old World mining population to town, and ethnic celebrations have become customary. Descendants of miners with Polish or Middle European names have become leading citizens. Oil has a presence, too. But none of these industries determine Sheridan's character in the way that its old cattle history does.

As Buffalo represents the post-boom cattle business, Sheridan represents the heyday of the cattle boom. It retains some of the aura of the great days before the blizzard of 1887–88. The low altitude (3,725 feet) and the presence of water from the mountains permit flowers and fruit trees that would perish farther south to flourish here. The first polo field in the nation (which remained open for many years) was a legacy of the Scottish-English influx. The preserved Brinton and Kendrick mansions are other mementos of Sheridan's tradition of high living. In 1893, the Burlington Railroad built a spur up to Sheridan, where Burlington owned and managed the grand old **Sheridan Inn**, in the spirit of the Adirondacks, with gambrel roof, dormer windows, and a big summer piazza. Considered the finest hotel between Chicago and San Francisco, dozens of famous people stayed here, starting

Oil derricks crowd the slopes of Wells Spring Valley in 1903.
(Courtesy, Hot Springs County Museum, Thermopolis)

with Colonel Cody. In the midst of another restoration, the National Historical Landmark is expected to reopen for guests in 2008 with 22 "mini-museum" rooms as well as meals and guided tours. *856 Broadway; 307-674-2178.*

It is appropriate that the dude ranch, that curious blend of the extremely Western and extremely Eastern, had its origins here in Sheridan, with **Eatons' Ranch** and the **Horton's HF Bar** (see page 337) still flourishing as the two oldest and most famous of their kind. There are now dude ranches all over the West, but Wyoming is where the best and most authentic dude ranches are.

Sheridan itself is the creation of one enterprising man, J.D. Loucks. The first settlement was a log house on Little Goose Creek, with a big corral in back reputed to be the hideout of "Big Nose" George Parrott, later—or so one story goes—killed in Rawlins and skinned by a man who went on to become the governor. Bad men surely did get about the country. A trapper, Jim Mason, built the first house of record in 1878, which was converted into a store and post office by a later owner (thus making it a Wyoming town) and called Mandel. It was bought by Loucks in 1882. He laid out a town plat on brown wrapping paper and sent this informal plan to Cheyenne with a $3 registration fee. On May 10 of the same year, the town was staked on a 40-acre plot and named after Loucks's commander in the Civil War, Union Gen. Philip H. Sheridan.

Lots sold for $2.50, which compares unfavorably (for the town coffers) to the $250 and more paid for lots in railroad boom towns. The town was incorporated in 1883, and Loucks, the only begetter, was, of course, mayor. He recorded only one person arrested there in the first two years of the town's existence. Nobody shot? What a contrast to centers farther south! By the end of 1883, there were 50. buildings, and soon, two rival newspapers: the *Sheridan Post* and the *Enterprise.*

Even before Sheridan existed, however, the area had its famous characters. Martha Cannary, better known as Calamity Jane, got her nickname on Goose Creek before the town of Sheridan was conceived. She was already a well-known scout by then, and was sent out with troops to quell an Indian uprising in the region. Her commanding officer, a Captain Egan, was shot. Calamity Jane (still just Martha then) rescued him, and when they got back to the fort he recovered and said to her, "I name you Calamity Jane, the heroine of the plains." That's the account found in her memoirs, at any rate. She didn't settle down in Sheridan, instead going on to become one of the West's most picturesque figures, particularly in Deadwood, Colorado, during the gold rush. But her first reputation was made in Wyoming.

The real history of Sheridan began with that flamboyant cattle boom of the 1880s. The influx and influence of the early cattle barons put a permanent stamp of high-living on the town. Along with the Bradford Brinton Memorial, the other principal sight in the area is the Kendrick house, Trail End, now a state-owned historic site and also on public display. Unlike the Brinton ranch, **Trail End** is definitely a town house, located up the hill on Clarendon Avenue, west of Main, in the center of the city. John B. Kendrick, immortalized by a plaque in the Cheyenne capitol, retired here after he had made his pile in cattle. He drove cows up from Texas in the late 1870s and became not only one of the state's great cattlemen, but a governor and U.S. senator. *400 E. Clarendon Avenue; 307-674-4589.*

Trail End was finished in 1913 and is very different architecturally from the Quarter-Circle A. It has borrowed not from Vermont, but from Tuxedo Park, New York—with dark woodwork, baronial-style decor, and heavy, handsome turn-of-the-century furniture. The Flemish exterior is surrounded by a garden in which is preserved the first cabin built on the site of Sheridan, in 1878. Once the old **Mandel Cabin,** it was reconstructed in 1976 by the Colonial Dames of Wyoming, active in Sheridan, preserving what was left of materials bought for $50 by Loucks in 1882. It was moved in 1883 to the corner of Main and Loucks

Streets and incorporated into a large building that became the city's first bank in 1885. The old cabin was shoved to the back of the lot and covered with clapboards and plaster—and was therefore preserved. The swift changes from 1880 to 1910, a mere 30 years, are admirably illustrated by these neighboring buildings, a cabin and a mansion.

On the way down the hill, Lewis and Dow Streets curve around Goose Creek (concrete-lined to protect the city from floods) and pass by a monument to Gen. George Crook, after whom Wyoming's northeastern county is named. It was here in Sheridan that Crook tried to substitute mules for horses before starting north for his ill-fated encounter with Crazy Horse and Sitting Bull on the Rosebud in Montana. The mules were unbroken, and the cavalrymen riding them were expected to break their own mounts on the spot. The result was a riot of bucking mules that is still remembered with pleasure in local history. The monument says nothing about this, of course.

To the south lies Alger Street and the **Fulmer Public Library**, surely one of the most beautiful modern buildings in the state, designed by Adrian Malone. The library contains a collection of paintings by Emil Gollings, one of Wyoming's most important artists, who ended his rather wandering career as a permanent resident of Sheridan. Sheridan's library is the best place in the state to see his work.

On Main Street itself, **King's Saddle and Rope Emporium** should not be missed. It's the greatest traditional center for cowboy gear in Wyoming. Not only does it sell saddles, clothes, sombreros, hackamores, and other Western paraphernalia, but behind the store, across the alley and through a black door, an annex houses a fine selection of ropes and riatas, as well as a famous collection of saddles. For anybody interested in Western lore, it's enticing and nostalgic. In this archetypal all-cowboy emporium, there's a big, framed photo of Queen Elizabeth II, commemorating her visit to Sheridan in the fall of 1984. She rested in the happy aroma of horses out in Big Horn, and of course she visited King's.

Nearby, at 151 North Main Street, is the famous **Mint Bar**, a hangout for local citizenry, with cattle brands and Charlie Belden photographs on the walls. The handsome red building at 117 North Main, formerly the Bank of Commerce, is now occupied by the **Book Shop**, which is the center of the town's literary life and features lectures and poetry readings. And there are several fine restaurants in the neighborhood, including the **Buffalo Bill Saloon** in the Sheridan Inn at 856 Broadway and the **Silver Spur** at 832 N. Main Street with cowboy portions. Altogether, Main Street is a parade of old business buildings adapted to modern usage.

The buildings are antique by Wyoming standards and are described in minute detail in a pamphlet, *Sheridan Main Street District Walking Tour,* available at the visitor center off Interstate 90. This whole exhibit of plains-style architecture, well preserved above the first-floor shop windows, has been enrolled in toto on the National Register of Historic Places—one of the few streets to be so honored. Sheridan also has a fine theater, the WYO Theater, presenting Broadway plays, nationally known entertainers, and local talent. The building, formerly called the Lotus Theater, was closed for a while until a group of locals set out to "Save the WYO," which they did, reopening it in 1989 (42 North Main Street, 307-672-9083).

This only scratches the surface of Sheridan's odd blend of cows and culture, Old West and new sophistication. The town's startlingly un-bloody history is rare for Wyoming.

■ OVER THE BIG HORNS TOWARDS CODY   *map page 112, A/B-1*

From Sheridan, Interstate 90 takes you briskly for some 15 miles to Ranchester (pop. 700) and U.S. Route 14. It is possible to detour around this bit of the Interstate by finding and taking Wyoming State Highway 331 west out of Sheridan,

Saddle bronc rider Larry Sandvick signs autographs.

then curving around by gravel roads north and west past the entrance to Wolf, the private post office of the Eaton Ranch. It's a beautiful trip across the golden, open foothills, but the chances of going astray are significant.

On Interstate 90, there's no problem finding your way to **Ranchester.** Ranchester is an old ranching center, and its name is another example of the Anglo-Western mixture of the area: it combines *ranch* with *chester,* the latter a common ending for many town names all over the British Isles, derived from the Latin word *caestra,* meaning "camp." The Connor Battlefield Historic Site is right in the middle of town, the scene of an 1865 clash between U.S. Troops and the Arapaho Indians (walking path, camping, fishing, picnic area and public restrooms).

From Ranchester, U.S. Route 14 heads west, past a historical sign pointing out the 1865 Sawyer Fight, through **Dayton** (pop. 678), an unspoiled ranching town where the great German painter Hans Kleiber had his cabin, before beginning the breathtaking ascent up that abrupt eastern flank of the Big Horn Mountains. The road up to the plateau is broad but constantly curving, climbing some 20 miles through forest and meadow, past lakes and streams, campsites and fishing spots, to **Burgess Junction,** in the middle of wide, open mountain meadows.

Here you have a choice of routes west to the Bighorn Basin and Cody. It's a difficult choice: **Alternate Route 14** takes off almost directly west through increasingly high, open country along the edge of timberline. Just before the highway begins its vertiginous descent, a small, marked road leads north to the Medicine Wheel (see page 135), one of Wyoming's most exciting and mysterious archaeological sites. **Regular Route 14,** on the other hand, turns almost due south through Granite Pass, and west through Shell Canyon, with its dramatic 120-foot falls and gorge.

*(opposite) Devil Canyon in Bighorn Canyon National Recreation Area
is a popular spot for local boaters.*

NORTHWEST CORNER
ABSAROKAS & YELLOWSTONE

Map page 183

Yellowstone
Nat'l Park

♦ **AREA OVERVIEW**

Wyoming's northwest corner, including Park County and the Absaroka Range, Yellowstone, and Jackson Hole, attracts far more visitors than any other part of the state. For many tourists, the northwest is the only reason they come to Wyoming.

From the Montana line down to the south tip of the Wind Rivers at South Pass, from the northwest corner of Yellowstone down through Jackson Hole and Swan Valley, this slice of the state is so different from Wyoming as a whole that it seems a separate province. Cody, Lander, Riverton, and fast-growing Jackson are the only towns of even modest size. Central to the complex is Yellowstone Park. There's nothing in the world quite like Yellowstone Country.

Weather: Below the Absarokas, wind and low precipitation keep snow from accumulating on the basin floor. The breeze also takes the edge off the summer heat. Yellowstone National Park is at high altitude (above 7,500 feet); therefore, its weather is unpredictable. Summers are warm, with temperatures in the high 70s. In winter, temperatures hover near zero throughout the day. At night in any given month, the temperature may drop close to freezing. Annual snowfall averages nearly 150 inches.

Food & Lodging: Guest ranches, the most attractive and characteristic accommodations, are concentrated in the northwest corner. Restaurants and lodging abound in Cody and Yellowstone.

■ The Absarokas *map page 183, B-2/3*

East of Cody sprawls the Bighorn Basin, with the Big Horn Mountains looming distant on the horizon. Cody itself, with a population of about 8,800, is the largest and oldest of Yellowstone's gateway towns. West of Cody stretches one of the country's most formidable mountain barriers, the **Absaroka Range**. It's not a single, serrated wall, like the Tetons or the Wind Rivers, but rather a mixed-up mass of wilderness, all part of the Shoshone and Bridger-Teton National Forests, occupied principally by bear (black and grizzly), moose, elk, deer, and a few mountain sheep. This barrier of almost random peaks can be explored and seen only by horse or on foot in summer, and on skis or snowshoes in winter. (Snowmobiles are allowed in some parts of the range, though why one would want to violate the wilderness with one of these machines is beyond the understanding of this author.)

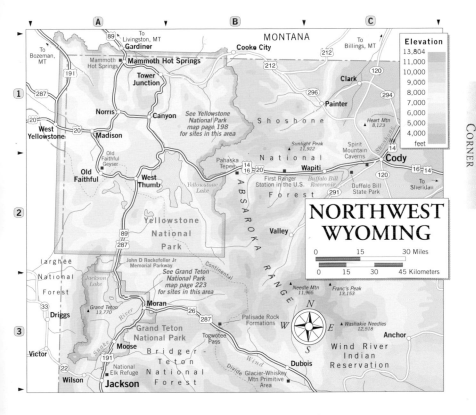

The Absarokas contain an incredible variety of scenery and many summits over 11,000 feet, including Sunlight Peak which overhangs beautiful, hidden Sunlight Basin and its choice dude ranches. To the south lies the highest of all, Frank's Peak (13,140 feet). Dominating the Wind River Basin are the Washakie Needles, north of Washakie's own Wind River Indian Reservation. There are many, many more peaks; some can be seen from roads, but most can't. They form a variegated, wide, and rugged barricade for a hundred miles from Montana down to the Wind River—beyond which rise the even more spectacular Wind River Mountains. Some of this great mountain area is protected by national parks and wilderness areas. The rest of it is protected (or exploited, as some environmentalists claim) by the National Forest Service. All of it is beautiful.

■ CODY   *map page 183, C-2*

One of the most famous and popular of the West's gateway towns is Cody, "East Gateway to Yellowstone." But Cody is more than just a gateway. As the name indicates, it is a memorial to the man who remains probably the most famous citizen of Wyoming: Col. William F. Cody, or "Buffalo Bill." Though he didn't found the town, and though he lived and worked all over the world during his active career, there's no doubt he's identified with his name-place. Scout and showman, buffalo slayer and friend of royalty, Cody left his stamp all over the town.

The town of Cody was actually started in 1895 by a group of entrepreneurs, near the DeMaris Springs, a thermal display that was first described by John Colter in 1807 and which has gradually lost its steam over the years. A company was organized to promote the town, and the organizers thought it might be a good idea to ask their friend Cody if he'd like to be president of the company. He was traveling with his Wild West Show at the time and was the best-advertised man in the West. Cody accepted and suggested that they name their new town after him. They agreed gladly, according to one founder, "since this did no harm to us and highly pleased the Colonel." They moved the town up the Shoshone River and convinced the Burlington Railroad to lay tracks to the town. When Park County was created in 1909, Cody became its seat. The first cabin there was built by a former Wyoming governor, Frank L. Houx, and well-known people have been flocking to Cody ever since. The first church was started with money raised at a poker game. The Colonel (so one story goes) sat in and won. The church's denomination was to be decided by the winner, and Cody said he guessed he was probably an

Beartooth Pass area, Shoshone National Forest

Episcopalian since his folks had originally come from Virginia (though he was born in Iowa). So Episcopalian it was.

◆ VISITING CODY

From its beginnings, the town of Cody capitalized on its Western character, as did Cody himself. It has always been a tourist center. Being on the way to Yellowstone helped, as did the colonel's worldwide reputation. One of the town's principal monuments is the Irma Hotel, built by Cody and named for his daughter. It was decorated with Remingtons, and it catered to everyone of importance who came through town. It has lost its Remingtons, but the great cherrywood bar still graces the sumptuous dining room, which is still very active. Along with the Plains Hotel in Cheyenne, it's a remnant of the days of Wyoming's great hostelries. *1192 Sheridan Avenue; 800-745-4762 or 307-587-4221.*

The principal attraction in town is a complex of museums under the umbrella of the **Buffalo Bill Historical Center,** which is housed in a magnificent stone building with great, high-pitched roofs, dominating the town from the western end of the main street. The BBHC's five very different, but equally fascinating, collections are housed in separate pavilions. *720 Sheridan Avenue; 307-587-4771.*

NORTHWEST CORNER

Buffalo Bill Cody with his family in front of the Irma Hotel in 1912. (Courtesy, Buffalo Bill Historical Center, Cody)

An 1875 poster romanticizes Buffalo Bill's adventure-filled life.
(Courtesy, Buffalo Bill Historical Center, Cody)

Food & Lodging in Cody

Buffalo Bill Village Resort. Contains two facilities: the Buffalo Bill Village Resort, 85 log cabins containing 184 rooms with contemporary decor inside; and the Holiday Inn Convention Center, a standard 2-story chain hotel. *1701 Sheridan Avenue; 800-527-5544 or 307-587-5544.*

Cody Lodging Company. Managing 50-plus properties in the area, including historic homes in town; great for families. *1302 Beck Avenue, Suite B; 800-587-6560 or 307-587-6000.*

Irma Hotel. Brass beds, period furniture, a huge restaurant, and an elegant bar given to Buffalo Bill by Queen Victoria. In summer, locals stage gunfights on the porch. Ask for historic rooms. The restaurant is a longtime favorite for stalwart but tasty meals. *1192 Sheridan Avenue; 800-745-4762 or 307-587-4221.*

Parson's Pillow. Innkeepers Lee and Elly Larabee serve a hearty breakfast in this former church—Cody's first, built in 1902. Four rooms, each individually designed. *1202 14th Street; 800-377-2348 or 307-587-2382.*

Proud Cut Saloon. Owner Becky Crump describes her steaks, burgers, and seafood as "kick-ass cowboy cuisine"; unusual sandwiches are also available for lunch at this tavern. Western decor with historic photos of Cody Country. *1227 Sheridan Avenue; 307-527-6905.*

Silver Dollar Bar & Grill. The tastiest hamburger in town. Rustle up a friend at night to come here and catch a rock band. *1313 Sheridan Avenue; 307-587-3554.*

Sunset House Restaurant. Steaks, pastas, salads, and seafood; seating in a lovely solarium. *1651 Eighth Street; 307-587-2257.*

Opened in 2002 as the fifth wing of the BBHC, the **Draper Museum of Natural History** gives visitors the chance to take a "virtual expedition" through mountain forests and valleys as they discover the natural forces that shaped Yellowstone and the surrounding region. The center also explores the influence of early explorers and modern ranchers.

The most famous of the BBHC collections is the **Whitney Gallery of Western Art,** one of the most prestigious collections of its kind in the country. It was established by Gertrude Vanderbilt Whitney, whose Whitney Museum in New York did much to foster the American realism movement that dominated the 1920s and '30s. Whitney's Cody museum fosters Americana as well—specifically, painting and sculpture associated with the Far West. The collection begins with early explorer-artists, like Catlin and Miller, and the landscapists Bierstadt and Whittredge. The high point is the museum's wonderful selection of works by Remington and Russell, along with semi-reconstructions of their studios complete with sketches and painting gear. Up through these masters, the art is magnificent. Unfortunately—perhaps because later patrons lacked Mrs. Whitney's acute and sophisticated taste—things go a bit astray as the collection progresses chronologically. Much of the later painting, though dynamic and colorful, is not on the same level as the earlier work. Still, the total effect of the collection is so overwhelming and evocative of the West that the slight post-Whitney decline doesn't make much difference—though a greater concentration on native Wyoming artists like Gollings, Will James, and Archie Teater would have been nice. The work of photographer Charlie Belden is displayed elsewhere in the museum.

The **Plains Indian Museum** stunningly displays brightly colorful Native American arts and crafts, mainly from the Sioux, Crow, Arapaho, Shoshone, and Cheyenne tribes. This section of the center alone is worth the price of admission.

Balancing the Whitney wing in front is the **Buffalo Bill Museum,** with a collection that ranges over the long and insanely active career of the great man, from his adolescent days as a champion Pony Express rider, to his performances before European royalty. It's a funny, fascinating, and outrageously glamorous panorama of the life of that extravagant, corny, and courageous figure.

The **Cody Firearms Museum** is one of the largest of its kind in the world and a mecca for gun lovers. The heart of the museum is the Winchester Collection, but you'll also find guns of other makes, a re-creation of a colonial gun shop, and a hunting lodge housing big-game trophies.

CODY AREA GUEST RANCHES

Along with cattlemen and cowhands, the population of Cody has for years been salted with distinguished dudes (like Mrs. Whitney)—some of whom have bought ranches and settled. Cody is also a well-established dude-ranching center.

Absaroka Mountain Lodge. Modern cabins with private baths in a quiet setting along a creek; dining room. Horseback riding, fishing trips, big-game hunting. *Open May 1–November 15. Wapiti, 12 miles east of Yellowstone; 307 587 3963.*

Bill Cody Ranch Resort. Operated by Buffalo Bill's grandson. Modern mountain cabins with baths, for a maximum of about 60 guests. Wilderness horseback riding. *Open summer only. 25 miles west of Cody on U.S. 14/16/20; 307-587-2097.*

Crossed Sabres Ranch. Weekly guest ranch. Rodeo, pack trips, square dancing. Family oriented. *Wapiti, 9 miles east of Yellowstone; 307-587-3750.*

Grizzly Ranch. Two modern log cabins. Pack trips. Family-style meals. *Open June–September. North Fork Route bet. Cody and Yellowstone; 307-587-3966.*

Hunter Peak Ranch. Rustic cabins with baths and kitchens, with meals available. Horseback riding, fishing, pack trips. *Open year-round. 23 miles east of Yellowstone's Northeast Entrance; 307-587-3711.*

Pahaska Tepee Resort. Buffalo Bill's 1904 hunting lodge, now with 47 rooms in 15 modern cabins, open May–October and December–March. Snowmobiles, horseback riding, cross-country skiing; spacious dining room and tavern. *2 miles east of Yellowstone on U.S. 14/16/20; 800-628-7791 or 307-527-7701.*

7 D Ranch. Reserve one of 11 modern log cabins by the week. Fishing, horseback rides. Excellent food, family style. *In Sunlight Valley, 50 miles northwest of Cody; 307-587-9885 or 888-587-9885.*

Shoshone Lodge. Sixteen log cabins with baths. Activities include fishing, horseback riding, pack and big-game hunting trips, and occasional square dances. Dining room. *In Shoshone National Forest, 4 miles from Yellowstone's East Entrance; 307-587-4044.*

BUFFALO BILL CODY

Col. William F. Cody or "Buffalo Bill" was one of the most remarkable men of his or any other era, a man who almost single-handedly established the aura of the Wild West.

Born to an Iowa farm family in 1846, William Cody started life like many others of his time. His parents moved to Kansas when he was six, but soon his abolitionist father, Isaac Cody, became embroiled in arguments with slaveholders intent upon making Kansas a slave state. While defending his views at a public meeting, Isaac Cody was stabbed in the back. He died of complications from the stabbing.

The 11-year-old Will Cody became the family's breadwinner. He joined the company of Alexander Majors, running dispatches between army supply wagons, with his $40 monthly wages going to his mother. On his first long wagon trek west, Cody met Wild Bill Hickok, perhaps the best gunfighter ever. On one of these excursions, the impressionable young Will stopped in at Wyoming's Fort Laramie, where he sat in awe as famed scouts Jim Bridger and Kit Carson reminisced. The experience was a turning point in Cody's life; he resolved to become a scout one day.

Cody's next job as a rider for the new Pony Express offered excellent training. At just 15 years of age he was already one of the finest horseback riders in the West, and a crack shot with a rifle. By the time he was 18, the Civil War had begun. Cody joined the Seventh Kansas Regiment, serving as a scout for the Union army. Afterwards, Cody briefly tried his hand at the hotel business, before heading west to briefly join Lt. Col. George Custer as a scout. In 1867, Cody found work hunting buffalo to supply fresh meat for railroad construction crews, a job that paid a hefty $500 per month and soon made him famous as "Buffalo Bill." Cody was one of the best hunters in the West.

After this stint, Cody finally got the job he wanted: chief scout for the U.S. Army in the West, a job packed with excitement and danger. The Indian Wars were on.

During these campaigns, the writer/preacher/scoundrel Ned Buntline began writing of Cody's exploits for the New York papers, giving Buffalo Bill his first taste of national acclaim. America had a new national hero. East Coast and European gentry began asking Cody to guide them on buffalo hunts. Cody's incredible knowledge of the land and hunting greatly impressed the men, but they were stunned to also discover in him a natural showman. During a trip to New York, Cody suddenly entered the world of high society and in a short while was on stage himself.

Suddenly, Cody was called back to the West, for the Sioux were again on the warpath after chafing under their forced reservation life. Shortly after he returned to guide Gen. Eugene Carr's forces, they learned of the massacre of Custer's men at the Battle of the Little Bighorn. In revenge, Carr's men set out to pursue Indians along the border between Nebraska and Wyoming. Under Cody's guidance the men surprised a group of warriors and Cody shot the chief, Yellow Hand, and scalped him, yelling "First scalp for Custer!"

Buffalo Bill's days in the real wild West were over, and he returned to staging shows, eventually starting his famed Wild West extravaganza. This was unlike anything ever done before. The Wild West Show was so successful that, at its peak in the late 1890s, it made Cody more than a million dollars in profits each year.

Even Sitting Bull, who had led the Sioux against Custer, joined the Wild West Show, selling autographed photos of himself. Amazingly, Sitting Bull and Buffalo Bill became good friends. Cody, who had earlier bragged of his many Indian killings, changed his attitude toward them, eventually saying, "In nine cases out of ten when there is trouble between white men and Indians, it will be found that the white man is responsible."

For the next decade the show continued to tour, gradually losing its originality as other forms of entertainment came along, especially movies. Cody used his money to buy the 40,000-acre TE Ranch in northwestern Wyoming. He helped establish the town of Cody, where he built the Irma Hotel in honor of his daughter. His hunting lodges of Wapiti and Pahaska Tepee (Pahaska was his Indian name) still stand today along the road to Yellowstone.

Unfortunately, Buffalo Bill seemed to have no comprehension of how to save money. His fortune slipped away and the Wild West Show went into bankruptcy. Three years later, in 1917, Cody died while visiting his sister in Denver and was buried on nearby Lookout Mountain.

Despite this pathetic ending, few individuals have ever lived such a diverse and adventure-filled life, and few could count so many people as friends. Cody's impact on American culture is still felt today, not just in the image of the West that he created and that lives on in hundreds of Western movies, but also in the Boy Scouts (inspired by his exploits), the town of Cody, and even in the dude ranches that dot Wyoming.

—Don Pitcher

(opposite) Buffalo Bill in 1872. (Courtesy, Buffalo Bill Historical Center, Cody)

A happy full day could easily be spent in the center. There are changing exhibits, a small cafeteria, a spacious gift shop, and two small, beautifully landscaped, statue-adorned side gardens for resting the feet (the most conspicuous statue, of Buffalo Bill by none other than Gertrude V. Whitney herself, is a bit away from the center, in a monument area adjacent to the grounds).

Another sight of the town, which itself is neat and nice but no longer picturesque, is the **Old Trail Town,** which houses a collection of pioneer relics. It's a bit north of the highway, on the strip west of town, and can be missed—but it's a must for those going toward Yellowstone. It consists of a long street of rescued ancient cabins, stores, sheds, and buildings of all kinds, all original, and most of them full of fascinating memorabilia. One of the oldest buildings is the original Hole-in-the-Wall cabin, once used by Butch Cassidy and the Wild Bunch, and not to be missed. *1831 Demaris Drive; 307-587-5302.*

■ THE ROAD TO YELLOWSTONE *map page 183, B/C-2*

The only road from Cody to Yellowstone is U.S. Route 20 (which includes routes 14 and 16). It is also the only highway crossing the mountains between U.S. Route 212, which wriggles along the Montana line, and U.S. Route 287, which runs between Jackson Hole and Lander in the Wind River Basin. From Lander to Cody as the crow flies is about 125 miles, and it's about 40 more from Cody to Montana. This expanse, which would hold most of the Eastern seaboard between New York and Baltimore, is crossed by just these three highways, and serves as another example of Western spaciousness.

U.S. Route 20 (14/16) goes up through the startling scenery of Shoshone Canyon. It passes by Buffalo Bill Reservoir, a project sponsored by the colonel himself, and runs into the mountains along the rushing Shoshone River, beneath fantastic, red-rock pinnacles with names like the Holy City, the Laughing Pig, and so forth. Despite these touristy names, it would be hard to exaggerate the effect of the pinnacles, especially when seen against an intense, blue Wyoming sky. The surrounding Shoshone National Forest is the oldest in the United States, created, like Devils Tower National Monument, under that most ardently conservationist of all American presidents, Theodore Roosevelt. (The fact that TR was a notable slaughterer of game has been held against him by modern environmental purists; but big-game hunters were early and active conservationists who fought to preserve animals for hunting.)

Along this magnificent forested valley known as the Wapiti is found a series of

Tower Falls *(1872), by Thomas Moran. (Collection of Gilcrease Museum, Tulsa)*

the state's best guest ranches (see page 190). These are a cross between the old, established dude ranches (which never took people off the road without references) and tourist cabin camps (which do). The compromise of the guest ranch is one of the chief charms of Wyoming, combining the convenience and availability of overnight stays and hearty meals with the pleasant surroundings of a regular dude ranch. Most offer comfortable, separate log cabins for sleeping and a big cabin for dining and relaxing. They have horses and guides for riding and fishing, and vary in style from comparatively modest to grandiose. One of the best, **Bill Cody Ranch Resort**, was even founded by a descendant of the colonel himself. Another fine option is **Pahaska Tepee**, just before you reach the eastern gate of Yellowstone. Its great, steep-roofed, main building is made of logs, and was once a Bill Cody hunting lodge.

By the time you approach Yellowstone's East Entrance, the road is full of curves and slow traffic. It wriggles past Pahaska and into a final jam of waiting autos, indicating that you have reached Yellowstone National Park.

■ WELCOME TO YELLOWSTONE *map page 199*

Most of Yellowstone is wilderness, best seen and appreciated on horseback or afoot. There's so much to see there that a month would be too short a time to inspect everything, though much of the scenery could be considered repetitive: hundreds of geysers and hot springs; dozens of waterfalls, canyons, and mountains; thousands of elk, bear, and bison; and even some museums. For the average traveler, a fairly complete, if crowded, survey of the famous sights can be made (just barely!) in two days, via the two circuitous roads, Upper Loop and Lower Loop. This guide sticks to these loops. If you stay on the route, stopping to gaze seriously at these sights, your two days will be happily filled. If you want to do more, you'll need more time and energy than a two-day round trip will allow.

If you want to stay overnight in one of the many and varied tourist facilities of the park, plan ahead and make reservations. A few of these lodgings are sights—practically natural wonders—in themselves. As you pass into the park at any of the five main gates, a ranger will be glad to hand you accurate and fairly detailed directions and data, and also to advise you on which facilities are booked up and which are possibly available. To keep up with the endless construction schedule, call 307-344-2117 for 24-hour road reports.

■ YELLOWSTONE HISTORY

As Shoshone was the first national forest, and Devils Tower the first national monument, so Yellowstone was the first national park. With 2.2 million acres, Yellowstone is one of the largest national parks in the country.

The first white man known to have seen the area was the ubiquitous John Colter. He came west with Lewis and Clark, left their expedition on the way back from the Pacific in 1806, and went into the wilderness to trap and explore. His hair-raising adventures took him into Jackson Hole from the south. He crossed the Hole and went over Teton Pass into Idaho and Pierre's Hole. In 1807, he passed into the Yellowstone country from the south, where he saw Yellowstone Lake, the falls of Grand Canyon of the Yellowstone, and various hot springs and geysers—but not Old Faithful and the main geyser basins, for which he was long given credit. The principal thermal display he seems to have described was the De Maris Springs, on which Cody was first founded. To the outside world, his descriptions were so unbelievable that he became known as a liar. Unlike other old-timers such as Jim Bridger, who rejoiced in this kind of reputation, Colter was aggrieved. He died in 1813 before he could be vindicated, his name immortalized as Yellowstone's first sarcastic nickname: Colter's Hell.

As early as 1827, a member of the Rocky Mountain Fur Company visited Yellowstone and published in the *Philadelphia Gazette* a rather detailed account of what he saw. He mentioned a large freshwater lake in the south, along which springs of hot water and others "resembling a mush pot" were playing. Jim Bridger passed through sometime in the 1830s. Bridger was a legendary teller of yarns; he loved to amuse himself and others with tales of such things as the canyon he crossed by walking on petrified air. As a result of his tall tales, few people believed Bridger's true accounts of the natural wonders he encountered in Yellowstone. He didn't do much to help Colter's case, either.

In the 1860s and 1870s, serious expeditions were made or attempted (Raynolds in 1859–60, De Lacy in 1863, et al). In 1870 and 1871 occurred the two surveys that figuratively and literally put Yellowstone on the map. The official Washburn expedition spent a month in the summer of 1870 making a careful, documented study, and made a report that "electrified the nation." For the first time, the public began to believe in Yellowstone. More decisive was the Hayden survey of the following year. This was the expedition that brought along William Henry Jackson and Thomas Moran, whose photographs and paintings of the beauties and wonders of Yellowstone so excited Congress. The park was created "for the benefit and enjoyment of the people." On March 1, 1872, President Grant signed the act of dedication.

It was some time before most Americans were able to enjoy their new park. Up to 1895, the annual visitor attendance remained less than 5,000. The park was still hard to get to, and hard to get *through*. Pack trips and stagecoaches were the only means of transport, and holdups of the stages were routine. Before 1886, the park was run by a civilian superintendent and a few "scouts." The first of these superintendents was Nathaniel Pitt Langford, of the Washburn expedition. For the next 30 years, a U.S. cavalry troop policed the area. Finally, in 1911, the secretary of the interior appointed a true superintendent. A corps of rangers was hired, and the park has been run under this system of management ever since.

President Theodore Roosevelt and Major John Pitcher of the U.S. Army in front of Liberty Cap in 1903. (Courtesy, National Park Service, Yellowstone National Park Collections)

The Northern Pacific railroad came to Gardiner, Montana, outside the park's north gate, in 1902. The Union Pacific arrived at West Yellowstone (also in Montana), outside the west gate, in 1907. Some 25,000 visitors saw the park in 1905, an early high point for tourism, but this was succeeded by an inexplicable nine-year slump. This slump was cured by the introduction of the first automobile in 1915, when the visitor tally leaped to more than 50,000. By 1929, there were 260,000 visitors. Now the number is in the millions, which has caused massive problems, even air quality problems. Cut the numbers? If so, how? Limit automobiles? Nothing has been done yet, and erosion caused by human traffic continues to be a severe problem at the major attractions. Coney Island must be less crowded than Yellowstone in summer, when traffic near the famous places slows to a crawl.

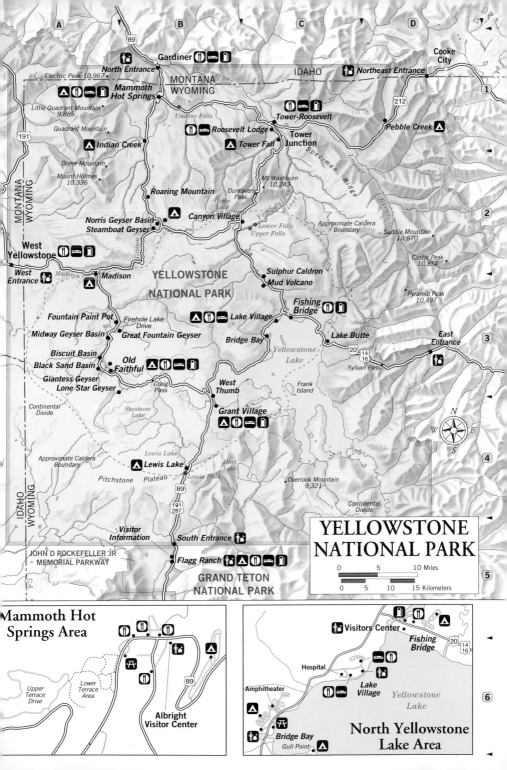

YELLOWSTONE
NATIONAL PARK

0   5   10 Miles
0   5   10   15 Kilometers

Mammoth Hot Springs Area

Upper Terrace Drive
Lower Terrace Area
Albright Visitor Center

North Yellowstone Lake Area

Visitors Center
Fishing Bridge
Hospital
Amphitheater
Lake Village
Bridge Bay
Gull Point
Yellowstone Lake

IMPRESSIONS OF GRANDEUR

Standing near the margin and looking down the canyon, an immense chasm or cleft in the basalt, with its sides 1,200 to 1,500 feet high, and decorated with the most brilliant colors, the rocks weathered into an almost unlimited variety of forms and here and there a pine sending its roots into the clefts on the sides as if struggling with uncertainty for existence, the mind of the onlooker is seized with impressions of grandeur. Mr. Moran exclaimed with a kind of regretful enthusiasm that these tints were beyond the resources of human art. The waters of the Yellowstone seem, as it were, to gather themselves into one compact mass and plunge over the descent of 350 feet in foam as white as snow. Upon the yellow, nearly vertical western side, the mist mostly falls, and for 300 feet from the bottom the wall is covered with a thick matting of mosses, sedges, grasses and other vegetation of the most vivid green, which have sent their small roots into the softened rocks and are nourished by the ever-ascending spray.

—Ferdinand Hayden, 1871

■ THE EAST ENTRANCE   *map page 199, C/D-3*

Coming from Cody, the first of these famous places is **Yellowstone Lake**. This is one of the largest, highest (7,731 feet), and most beautiful bodies of water in the country (of its kind, of course; it's not in the same league as the Great Lakes). On a clear day, especially on first sight as you descend from Sylvan Pass, the effect of a vivid sky reflected on the still surface is overwhelming. The **Lake Butte** viewpoint is reached by a short, steep road to the right, just before you reach the lake's shore. The view from above gives you a full sweep of the lake and a glimpse of the Tetons far to the south and west.

Once you reach the lake, the highway curves along the shore, through open meadows decorated by lazy hot springs and grazing bison, till it reaches **Fishing Bridge**, which crosses the river at the lake's outlet. At one time this bridge was lined with fishermen, but now fishing is prohibited. The stream is the beginning, though not the source, of the mighty Yellowstone River, which rolls down to the Missouri and Mississippi Rivers and on to the Gulf of Mexico. Just beyond the bridge, the road merges into the Lower Loop. The natural thing would be to turn south and continue the drive along the beautiful lakeshore; but in order to cover the whole circuit of the park without repetition, our route turns north.

(opposite) The colorful walls of the Grand Canyon of the Yellowstone.

■ Yellowstone Lake to Tower Junction   *map page 199, C-2/3*

Heading north along the limpid and placid young Yellowstone River (once full of hip-booted fishermen, but now closed to fishing in this area), you come to **Hayden Valley**, a peaceful, wide, grassy meadow, and one of the park's most beautiful spots. In addition to its natural beauty, the valley offers thermal features and wild game. In the **Mud Volcano** area, **Dragon's Mouth** and **Black Dragons Caldron** are big water-and-mud hot springs that belch and roar and splash about and stink in a splendidly repulsive way, to the delight and horror of all children. The valley's buffalo population is a recent phenomenon. The common roadside excitement used to be spotting bears, but in the interest of restoring the animals to a more natural existence, the National Park Service has persuaded the bears to move off the road and into the woods (where they belong) by closing off garbage dumps. Bison, which used to be pretty much confined to the Lamar River Valley, have increased in number, and have now taken the place of bears as tourist pets and spectacles. Tourists used to be warned about the dangers of bears; now it's the dangers of bison. The only thing that hasn't changed is the idiocy of travelers who don't realize that wild animals are indeed *wild*. Meanwhile, the bird population of Hayden Valley remains spectacular. You'll see such commonplace visitors from California and Utah as gulls and pelicans, and, if you're lucky, such native rarities as trumpeter swans. The valley is, of course, named for Ferdinand Hayden, whose 1871 expedition inspired Congress to create the park.

Soon, the pastoral serenity of the Hayden Valley gives way to dark canyon walls and rough water, and you come to the **Grand Canyon of the Yellowstone**, with its two spectacular falls. It's one of the world's most colorful wonders, and enough all by itself to justify creation of the national park. The **Upper Falls** (109 feet) is the lesser of the two, but it is still grand and is the more accessible one. A path from the parking lot leads right to the point where the powerful, dark water topples over the cliff with a roar and spume of spray that catches the sun in rainbows. The **Lower Falls** (308 feet) is more spectacular, but is best seen from a distance, looking up the multicolored canyon. You can drive along either side of the canyon and get numerous variations on its beauties from viewpoints labeled **Inspiration Point** and **Artist Point**. The artist first inspired to paint the falls was, of course, Thomas Moran—and nobody since has done it better. William Henry Jackson took the first black-and-whites; they're splendid, too, but color is of the essence.

Canyon Village is a big, homely, modern center for everything from souvenirs to food and lodging. Built around a vast parking lot that has been much improved over the years by the growth of pines, it is typically crowded in season. The cabins, in their pine-shaded "villages," are simple but comfortable and tasteful. The food in the main restaurant is good, the shops enormous and richly stocked. The center is so large that it seems to be able to handle the huge crowds. But it can't possibly be called "scenic." There used to be a beautiful hotel here, one of the most magnificent in the park, but the earthquake of 1959 damaged it (and it was probably already losing money), so it was torn down just before the revival of art deco would have made it a historical monument. A great loss to architecture, and to tourism.

At Canyon, you could go due west on a boring, straight road through burned timber and without sights, to Norris Geyser Basin. But our route continues north on the Upper Loop, passing into open country after crossing **Dunraven Pass**.

Mount Washburn is the central feature of this new landscape, so much more scenic than the endless lodgepole plateau that occupies (or occupied before the fires of '88) most of the southern half of the park. Washburn is only 10,243 feet high, which in this part of Wyoming is just a hill. It is approached from the south by Dunraven Pass (8,859 feet), which also isn't much of a pass, but has fine views to the south of still-unburned forests, though there is a considerable amount of burnt ground on the north side. Along with Hayden Valley, Mount Washburn is a memorial to the leaders of the seminal expeditions of 1870–71. Oddly enough, Mount Washburn is one of the park's highest summits that's visible from the road. For although the level of the park is high—most of it between 7,000 and 8,000 feet—none of its peaks compare with the Absarokas or the Tetons. A road goes part of the way to Mount Washburn's summit from the north side, but the lookout on top is reachable only by trail (look for signs warning of grizzly bears).

Tower Fall is the next principal point of interest. Though less impressive than the falls of the Yellowstone River, it is attractive: a slender column of water emerging from a fantastic cluster of yellow rock spines. After falling 132 feet, Tower Creek flows off in a sleek canyon to join the Yellowstone River. Shortly after Tower Fall, the **Calcite Springs** overlook of the Yellowstone Grand Canyon appears. The springs aren't much to look at, but the gorge they are in is awesome—not colorful like the more famous southern part of the canyon, but grand, deep, and somber.

(following pages) Bison along Firehole River near Old Faithful.

■ TOWER JUNCTION TO MAMMOTH   *map page 199, B/C-1*

At Tower Junction, the Upper Loop turns west to Mammoth Hot Springs. To the right, due east, U.S. Route 212 goes over a spectacular pass and through the northeast gate toward Cooke City and Red Lodge, in Montana. Along the way the road passes the park's old buffalo range, the lush valley of the Lamar River, now home to wolves. This area, especially around Cooke City, was devastated by fire. Sometime in the late 1830s, long before the Yellowstone fires of 1988, trapper Osborne Russell passed through the Lamar Valley and noted the area's beauty:

> There is something in the wild romantic scenery of this valley which I cannot . . . describe; but the impressions made upon my mind while gazing from a high eminence on the surrounding landscape one evening as the sun was gently gliding behind the western mountain and casting in gigantic shadows across the vale were such as time can never efface from my memory.

These roads lead through open meadow and mountain scenery ablaze with wildflowers in midsummer. Striking, odd-shaped peaks surround the valley on every side, most notably the jagged crags to the east. Fortunately, the area to the west was only lightly touched by fire.

Along the road to Mammoth Hot Springs stands the relatively ancient (1906) and honorable log cabin camp of **Roosevelt Lodge Cabins**, initiated by Teddy himself and still retaining the air of a hunting lodge and dude-ranch outfit. There's a fine main lodge for meals, and many nice, smaller cabins for sleeping; unfortunately, the cabins are popular and hard to get into. Advance reservations are suggested; *307-344-7311 or 866-439-7375* (also see page 334).

Soon you come to another park oddity: the **Petrified Tree**. It's just that—the remains of a whole tree trunk standing in a pretty, somewhat fire-scarred valley off the highway. Elsewhere in the state there are more extensive exhibits of the kind, notably one on the Laramie plains, but they are less accessible.

Farther along are the Wraith and Undine Falls. **Wraith Falls** is a good half-mile trail trek south of the highway. **Undine Falls** is right on the road, to the north. Both are pretty, but Undine is a lot easier to see than Wraith.

(opposite) The travertine terraces of Mammoth Hot Springs.

◆ MAMMOTH HOT SPRINGS   *map page 199, B-1*

Mammoth Hot Springs is the capital of Yellowstone. It's park headquarters, and there's a staid little village of old-fashioned stone houses where park personnel live under a canopy of old-growth trees, the whole resembling an old military post (which it once was). The vast **Mammoth Hot Springs Hotel** has been modernized with 140 cabins, a few with hot tubs, and is now very stylish-looking. One restaurant serves regional cuisine; the other spacious dining room offers cafeteria-style food. *Xanterra Parks and Resorts; 307-344-7311* (also see page 334).

Mammoth was the busiest entrance to the park when the majority of visitors came by railroad, before the automobile took over and the railroads ceased passenger service. A big, stone gateway at the North Entrance celebrated the touristic preeminence of this entryway, and the size of the hotel's north entrance is accordingly immense. The hotel is still enormously crowded and busy. It is fronted by the massive terraces of Mammoth Hot Springs, which in the early 20th century was the park's foremost thermal display, as well as the premier tourist center. But things aren't what they used to be: most of the terraces are dry or only faintly steaming. Still, there are two sufficiently active ones, **Minerva** and **Palette Spring**. Minerva, on the lower end of the terraces, and Palette Spring, accessed from the uphill trails, are fine, fully flowing, multicolored terraces with hot water cascades. Paths and steps still lead all over the great white sepulchers of defunct terraces. The terraces have a melancholy grandeur and the springs show faint signs of residual life, but the walk is long and the steps are steep.

Horace Albright Visitor Center, near the hotel, is the central information source for the whole park; it's open daily year-round. The center offers information about the park, ranger-led walks, films and videos, and exhibits about Indians and explorers who first came across the area's astounding sights. Notable are 23 watercolors by painter Thomas Moran, as well as his easel, chair, and painting accoutrements; and 26 photographs taken by William Henry Jackson as part of the 1871 Hayden survey. Jackson's huge 8x10 camera, similar to the one used on the Hayden expedition, is also here, a reminder of how cumbersome it must have been to take these photographs. *Call the main switchboard at 307-344-7381.*

Terrace Loop Drive gives a grand panorama of the springs to the south, including one fairly active terrace on the very south end of the complex. Swinging into the woods, the road passes all sorts of fascinating, semidefunct, curiously misshapen, separate outgrowths.

■ MAMMOTH TO NORRIS   *map page 199, B-1/2*

The 21-mile road south from Mammoth to Norris is the homeliest stretch of travel in the park (except for the link from Canyon to Norris). In contrast to the road from Canyon Village to Mammoth, this one passes through forest and low hills, following the rather mousy Obsidian Creek through its willow valley much of the way. There's nothing particularly interesting or beautiful to see along the route; it's true that you can see the snow-capped Gallatins to the northwest, and that there are elk visible along the way, but the only two sights, Obsidian Cliff and Roaring Mountain, don't really amount to much. Also, this area was more devastated by fire than any other section of the park visible from the loop roads. There are burnt patches at Dunraven Pass and elsewhere, but nothing quite like this. But the natural cycle continues and young trees now dot the burned forest floor.

Obsidian Cliff, on the east side of the road, is made of shiny black obsidian, a glassy volcanic stone prized by Native Americans as a material for arrowheads and other blades.

Roaring Mountain is a good deal farther south. It has long ceased to roar. When it blew in 1902, killing many trees, it did roar and smoke, but now it's a bare, white sulphur cliff with several feeble steam vents still active.

For thermal variety and profusion, nothing matches **Norris Geyser Basin**. Probably a full day could be happily spent looking and waiting for the eruption or mere bubbling up of each and every geyser and hot spring there. There are two large thermal areas at Norris: the Back Basin, south of the entrance near the visitor center, and the Porcelain Basin, to the north.

The complete circle of **Back Basin** is longer, but it has fewer events, spaced farther apart. They are big events, however: notably **Echinus Geyser**, which goes off in a splendid, if diffuse, fashion every hour or so—it's become erratic of late); and **Steamboat Geyser**, which performs modestly but more or less continuously. Steamboat can erupt tremendously, though, as it did in May 1989, to become the tallest geyser in the park—and on the planet, for that matter. The Norris Geyser Basin has been active at all times through the years, but the program varies dramatically. Former spectacles dry up, and new ones (mostly geysers) surge forth. Meanwhile, other less active springs and holes keep right on steaming and bubbling.

Porcelain Basin is far more crowded with thermal events (and people) than Back Basin. It's a wide pink-and-white valley where a constant, rather minor tur-

NORTHWEST CORNER

moil of spouting and steaming transpires. Printed guides are available in boxes near the visitor center, and the rangers are very helpful.

At Norris, how much you see is a matter of persistence, appetite, endurance, and time. If you're a thermal nut, this is the place. Otherwise the Echinus and a few other sights might suffice.

■ NORRIS TO OLD FAITHFUL   *map page 199, B-2/3*

At Norris, the Upper Loop ends and the Lower Loop begins, and the dull 12-mile umbilical cord to Canyon Village takes off east. The Lower Loop goes down from Norris to Madison Junction, 14 miles along the handsome gorge of the **Gibbon River**. It, too, has falls. However, this lovely area has also been wracked by fires and mud slides caused by flooding rains.

At Madison Junction is a small museum and campground. From there, a road runs west along the **Madison River**, one of the famous fishing streams of the West, and through mountain scenery to West Yellowstone, Montana. The Lower Loop continues south to Old Faithful, passing all sorts of pools and geysers en route.

Just beyond Madison Junction, before you get to these geysers, there's a short, scenic detour up the gorge of the **Firehole River**, with its fine cliffs, splendid rapids, cascades, and a big, surprisingly warm swimming hole in the river, where kids cavort. The water temperature is moderated by hot springs.

After this diversion and your return to the highway, it's hot water all the way. Among the myriad thermal features along this route, the most interesting are the Fountain Paint Pots, the hot-spring pools of Midway Geyser Basin, and, finally, Old Faithful itself.

Fountain Paint Pots, in the Lower Geyser Basin, is sort of a *Traveller's Digest* of thermal phenomena. It has one or two of everything. There is a beautiful, blue, hot-spring pool; some hot, roaring steam vents, called fumeroles; an area of pink, plopping mud-geysers; and several small but active water-geysers. Nothing stupendous, but a bit of everything. Here, a lazy tourist has the opportunity to see all the main varieties of thermal display in one place.

Shortly beyond the Fountain Paint Pots, the one-way Firehole Lake Drive heads back north, passing **Great Fountain Geyser**. Farther on, at Midway Geyser Basin, are two immense, steaming, wonderfully colored hot-spring pools. The one closest to the road, **Excelsior Geyser Crater**, was a great geyser that blew up not so long ago, leaving a deep cavity full of blue water. Behind the crater, toward the hills, is

(opposite) Winter turns Castle Geyser into an otherworldly masterpiece.

the equally full and gorgeously colored **Grand Prismatic Spring**. There are many other smaller, less interesting pools, but these two are the prime attractions.

The **Biscuit** and **Black Sands Basins** are more of the same (except that thermal displays are never exactly the same); any attempt to list them all would lead to confusion and perhaps insanity, especially as they keep changing from year to year.

◆ **OLD FAITHFUL**   *map page 199, A/B-3*

The supreme attraction of this whole thermal region is, of course, Old Faithful. This is undoubtedly the world's best-known thermal outburst. Though other geysers are, or have been, larger, nothing approaches the grandeur—or the familiarity—of aptly named Old Faithful. Though it is named for its regularity over the decades, lately there has been a rather suppressed rumor of some fickleness; nonetheless, its regularity is still remarkable, and the always impatient anticipation of hundreds of spectators during the season is faithfully rewarded by its 140-foot explosions of roaring, steaming water, shooting up in a shapely fountain.

Old Faithful is not the only spectacle in the vicinity. A rival in grandeur is the manmade **Old Faithful Inn**. This vast hall, like a fairy-tale giant's castle, dates from 1903. To celebrate its centennial, major renovations were undertaken and continue, though most of the lodge remains open. It is still awe-inspiring, especially the six-story interior grand hall, with intricate log-work and huge stone fireplaces. It claims to be the largest native-log structure in the world (designed by a R. C. Reamer of Seattle, with something Swiss in mind) and is still very much an active hotel, with dining rooms, shops, annexes, and all sorts of accommodations at different price levels. The fire of 1988 came perilously close, but didn't touch the lodge, although some service buildings burned. *307-344-7311* (also see page 334).

Roundabout the inn spreads one of the largest and most active of Yellowstone's geyser basins, **Upper Geyser Basin**. By comparison, Norris is profuse, busy, and cheerful; the Midway Basin pools, calm, soothing, and richly colored. Old Faithful's Upper Geyser Basin is grand and awe-inspiring, a wide valley of white volcanic ash, full of the gnarled cones of other punctually famous geysers, and studded with steaming hot springs. To catch some of these other geysers you may have to wait hours, weeks, months, even years. A few are seen only with the greatest of luck and planning. **The Giantess**, for instance, habitually sits dormant for six to eight months before blowing—up to 200 feet in the air for four hours. Other features are more amenable, such as the non-eruptive springs known as the Teakettle, the Pump, Spasmodic, and Summit. Long paths take you all about the

(opposite) The Morning Glory Pool is one of Yellowstone's most famous thermal features.

NORTHWEST CORNER

basin and to other thermal areas, notably the nearby **Lone Star Geyser** and the far-off **Shoshone Geyser Basin** along Shoshone Lake, to the south.

■ OLD FAITHFUL TO WEST THUMB   *map page 199, A/B-3*

As you go over **Craig Pass** (8,261 feet) on the road to West Thumb, you get a glimpse of **Shoshone Lake**, far below and to the south, looking as though it had been totally bypassed by the fire of 1988; the fire spared a swath (running southwest to northeast) east of Old Faithful.

West Thumb, on Yellowstone Lake, is the place noted in the 1827 *Philadelphia Gazette* accounts of active mud geysers. There are still hot springs along the shore and even *in* the lake itself, but as at Mammoth, there has been a decline. The mud pots that used to pop and burble have subsided. An old sign described them as being "likened to a bowl of porridge," and the *Gazette* said the springs resembled a "mush pot." They no longer plop, but the residual springs are highly colorful, and the wide, blue lake beyond is, when in a good mood, as beautiful as ever.

These thermal areas are capricious. Earth tremors, like the serious one in 1959 that killed people on the edge of the park, disturb geysers and upset springs.

(above) The Old Faithful Inn's six-story interior grand hall contains intricate logwork and huge stone fireplaces. (opposite) One of the most impressive sights in Yellowstone is Echinus Geyser in the Norris Geyser Basin.

Sometimes thermal features just get tired and fade away, as did the De Maris Springs, once active near Cody. And sometimes they get *more* active: Norris Basin seems feistier than ever.

From West Thumb, the Lower Loop Road turns north along the shore of the lake toward the junction at Fishing Bridge. This particular stretch of shoreline was completely spared by the fire and is its old pristine self. Sights include a **natural bridge,** to the west. One of the remaining grand hostelries of the park, **Lake Yellowstone Hotel,** still stands on the shore at **Lake Village**. Neither Nordic nor Western in style, it's the model of a Great Lakes–style inn: a yellow neo-Colonial, built in 1889. It has an especially comfortable, delightfully old-fashioned atmosphere (though recently it's been tastefully redecorated). You can imagine evenings sitting on a front veranda, the ladies rocking, the gentlemen smoking pipes, and someone strumming a mandolin. The hotel is open from mid-May to late September. *Yellowstone Central Reservations; 307-344-7311* (also see page 334).

■ WEST THUMB TO JACKSON HOLE   *map page 199, B-3/4*

Just south of West Thumb, on a short detour east, is ugly **Grant Village**, with its scattering of buildings and parking lots along with a marina and campground; it was desperately threatened by fire in 1988. Then you begin a gradual decline from the Pitchstone Plateau, which occupies most of the southwest corner of Yellowstone, passing **Lewis Lake**, a favorite fishing place, and somber **Lewis Canyon**. These are the principal sights en route, along with pretty little **Lewis Falls**, close to the lake's outlet. Unfortunately, this area is far from untouched by the fire: Lewis Canyon, in particular, was badly burned, and much of Lewis Lake's shoreline was ravaged, though the stretch along the roadside miraculously escaped the flames. But new green growth has gained a strong foothold since then.

Finally, you exit Yellowstone through the south gate onto the **John D. Rockefeller Jr. Memorial Parkway**. The road's name recognizes one of the most extraordinary and generous conservationist efforts in the history of America: the rescue of the Jackson Hole valley floor from predatory commercialism by the timely purchase of private lands for their inclusion in a national park. Local activists (who thought of the idea), Horace Albright (who got Rockefeller personally involved), and, eventually, the governments of the state and nation brought about the creation of Grand Teton National Park in 1950 (see page 226).

The result of this long effort lies at the end of the memorial highway. The first upsurges of the Tetons come into view as soon as you leave Yellowstone, becoming more and more visible and exciting as you head south. When you reach extremely long Jackson Lake itself, you have entered Jackson Hole, though the valley proper doesn't begin till you reach the Snake River below the dam.

■ YELLOWSTONE WILDLIFE

Everyone's favorite place to see wildlife is Yellowstone Park. Bison and elk are the most commonly seen large mammals, creating long traffic jams as folks get out to take photographs, but visitors also frequently observe coyotes, moose, mule deer, and river otters. Other more secretive animals, such as black and grizzly bears, bighorn sheep, striped skunks, red foxes, bobcats, porcupines, and beaver, are sometimes seen. Ask where to look at the visitor centers. In late 1994, wolves were introduced into Yellowstone, and now visitors travel for the express purpose of hearing their haunting songs.

◆ ELK

More than 30,000 elk graze in Yellowstone alone, with many more in surrounding areas. Another extremely popular place to see them is the National Elk Refuge, just north of Jackson, the winter range of a herd of more than 7,500 elk. Visitors traveling by horse-drawn sleigh can actually ride through their midst. With bulls weighing up to 900 pounds and cows up to 600 pounds, they are some of the largest antlered animals in the Americas. The bulls' massive antlers are a favorite of collectors and of Asian aphrodisiac manufacturers (the elk shed their antlers naturally each spring, then grow them back again in the summer and fall). An antler auction in Jackson each May attracts hundreds of buyers willing to pay more than $14 per pound.

◆ GRIZZLY BEARS

Grizzlies are large brown bears that once ranged throughout the Northern Hemisphere. When Lewis and Clark crossed the Rocky Mountains in 1804, they found grizzlies common along the upper Missouri River, especially at Great Falls, where dozens congregated to fish. Unfortunately, as settlers arrived they quickly came to view these massive and powerful creatures as a threat to themselves and to their stock. They shot, trapped, and poisoned them, nearly to the brink of extinction outside of Alaska and western Canada. In the lower 48 states, they now exist in only the most remote parts of Montana, Wyoming, Idaho, and Washington. In Wyoming,

NORTHWEST CORNER

their numbers have increased markedly, with perhaps as many as 500 or more in Yellowstone and the surrounding national forest lands. In recent years, they have returned even to Grand Teton National Park and the Wind River Mountains to the south, where just a decade ago their presence was rare or unheard of.

For many years both grizzly and black bears were common sights along Yellowstone's roads and at the garbage dumps, where grandstands were set up so that visitors could watch the bears. When the dumps were finally closed in the 1970s, the bears were suddenly forced to find more natural food sources. This sudden change led to a number of encounters between humans and bears, including maulings that killed two people. The incidents have declined as people have become more careful with their food and garbage, and as the bears have begun to relearn their old feeding patterns.

Grizzly encounters are rare and frightening experiences for most people. The adult males can weigh more than 500 pounds. Surprising a bear, especially a sow with her cubs, is the last thing you want to do. When in bear country, talk loudly or sing, or carry bear bells to warn them of your presence. Most bears hear or smell you long before you know they are present, and hightail it away.

◆ BISON

Bison (commonly called buffalo) are the veritable symbol of the old frontier. Often weighing up to 2,000 pounds, they are also the largest land mammal in the New World. An outline of one graces Wyoming's state flag, and it was declared the state mammal in 1985. With their massive heads, huge shoulder humps, heavy coats of fur, and oddly small posteriors, buffalo are certainly one of the strangest animals anywhere. They look so front-heavy as to seem unstable. This impression is, of course, false, for buffalo are remarkably well-adapted to life on the plains. They use their strong sense of smell to find grass buried in deep snowdrifts, which they sweep away with a sideways motion of their heads. They are also surprisingly fleet of foot, as many careless Yellowstone photographers have discovered. In addition, they are one very tough critter. In 1907 a buffalo was pitted against four of the meanest Mexican bulls at a Juarez, Mexico, bullring. After knocking heads several times with the buffalo, the bulls fled and were saved only when bullfighters opened the chute gates to let them escape.

NORTHWEST CORNER

(opposite) Top: Elk herd near Indian Creek. Bottom: Bison and calf in Yellowstone.

◆ WOLVES

The wolves are back! One of the most exciting developments for visitors to Yellowstone National Park has been the successful reintroduction of wolves, making this one of the few places in the lower 48 states where these animals can be viewed in the wild. Wolves once ranged across nearly all of North America, but white settlers regarded them—along with mountain lions, grizzly bears, and coyotes—as threats to livestock and as unwanted predators upon game animals. Even in Yellowstone, wolves were hunted and poisoned by both the Army and the National Park Service. By 1940, the wolf was probably gone from the park, though a few turned up briefly again in the early 1970s. Until 1995, wolves could only be found in parts of Canada, Alaska, northern Minnesota, Isle Royale, and Glacier National Park. With a more enlightened attitude in recent years, conservationists began pushing for the reintroduction of wolves to Yellowstone, considered one of the few remaining areas in the lower 48 that could support a viable wolf population. Without wolves, it was argued, elk, deer, and bison populations had grown too high, potentially throwing the entire ecosystem out of balance.

Despite dire predictions from local ranchers who feared that wolves would decimate sheep, cattle, and elk herds, the National Park Service began reintroducing Canadian-born wolves in 1995. So far, things have gone better than almost anyone predicted, and the Yellowstone ecosystem now supports as many as 1,000 individual wolves. A few wolves have been shot by ranchers when caught killing sheep, but most of them have remained within the park and surrounding public lands. While the return of the wolf to Yellowstone has created a buzz of excitement for visitors and environmentalists alike, the program remains controversial and a particularly sore subject with the Wyoming State Legislature, which as of 2007 was still grapppling with a management plan that the U.S. Fish and Wildlife Service could stomach and thus remove wolves from the Endangered Species List. In the meantime, the park will continue with the reintroduction management plan, and the wolves will remain—albeit in limbo—free to roam through Yellowstone, blessing visitors once again with the haunting beauty of their plaintive howls resounding through the woods.

(opposite) Tower Fall.

JACKSON HOLE
& GRAND TETON NATIONAL PARK

Map page 223
Grand Teton National Park
& Jackson Hole

◆ **AREA OVERVIEW**

Jackson Hole lies in the flats that begin where the Snake River flows south from the Jackson Lake Dam. The name applies as well to the whole mountain area surrounding the valley, including the Teton and Gros Ventre ("GROW-vont") Ranges. (*Gros Ventre* means "big belly" in the language of the French-Canadian trappers; the same trappers called the Tetons *les Trois Tetons,* meaning "three tits.") By the larger measure, the Hole begins where the Snake runs into Jackson Lake, at Grand Teton National Park's northern boundary.

Jackson is the name of the lake and town, Jackson Hole the valley and the area. No wonder some people get confused. It's all perhaps too much of a memorial to David E. Jackson, an otherwise undistinguished early local trapper.

Weather: Jackson Hole is slightly lower in elevation than Grand Teton National Park. As a result, in September, October, and March through May, when it is raining in Jackson Hole it is snowing in Grand Teton National Park. Winters in Jackson can be brutally cold, with temperatures falling below zero any time from late November through early February.

Food & Lodging: Restaurants in Jackson Hole cater to every taste—from a New York–style cafe like Kashman's, where you can enjoy fresh bagels and a latte, to Bubba's Bar-B-Que, where the ribs are highly recommended.

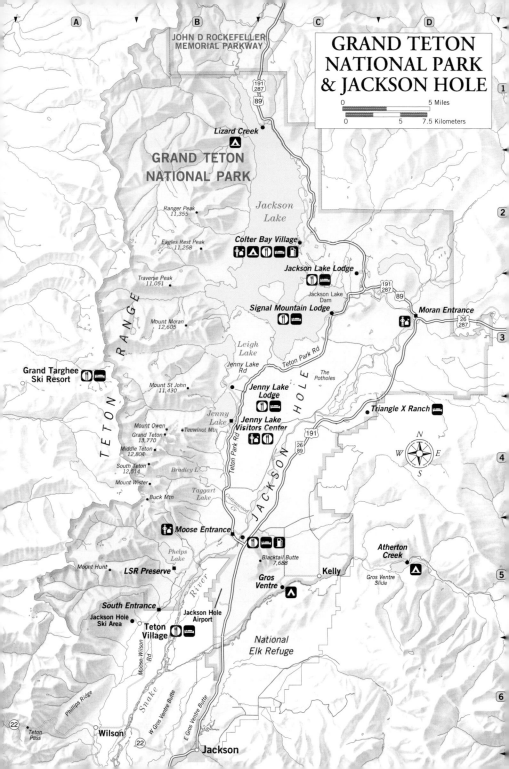

■ History

All of Wyoming was involved in the fur mania, but no section more so than Jackson Hole. Up through the 1840s, traders and trappers bustled through the Hole, much like today's tourists. The first white man to see it was John Colter—a trapper, of course. Colter, the same one whose tales of the Yellowstone were not believed, probably passed through in 1807. Although Colter himself kept no records, a map printed in Nicholas Biddle's history of the Lewis and Clark expedition, published as early as 1814, has a dotted line across a map of the area marked "Colter's route in 1807," and Jackson Lake is labeled "Lake Biddle," after the author of the book. (Not really the author so much as the transcriber-editor, since the material came directly from the original writings of Lewis and Clark.)

Jackson Hole became the crossroads for trappers traveling between Wyoming and Idaho from the 1820s through the 1840s. David E. Jackson frequented the region for years, though nobody can be quite sure when his name was first attached to it. William Sublette supposedly christened it in 1829. It was probably called "Jackson's Hole" even before then, and it appeared so in a book dated 1837.

Beaver Dick Leigh and his wife, Jenny, with their children in Jackson Hole. (Photo by William H. Jackson, courtesy, National Park Service, Yellowstone National Park Collections)

For many years, Menor's Ferry offered one of the only ways to cross the Snake River in Jackson Hole. (Courtesy, Jackson Hole Historical Society and Museum)

All this activity simmered down when the fur trade died. The beaver were then left in peace, and for more than 40 years the valley was relatively empty of humans except for Indian summer camps (of which teepee rings still exist as evidence) and fall hunting. White hunting parties came through later, but the first permanent homestead was not established until 1884. By 1889, some 40 settlers were living in the valley, and in the fall of that year the first wagon train crossed Teton Pass bearing five Mormon families, including members of the Wilson family. The community of Wilson at the foot of the pass was for decades—and still is—the valley's "second city," Jackson being the metropolis.

Negotiating Teton Pass remained an adventure, particularly after snowfall, until the mid-20th century. Nowadays, thousands of cars stream over it, but still more use the other, newer highways. The Hole now regularly fills with a transient population greater than its permanent population, in both the summer and winter seasons. Jackson Hole can no longer be called lonely; but beautiful it certainly still is.

JACKSON HOLE

The Creation of Grand Teton National Park

Unlike most Western national parks that were created from wilderness by the government, Grand Teton National Park is a homegrown product, the result of local effort.

After World War I, the beauty of the old, secluded Jackson Hole began to be tarnished by the booming commercialization of the Roaring '20s. A group of Jackson Hole idealists, violently opposed by a group of local entrepreneurs, gathered to discuss ways of preserving the valley from exploitation. It became obvious that the only agency powerful enough to provide that sort of protection was the National Park Service.

Yellowstone Park was a next-door neighbor, but Yellowstone was exactly what the idealists did not want. A meeting in 1923 with Yellowstone's superintendent, Horace Albright, confirmed that he wanted to extend the park's boundaries to include the Hole. The locals hated the spectacle of yellow buses, gaping tourists, and huge hotels. They wanted to keep the Hole a place of untouched natural beauty, with a small population of ranchers and sympathetic summer visitors.

When the idealists sought a benefactor to buy up private land and turn it over to the Park Service, they chose John D. Rockefeller Jr., who had already contributed generously to the Acadia and Great Smoky Mountains National Parks. When J.D.R. visited Yellowstone in 1926, Horace Albright showed him around Jackson Hole and pointed out examples of the progressive deterioration there—dead timber on the shores of Jackson Lake, cheap commercial excrescences around Jenny Lake, and uncontrolled, messy automobile camping sites. Rockefeller got the message.

A camouflaged company called the Snake River Land and Cattle Company was organized to buy up properties in the north end of Jackson Hole. No one was supposed to know who the buyers were, as the name Rockefeller would boost prices. Against the advice of the project's initiators, the Rockefeller organization chose as its purchasing agent the most prominent local banker, who knew the real estate situation because so many ranchers were deep in debt to his bank. The banker was also a leader in the movement against conservation and for "progress." The bank's outstanding ranch mortgages were quickly cleared up, after which he resigned as agent and publicly exposed Rockefeller and his plans. Prices immediately rose, and a very active and vocal resistance to the plan emerged. The matter became one of local, then national, politics. The battle raged for two decades. U.S. senators came to investigate; constant hearings were full of bitter debates between supporters and detractors.

Vintage postcard of Tetons and the Snake River.

Since the actual Teton Range was already national forestland, it was easy enough to convert it into a Grand Teton National Park, which happened in 1929. This preserved the peaks and lakes from any further exploitation, but the valley floor was still threatened. In 1943, Franklin D. Roosevelt created a Grand Teton National Monument, which took in the whole upper valley, including many of the properties by this time owned by Rockefeller. J.D.R. was becoming impatient. Horace Albright, now director of the whole National Park Service, and Harold Ickes, Roosevelt's secretary of the interior, were hard at work influencing the president and trying to keep a discouraged J.D.R. from selling out his holdings.

The move to create a monument, however, roused a real storm of fury. National monuments could be created by direct presidential fiat, unlike national parks, which were created by Congress. But national monuments were supposed to be small sites, not thousands of acres of rangeland. Anti-Roosevelt politicians, who had no particular interest in conservation, took the opportunity to create an anti-Roosevelt crusade.

When the national monument became part of Grand Teton National Park in 1950, the battle was won. Rockefeller donated his lands (but kept ownership of all the park concessions), and the Park Service took over. Though Rockefeller and Albright get their much-deserved praise for this salvation, the locals who started the whole idea are forgotten.

JACKSON HOLE

(following pages) As the sun rises, a full moon sets over Mount Moran and Jackson Lake.

■ ALONG JACKSON LAKE

As you travel from Yellowstone south on U.S. Route 191/89, the first view of the Tetons, their sheer faces rising over the water, captivates you from across Jackson Lake. Among the most familiar of all American photographs is that of Mount Moran reflected in Jackson Lake, taken by William H. Jackson. (This combination of names ought to celebrate the friendship of the two artists—Thomas Moran and William Jackson—who first put this corner of the state on canvas and film, or rather, on plate. A pity the lake is named for the wrong Jackson.)

◆ COLTER BAY VILLAGE   *map page 223, C-2*

The road then passes the well-known Flagg Ranch and Leek's Marina, née Leek's Camp (two Old Wyoming fishing, hunting, and overnight camps) before hitting the big, handsome Rockefeller complex of Colter Bay Village. The complex is centered around a marina and a street of stores, a splendid restaurant called the Chuckwagon, and other conveniences; surrounding these are an extensive camp of old cabins moved from older resorts around Jackson Hole. Colter Bay also has a small but excellent museum (displaying mostly Indian artifacts) and an outdoor church, where weekly services are held in summer. *8 miles northwest of Moran on U.S. 89/287; 800-628-9988 or 307-543-3100.*

◆ JACKSON LAKE DAM   *map page 223, C-3*

The Jackson Lake Dam was built under difficult conditions in 1910–11 on the site of a feeble earth dam. The tale of its building is grippingly and amusingly told by Eliot Paul in his somewhat fictionalized *Desperate Scenery* (1954). The book gives an overdramatized account that is much too pro-dam and anti-local, but it certainly gives a vivid picture of the engineering feats of the dam's construction from the perspective of a superb writer who just happened to be there. Locals, particularly conservationists, were violently opposed to the project. For one thing, the water didn't help Wyoming at all. It was piped to Idaho's potato farmers. For another, the dam ruined the shores of one of America's most beautiful big lakes for years and years. Dead timber, killed by the rise of the water, disfigured the lake until the Civilian Conservation Corps came along and cleared away the debris in the 1930s. Now it's beautiful again, if not quite natural, and there are beaches for swimming and other water activities. (There are marinas at both Colter Bay and Signal Mountain Lodge.) Just the same, Jackson Lake is, and always will be, an ambivalent example of exploitation on a grand scale. Potatoes are a good thing, and the lake is still beautiful. But at what cost?

◆ **Jackson Lake Lodge** *map page 223, C-2/3*

Just before you get to the dam, you get a view of Jackson Lake Lodge, up on a bluff with an overwhelming panorama of the Tetons. This grandiose Rockefeller enterprise is in the spirit of the great hotels of Yellowstone, like Old Faithful Inn. It is, however, very much in the modern style, with the main lobby's enormous plate-glass expanse looking out on lake and mountains; a huge dining room; luxurious cabins furnished in attractive Western style; and even a big swimming pool, open to the public for a fee. There's also a snappy new bar with a Teton view. It is not what's known in the West as "rustic"—that is, homey, and primitive, and built of logs. J. D. Rockefeller himself liked to contemplate the scenery from **Lunch Tree Hill,** a little knoll north of the lodge, to which a trail leads. The knoll is marked by a memorial plaque. *5 miles northwest of Moran on U.S. 89/287; 800-628-9988 or 307-543-3100.*

◆ **Signal Mountain Lodge** *map page 223, C-3*

South of Jackson Lake Lodge, the road forks south. The main highway, U.S. Routes 26 and 287, goes east towards Moran Junction, Togwotee Pass, and Lander. Teton Park Road, which runs down the west side of Jackson Hole, follows the lake shore, passing Signal Mountain Lodge, one of the more attractive lakeside resting places. Shortly beyond the lodge, a side road cuts east, heading up the rather steep **Signal Mountain**. From the top of this peak are epic views north, east, and south. Particularly vivid at sunset, the wide, gray, sagebrush valley floor stretches south on both sides of the wriggling Snake River, and the great heights of the Gros Ventre mountains loom eastward. It was from Signal Mountain that William H. Jackson took the first photograph of Jackson Lake, in 1877. The photograph was dimmed by the residual smoke of a forest fire, and burnt trees on top of Signal Mountain were visible in the photograph. Views of the lake and the Tetons are part of the appeal of **The Peaks** restaurant, which serves buffalo sirloin and many fish dishes. *Teton Park Road, 4 miles west of Moran; 307-543-2831.*

■ **The Lakes at the Foot of the Tetons** *map page 223, B-3/4*

Teton Park Road soon leaves the timber and starts across the sagebrush flats toward the Tetons. From this angle you get spectacular new views of the principal peaks at their most pointed. From every direction, Grand Teton (13,770 feet) changes character. From this northern side, it is a sharp spire; from due east, a rather smoothly shaped but elongated half-dome; from the south, a hulking, almost square-topped, rugged mass.

The fact that Gannett Peak in the Wind Rivers beats out Grand Teton as tallest in the state by a mere 34 feet is a bitter pill for local chauvinists, but it's sweetened by the knowledge that Grand Teton is world-famous and universally photogenic.

At the foot of the abrupt wall of the Tetons is a chain of glacial lakes, each one different, that are among the park's chief glories. Leigh, String, Jenny, Bradley, Taggart, and Phelps Lakes are all preserved in their virgin state, saved from the fate of Jackson Lake—but only because of the vigilance of local people who found out and exposed plans to desecrate them by dams (and from 1929 onward, by the National Park Service). Leigh, String, and Jenny are approached by a detour road that cuts west from Teton Park Road at North Jenny Lake Junction.

Trails from the parking area at String Lake lead to Leigh Lake and up toward the mountains. **String Lake** is something of a misnomer, since it's not really a separate lake so much as the somnolent outlet of Leigh Lake, suitable for canoeing. You lose the crowds quickly as you walk north toward Leigh Lake. **Leigh Lake** is the most beautiful of all the park lakes, with many timbered bays and promontories reachable by trail, and magnificent views of the peaks, especially Mount Moran.

The detour road, one-way after String Lake, continues south, passing the handsome **Jenny Lake Lodge** (also see page 334). Once the Tony Grace dude ranch, it is now a luxurious Rockefeller cabin-camp with one of the best restaurants in the valley attached to it (not cheap or easy to get into; reservations recommended). Prices for staying at the lodge include horseback riding, cycling, breakfast, and a six-course dinner at the excellent restaurant. The road then goes alongside **Jenny Lake**—round, deep blue, right under Grand Teton—the most accessible and frequented of these smaller lakes. Facilities include a campground, store, docks, and boat service across Jenny Lake, from where you can hike to **Hidden Falls**—rushing, white, ice-cold, and anything but hidden. *Jenny Lake Road; 800-628-9988 or 307-733-4647.*

Reaching the two smaller lakes farther south, Taggart and Bradley, requires a certain amount of tramping (especially Bradley). **Taggart Lake** suffered a fire around its eastern approaches in 1985, and the area now gives the hiker some idea of just how slowly fire-damaged forests recover. Much of the blackened timbers, lodgepole pine for the most part, has fallen and lies hidden under a new, green and burgeoning forest of aspens, bushes, and teenage lodgepoles. One odd advantage of the fire damage is the extensive new view of the nearby Tetons and the farther Gros Ventre peaks. Luckily, Taggart's shores remain almost totally untouched.

(opposite) Barn in Mormon Row area, with view of the Tetons.

The Lure of the Tetons

Rising abruptly from the valley floor like a wolf's jagged molars, the mighty Tetons beckon climbers from around the globe. The youngest of all the Rocky Mountain ranges—which average around 50 million years old—the Tetons ascended less than 10 million years ago and continue to rise, in some cases more than 7,000 feet above the valley floor. The valley, meanwhile, continues to sink.

With no intervening foothills and with spectacular lakes at their feet, the Tetons, only 40 miles long and perhaps 15 miles wide, are supremely accessible. Almost every peak can be scaled in a single day, on trails that range from novice to expert level. High-angle routes on excellent rock, mixed alpine climbs involving steep snow and ice, and abundant wildlife make the Tetons a place for discovery and adventure. In their comprehensive book *A Climber's Guide to the Teton Range,* Leigh Ortenburger and Reynold Jackson declare the challenges of Teton climbs "unmatched below the Canadian border."

On August 11, 1898, William Owen, Franklin Spalding, John Shive, and Frank Peterson became the first party known to reach the top of Grand Teton, at 13,770 feet the range's highest and Wyoming's second-highest peak. These days, 38 technical rock-climbing routes lead to the Grand's summit. In good weather, the traditional Owen-Spalding route remains the easiest way to reach or descend from the crest.

In 1931, the legendary climber Glenn Exum made the first ascent, alone and without a rope, of the south ridge of the Grand. This area, now called Exum Ridge, is the mountain's most popular route. Recognizing that climbing could be an empowering experience for both climber and guide, Glenn started the **Exum Mountain Guides** (307-733-2297, www.exumguides.com) school with Paul Petzoldt, another accomplished guide. Their company and the also world-renowned **Jackson Hole Mountain Guides** (307-733-4979, www.jhmg.com) offer superb instruction and guided climbs through the Tetons.

— Jeanne Ball

Bradley Lake is *truly* hidden, secluded in its own cup of forest foothills, separated from Taggart by a high, wildflower-covered moraine. The trail to the lake is moderately steep and requires some stamina, and like all park trails is clearly marked with mileage.

All these trails continue up into the mountains beyond. Miles of scenery; views of the valley below and the peaks above; tumbling, icy mountain streams cascading down from hidden, small glacial lakes; and all sorts of flowers and growth alongside the trail are revealed to travelers on foot or horseback as they climb above the cliffs and canyons. Then come the peaks themselves, a treat for mountain climbers. Grand Teton is the prime target here—the most popular of Teton climbs. The routes and variations are thoroughly worked out and properly guided, so the risk is minimal. This can't be said of some other peaks, and foolish people who scorn guides and don't follow instructions fall off every year.

Phelps Lake, southernmost of the chain, is semiprivate. The land around the outlet is the JY Ranch, the first dude ranch in the valley (circa 1907) and for years one of the most prestigious. The Rockefellers then owned it for many years, but the family recently donated it back to the park and it opened to the public in late 2007. Park trails go up along its northern side and into **Death Canyon**. This most conspicuous of the Teton Range's canyons leads up from the west end of Phelps Lake and is a favorite camping and packing area. The name seems appropriate to the great, solemn cliffs at the entrance, which look like Hittite or Egyptian gods. But no one really knows what the name signifies. There are old tales of mysterious noises—horses running where there were no horses—and rumors of rustlers ambushed and killed; but none are worthy of the setting and the name. Nothing sinister has happened up there lately.

Altogether, the Tetons and their lakes, trails, canyons, and climbs are enough to keep a healthy hiker or horseback visitor happy for weeks.

■ MOOSE   *map page 223, B-5*

The Jenny Lake detour joins Teton Park Road at South Jenny Lake Junction. Passing along an odd, forested protrusion from the flats called **Timber Island** (where it's quite easy to get lost, despite its narrowness), Teton Park Road crosses Cottonwood Creek and goes down a bench to Moose. Here, it crosses over the Snake River to join U.S. Route 191, which has been running down the east side of Jackson Hole.

Moose was once the crossing point of the old Menor's ("mee-ners") Ferry, for years the only way across the Snake between Wilson, way to the south, and

Moran, way to the north. The Snake River at this particular point is, for a change, concentrated in one smooth, deep channel. Besides the ferry, there was a store and a few cabins. Now it's the site of the Moose Post Office, official headquarters, and new, grand, airy visitors center for Grand Teton National Park, with a tourist desk and a big exhibition area. Along the river are preserved mementos of the old days. Of these, the most popular is the pretty little log **Chapel of the Transfiguration**, with its plate-glass window framing Grand Teton behind the altar. This was copied from the famous mission church at Ethete, on the Wind River Indian Reservation, but it must be admitted that the scene so framed is far more dramatic in Moose. The summers-only congregation is not Indian, but a total spectrum of visitors passing through, of nearly every Protestant denomination. You no longer see horses tied to the fence outside as you did in bygone days, when some prestigious dude ranches, now defunct, were nearby. A trail leads from the church's crowded parking lot to the river, where is preserved the old Menor cabin and a replica of **Menor's Ferry**. Two cantankerous bachelor brothers, Bill and Holiday, lived on opposite sides of the river and refused to speak for years. Bill operated the ferry.

Nearby is also preserved the **Maud Noble cabin**. Miss Maud was a Philadelphia spinster of high degree and great presence, who ran away west with the family coachman, Sidney Sandell. He was a lively little Cockney, who for years ran the store at the ferry. She always called him "Sidney." He always called her "Miss Noble." She looked like George Washington, with snow-white, cropped hair and severe black riding clothes. The cabin is preserved not so much in memory of this odd companionship, as it is for the site of a seminal meeting in 1923. Horace Albright, then superintendent of Yellowstone Park, and a group of local conservationists got together to organize a plan of action to preserve the valley. Albright simply wanted to extend the boundaries of Yellowstone. The locals objected strongly. They didn't want to see their valley become another mass tourist attraction, with big hotels and yellow buses packed with visitors wearing knickers and golf caps—the preferred ensemble for tourists, especially women, in those ancient days. They had in mind some sort of preservation of Jackson Hole exactly as it had been before the contaminations of the twenties, as a "museum on the hoof"— a romantic and impractical hope of preserving the past into the present. The meeting was a failure, but these former antagonists got together later on, and in a battle that lasted for decades finally saw the creation of the enlarged Grand Teton Park in 1950.

(opposite) A rainbow arches over Rosie's Ridge near Moran.

Though Grand Teton is no museum on the hoof, but rather a big, crowded national park, there still is a difference between it and Yellowstone. Yellowstone remains strictly a mass operation. Grand Teton is much more individual, informal, intimate, and oriented toward youth, action, nature study, science, and art. People aren't just crowding around geysers. They climb mountains, watch birds and big game, ride horses and hike on trails, and raft down the Snake. Just the same, it's a big bustling park, and not what the idealists of 1923 had in mind.

A big bridge, no longer a ferry, now crosses the Snake at Moose. On the other side is **Dornan's**, a private enclave founded and owned by the daughter and son-in-law of Joe Jones, one of those local dreamers. An outdoor chuckwagon eating place serves breakfast, lunch, and dinner through the summer. It is adorned with teepees for bad weather, with the river alongside and spectacular views of the Tetons to the west. Stores carry sundries and specialties, and a most pleasant bar now has an excellent restaurant and superb wine shop. Upper and lower outdoor decks open to a grand view of the Tetons. *307-733-2415*

■ BACK ROAD FROM MOOSE TO TETON VILLAGE   *map page 223, B-5*

The slowly improving Moose-Wilson Road turns southwest at the Moose post office and heads towards the Tetons, up the bench, and then due south down the west side of Jackson Hole to Teton Village, just outside the park boundary. It's a narrow road, paved most of the way, between the river and the foothills, going through aspens, willows, and pines, and past various hidden ranches, including the JY, which the Rockefellers donated to Grand Teton National Park in 2001. It's a road that can be recommended scenically, but not as a traffic artery. Too many people use it for slow-going comfort, and curves threaten collisions. Additionally, the new southeast entrance station, completed in 2001, often delays traffic for 10 minutes or more in both directions. No trailers or campers of any kind are permitted.

When you emerge into sunlight, you are faced by the grandiose, absurdly neo-Swiss **Teton Village**, full of broad, overhanging roofs and balconies and year-round Christmas lights. This importation of the spirit of Colorado (á la Vail) into Wyoming is Jackson Hole's principal ski resort, with lifts (including a new gondola and, coming soon, a new summit tram), runs, and hotels. It is all modern and occasionally awful, but also amusing and successful, especially in winter. In summer, it's very active, too. The hotels cater to different budgets, with varying degrees of competence. The principal summer attraction is the

Grand Teton Music Festival, hosted by the Grand Teton Festival Orchestra. The festival is a solid, two-month-long schedule of musical activities, ranging from full orchestral concerts each weekend to a great variety of chamber and solo performances during the week. Various famous soloists, orchestras, small ensembles, and choruses perform as guests, diversifying the summer programs. This festival has become one of the chief pleasures of the valley's summer life. *Walk Festival Hall. July–August; 307-733-1128* (also see page 344).

South of this enterprise lie other attractions, including many restaurants. Along the river, you still see beautiful, big private ranches, green with hay, aspens, and cottonwoods. Down the road is a million-dollar extravaganza called Teton Pines. This is Jackson Hole's only gated community and where Vice President Dick Cheney resides. Its enormous main building looks like a beautifully decorated airport, with a beautifully decorated restaurant overlooking beautifully decorated condominiums. You could fly in from L.A., play golf, fly out, and never know you'd left home. There is, of course, a fine view of the Tetons. This is an extreme manifestation of the new Jackson Hole—of far-flung millionaires and billionaires from all over, who have built massive mansions and swimming pools so that they can enjoy the simple life of the Old West. Oddly, albeit fortunately, many of them are full of local spirit and support for conservation, the arts, and everything worthwhile. It's all a little confusing. Things sure ain't the way they used to be.

(For Food and Lodging in Teton Village see page 247.)

■ TETON PASS   *map page 223, A-6*

After leaving Teton National Park the Moose-Wilson Road turns into what locals call the Village Road, which runs into Wyoming State Highway 22. Approximately five miles south is the entrance to "the Aspens" and the **Westside Store and Liquor Shop,** which has an excellent selection of fine wines from around the world. Nestled in the same enclave adjacent to the Jackson Hole Racquet Club on Teton Village Road is **Stiegler's** restaurant, an elegant setting for outstanding German-Austrian dishes and game. The elk medallions are terrific. Past the Teton Pines, two good restaurants lie on the left side of the road before it reaches Highway 22. **Q Roadhouse Barbeque,** the new hot spot on the Village Road, also offers steaks. **The Calico** is a friendly fire-

(following pages) The Tetons and Oxbow Bend.

GRAVITY ADDICTION

Swift. Deep. Silent. Witnessing a tactical strike by a member of the Jackson Hole Air Force is always impressive. "Hucking carcass," as snowboarders call it, some 40, 50, even 80 or more feet off summit cliffs and cornices and landing perfectly to speed down steep, narrow gullies and near-vertical terrain is the hallmark assault of the elite airborne skier. Jackson Hole's three ski resorts, along with Teton Pass's "earn your turns" backcountry, provide a vast training area. Grand Teton National Park's forbidding, wild, "if you fall you die" peaks afford the elite their proving ground.

Limitless wilderness, variable conditions, and challenging topography combine to render Jackson Hole a skier's preferred destination. It's therefore no surprise that many of the nation's best extreme skiers, snowboarders, and racers cut their teeth in the Tetons. Bill Briggs, who on June 16, 1971, with a fused hip, became the first person to ski Grand Teton, was perhaps the first to epitomize the Jackson Hole skier's extreme prowess. Today, Exum climbing guide Stephen Koch has established some of the most difficult descents in the Tetons and is on his way to being the first person to snowboard each of the seven continent's highest summits. Yet this aggressive, adrenaline-pumped gravity addiction is a modern phenomenon in Jackson Hole's ski history.

In *Teton Skiing: A History & Guide to the Teton Range*, Tom Turiano notes that, according to 1800s frontiersmen's journals, some of the earliest Teton explorations were conducted in winter on long, ski-like "snowshoes" made by Indians. Early homesteaders, miners, and trappers used skis as tools, as did the U.S. Postal Service beginning in 1892 to deliver mail between Teton Valley, Idaho, and Jackson Hole.

Recreational ski touring in Jackson Hole began in the 1930s. One Teton Pass mail skier, Fred Brown, trailblazed much of the area. In 1935, he joined Paul and Curly Petzoldt to achieve the first descent of Rendezvous Peak, today Jackson Hole Mountain Resort's centerpiece. Skiing and mountaineering blend well, and on December 19 of that same year, Fred and Paul scored the first winter ascent of Grand Teton. Olympic skier Betty Woolsey arrived in Jackson Hole in 1936 and later bought Trail Creek Ranch, today an established cross-country and skate ski touring destination located in Wilson at the foot of Teton Pass. Woolsey's superb skiing ability and adventurous spirit spurred her to be the first to explore vast tracts of previously unskied territory, even after lift service vacated the backcountry.

Neil Rafferty was responsible for drumming up support for the area's first ski lift, "Old Man Flat rope tow," established on Snow King in 1939. Rafferty later installed Snow King's, and the valley's, first chair lift in 1946. About that same time, Paul Petzoldt hoped to establish a lift-service ski area on Rendezvous Mountain, but failed to secure the base property necessary. In 1964, Paul McCollister bought the property and began the task of making Petzoldt's dream a reality, opening the now world-class Jackson Hole Ski Resort in the winter of 1965. Over the pass, in Alta, Wyoming, tremendous financial support from Idaho and Wyoming residents alike opened Grand Targhee Ski Resort in 1969.

Today, Teton backcountry skiing is more popular than ever. Free-heeled, "telemark" extreme-skiers shred terrain once reserved for alpine experts only, while snowboarders boot pack to hidden summits. Avalanches, however, cull mountain enthusiasts each winter. Prerequisites to skiing anywhere in the Tetons are proper skill and gear, particularly in the backcountry. Gravity can be fun, but beware.

For more information about skiing or snowboarding in Jackson Hole, contact:
Avalanche Hotline: *307-733-2664.*
Snow King Resort: *800-522-5464 or 307-733-5200. www.snowking.com*
Jackson Hole Mountain Resort: *888-333-7766 or 307-733-2292.*
www.jacksonhole.com
Grand Targhee Resort: *800-827-4433. www.grandtarghee.com*

— Jeanne Ball

side bar offering a variety of microbrews, fine wines, and spirits while its restaurant serves gourmet pasta dishes and pizzas.

Highway 22 itself runs west from Jackson over Teton Pass, which at one time was the one viable way into the Hole and the only real link with the outside world. Teton Pass was famous for its difficulties. Nowadays, it leads easily up over the tail-end of the Tetons to Victor, Idaho, once a backwater farming town, but now Jackson's burgeoning bedroom community. This route is also the only link with **Alta**, an odd little once-lost fringe of Wyoming that lies on the west side of the Tetons. From Victor, take Idaho State Highway 33 due north, then turn east after Driggs, Idaho, to the secluded **Grand Targhee Resort**, Wyoming, nestled under the west side of the Tetons in the Targhee National Forest. Grand Targhee is a lesser known world-class ski resort, where the Teton view outclasses that of the more famous Jackson Hole Mountain Resort. It was from this Alta side that Moran did his Teton range sketches—the first in history.

Back on Highway 22 at the eastern end of Teton Pass—in Jackson Hole—is the growing community of **Wilson**. Named for the family that moved here en masse in 1889, the town is no longer a small center for neighboring cattle and dude ranches, but rather a trendy haven for the Forbes 500 set. Not surprisingly, houses are seldom available for under a million dollars and the Wilson zip code desirability surpasses all others—including Aspen and Sun Valley—as the most sought-after haven for the rich and famous. A fascinatingly detailed history of Wilson and the Teton Pass by Doris B. Platts traces the story from trapper days up to 1940, with biographies of settlers and endless anecdotage. Another excellent and colorful history of the Pass, written by Virginia Huidekoper, can be purchased at **Hungry Jack's** store in Wilson at the base of the Pass. *307-733-3561.*

■ JACKSON   *map page 223, B-6*

Going east from Wilson, the road soon reaches the outskirts of Jackson and its present-day welter of commercialism. For years, since its founding at the turn of the century, Jackson was a dusty little cow town built around a dusty open square surrounded by a fence, to which were hitched dusty cow ponies (covered in mud and snow during the winter). No longer. Now it's a little metropolis overwhelmed by tourists. The town's central square has become a green, tree-shaded oasis, with **elk-horn arches** leading into it. It is surrounded on all four sides by a medley of specialty shops—a few still in the old buildings, but transformed—with the old plank sidewalks intact. The shops house everything from cowboy boots to art galleries, the effect overwhelmingly that of expensive tourism.

Away from the center of town, south toward Snow King and its ski lift, Jackson's original character and charm abound in the casually mixed, old residential section, with its residual log cabins and old houses hidden in big trees, with bright flowers out front. However, farther south of town is the horrendous strip of rampant, unregenerate commercialism. There, modern times have conquered, as the founding fathers of the Grand Teton Park feared they would all over the Hole, with the usual mix-up of supermarkets, stores, and motels run riot. In South Park, site of the valley's principal ranch and hay fields, new tract houses disfigure the landscape with gray-brown suburbia. This is entirely the product of Wyoming's latest boom: tourism. Like other booms, it too is hard at work disfiguring Wyoming's most precious asset—scenery—but with much, much less excuse than coal, oil, or reclamation dams.

However, in central Jackson you can certainly enjoy yourself, and it does have a dignified charm. Many restaurants are good, ranging from plain to superlative. The shops are enticing, if not cheap. Four theater companies offer comedies and dramas, and the **Silver Dollar Bar** of the handsome **Wort Hotel** still has its name

Jackson in 1907 consisted of little more than a couple of farmhouses and shops.
(Courtesy, Jackson Hole Historical Society and Museum)

sake coins imbedded in the bar. Nightlife usually riots at the Wort and elsewhere roundabout the square, though the open gambling of the thirties and later has gone—some think to the detriment of atmosphere (if not of pocketbooks). Things are still going on in winter during the skiing season, so the town jumps both day and night, summer and winter, except on Sundays. *50 N. Glenwood (at Broadway); 800-322-2727 or 307-733-2190* (also see page 335).

There are many excellent art galleries and a grand new **Center for the Arts** with a 525-seat theater for music and plays (265 South Center Street; 307-733-4900). There are also fine museums. The **National Wildlife Art Museum** is three miles north of Jackson on Highway 89, overlooking the National Elk Refuge. Just the view of the building, looming like a giant's creation on the hill, is awesome. There are 12 galleries in the high-ceilinged, impeccably designed building, featuring every major wildlife painter from Carl Rungius and Charles Russell to Conrad Schwiering. There's even a bison gallery and a recreation of John Clymer's studio. This world-class facility is located in the perfect setting, directly across the street from the National Elk Refuge. Wildlife viewing with binoculars or scope is superb during annual spring and fall migrations. *North of Jackson at 2820 Rungius Road; 800-313-9553 or 307-733-5771.*

Jackson's 1920 local election created the first all-woman town government in America. (Courtesy, Jackson Hole Museum and Teton County Historical Society)

JACKSON HOLE

FOOD & LODGING IN JACKSON AND TETON VILLAGE

Bubba's Bar-B-Que. Expect long lines for the mouth-watering smoked and roasted meats at this local favorite. *515 W. Broadway, Jackson; 307-733-2288.*

Jedediah's House of Sourdough. At breakfast or lunch, try the special "sourjacks," sourdough flapjacks. *135 E. Broadway, Jackson; 307-733-5671.*

Mangy Moose. A favorite for the après-ski crowd and has an excellent salad bar. *Teton Village; 307-733-4913.*

Million Dollar Cowboy Bar. With saddle-stools and knotty pine decor, the Cowboy Bar, which dates back to the 1930s, features live music upstairs and a steakhouse downstairs. *25 North Cache Street; 307-733-2207.*

Nora's Fish Creek Inn. The local breakfast hang-out for all kinds of outdoor enthusiasts. *Wilson; 307-733-8288.*

Rendezvous Bistro. The scene for the young and hip, with fairly reasonable prices, an oyster bar, and nightly specials. *390 South Highway 89; 307-739-1100.*

Snake River Grill. Immense log interior with the fanciest Western specials you can imagine. *84 E. Broadway, Jackson; 307-733-0557.*

Sweetwater Restaurant. Mediterranean dishes ranging from French pastries to Greek classics in a cozy old cabin that's been renovated and expanded. *85 King Street (at Pearl), Jackson; 307-733-3553.*

Alpenhof. Pseudo-Austrian decor, next to tram. Dietrich's Bar and Bistro is great for a nightcap. *3255 W. McCollister Drive, Teton Village; 800-732-3244 or 307-733-3242.*

Painted Porch Bed & Breakfast. Red and white farmhouse (ca. 1901), with four porches and a few Japanese soaking baths for guests to enjoy. One suite and one room; large breakfast. *3680 N. Moose-Wilson Road, Jackson; 307-733-1981.*

Rusty Parrot Lodge. Convenient, quaint in-town location where attention is paid to details. Private massage available. *175 N. Jackson Street, Jackson; 888-739-1749.*

Wort Hotel. Though dripping with history, this brick Victorian feels up-to-date. A fireplace in the main lobby keeps loungers toasty. Warm yourself with a whisky at the Silver Dollar Bar. *50 N. Glenwood (at Broadway), Jackson; 800-322-2727.*

JACKSON HOLE

Also fascinating, with far more local emphasis, is the **Jackson Hole Historical Museum**, much better organized and displayed than most places of its kind (every town in Wyoming has one), with strikingly presented local history ranging from prehistoric days to the present. It's now on the corner of DeLoney and Glenwood Streets. This charming museum is a one-man foundation by old-timer Slim Lawrence, who collected most of the material himself and founded the museum. *105 N. Glenwood; 307-733-2414.*

There is also the **Jackson Hole Historical Society,** with exhibits and an extensive selection of local writing. *105 Mercill Avenue; 307-733-9605.* The **Jackson Hole and Greater Yellowstone Visitors Center,** operated by a coalition of public agencies and private nonprofits, has wildlife displays and observation decks overlooking the National Elk Refuge to the east. *532 North Cache Street; no phone.*

While Jackson continues to experience residential and commercial growth at a rapid pace, the town planners strive to preserve its historic character. Tourists and residents alike are drawn to Jackson's many outdoor pursuits—fly-fishing, whitewater rafting and kayaking, mountain biking, cross-country and downhill skiing, hunting, and backcountry pack trips. Ninety-seven percent of Teton County, Wyoming, is public land protected as National Forest, National Park, or Wildlife Refuge. The Snake River corridor boasts the largest population of nesting bald eagles in the Lower 48. In a place where natural beauty abounds, Jackson Hole offers the outdoor enthusiast endless possibilities.

■ JACKSON TO MOOSE   *map page 223, B-5/6*

Heading north again from Jackson on U.S. Route 191 (which is also Routes 89 and 26), you pass along the west edge of the **National Elk Refuge**, where the local elk are fed in the winter and may be viewed migrating in spring and fall. Winter visitors have enthusiastically watched recently returned wolves feeding on carcasses and a resident mountain lioness raising her cubs in a nearby crag. Winter refuge sleigh rides to view feeding elk up close are available. Inquire at the visitors center located adjacent to the Refuge's south end off the main highway. A veritable aviary—from trumpeter swans to common goldeneye—also finds refuge on the Refuge.

After passing a smattering of gas stations and stores across the road, the highway rises and leaves Jackson. You are back out on the flats. The Tetons again command the view. Soon you re-enter Grand Teton National Park. Numerous turnouts

(opposite) Jackson's famed Cowboy Bar attracts both locals and tourists.

along the road permit you to gaze and photograph. Then you cross the **Gros Ventre River**, flowing down from the northeast. Right after the bridge, there's a crossroad known as Gros Ventre Junction. Here, if you're lucky, a herd of resident bison may capture your gaze if you're passing through any time in late spring or early autumn. Antelope and moose also commonly occupy this area.

At this junction, one road goes northeast to the tiny town of **Kelly**, and continues to the site of the **Gros Ventre Slide** and its residual lake. There are no services available in Kelly, which has attracted artists, writers, climbers, and hearty yurt-dwellers. The cataclysm that created Slide Lake was, first, a great landslide down the rump of **Sheep Mountain**. Named for its sheep, but nicknamed the Sleeping Indian because of its profile, Sheep Mountain is the principal protuberance of the Gros Ventre Range. In 1925, a mass of earth slid across the Gros Ventre River and swooped up the opposite side, forming a lake. In 1927, this lake burst through its dam and roared downstream, destroying Kelly (since rebuilt), devastating ranches, taking out bridges, and drowning several people. What was left was the huge gouge of the slide, the remains of the dam, and its reduced lake. The road goes up along all this, and then rather precariously on into the secluded valley beyond, with its few choice ranches and surrounding wilderness.

Slide Lake and the devastating Gros Ventre Slide of June 1925. (Courtesy, Jackson Hole Historical Society and Museum)

Dude and Guest Ranches

◆ Grand Teton National Park

Flagg Ranch Resort. Cabins, campground, restaurant. Snowmobiling, scenic float trips on Snake River. *Open May–Oct., Dec.–Mar. 2 miles south of Yellowstone's South Entrance, on Snake River; 800-443-2311 or 307-543-2861.*

Moose Head Ranch. Family-run ranch. Room for 40 in modern cabins with porches; gourmet meals. Fly-fishing on Snake River; horseback riding. *Open June–Aug. In Grand Teton National Park; 307-733-3141 (summer) or 850-877-1431 (mid-October to mid-May).*

Triangle X Ranch. Main lodge with dining room and cabins with showers. Horseback riding, pack trips, square dances, and Dutch-oven suppers. Views of the Tetons. *Open summer only. In Grand Teton National Park, 26 miles northeast of Jackson, 1 mile off U.S. 89/191/26; 307-733-2183.*

◆ Jackson Area

Darwin Ranch. Small private valley. Only 12 guests at a time; trails, fine horses, hunting. *In Gros Ventre Wilderness, east of Jackson Hole; 307-733-5588.*

Diamond D Ranch & Outfitters. Pack trips, fishing, and fall big-game hunts. Snowmobiling and cross-country skiing in winter. *Open year-round. 22250 Buffalo Valley Road, 12 miles east of Moran Junction; 800-233-6299 or 307-543-2479.*

Heart Six Guest Ranch. Modern cabins for 50, overlooking Buffalo River and Tetons. Horseback riding, fishing, snowmobiling, hunting; cookouts and children's programs. *Open year-round. 35 miles north of Jackson; 307-543-2477.*

Lost Creek Ranch. Exclusive ranch: heated pool, tennis, skeet range, horses, health spa. *Open May–Sept. Moose, 20 miles north of Jackson; 307-733-3435.*

R Lazy S Ranch. Central lodge and log cabins for 45. Fishing in pond and Snake River; horseback rides. *Open June –Sept. 1 mile north of Teton Village; 307-733-2655.*

Turpin Meadow Ranch. Twelve cabins; horseback riding, fishing, pack trips, evening entertainment; hunting trips in fall; snowmobiling in winter. *Open year-round. Outside Moran, on the Buffalo River; 307-543-2000 or 800-743-2496.*

A second road at Gros Ventre Junction takes off west from the highway to another of the Hole's modern Shangri-las. This is **Jackson Hole Golf and Tennis Center**, sponsored by Rockefeller interests, with a beautifully manicured golf course, big swimming pool, tennis courts, and a restaurant, the **North Grille.** These facilities are generally open to the public—at a price—and you'll need to make reservations in advance at the restaurant. President Clinton enjoyed a few rounds of golf here during his visit in 1999. Around and amid the wanderings of the green golf course are various developments called "estates" (of a few acres), with sumptuous, multi-million dollar modern villas on them. Once again, the new Jackson Hole with a vengeance. *307-733-7788.*

One of the most astoundingly beautiful villas is that of the well-known artist, Joanne Hennes, a key figure in Jackson's hyperactive art world. As it's her show-room and studio, as well as her home, you can visit it. The estate is certainly one of the most originally landscaped garden spots in Wyoming, or anywhere. Once-humble ranch ditches have been converted into a paradise of pools, fountains, small waterfalls, bridges, tree groves, lawns, and flowers, native and exotic. To find the villa, take Spruce Drive west from the south side of the clubhouse complex. Larkspur Drive is the second road to the left, and the studio is at the end.

John Jakubowski and Shanna Driscoll enjoy amenity-free country living in their small Wilson cabin. (opposite) The view across Antelope Flats to the Tetons.

MEMORIES OF SPRING

It would take thousands of words, hundreds of pictures, to tell about the rich variety of life in this river-bottom world along the Snake River, and still its spirit could not be captured. It is, so far, an area nearly untouched by man. For our small part of it we are so grateful that through all the years that it was a dude ranch Buster and Frances and their guests were careful never to disturb any wildlife, not even to pick many wild flowers.

So that now, on an afternoon in May, Bob and Mickey and Olaus and I can make our way through the woods and come to a spot where we all kneel and look, and Olaus and Bob take some pictures. Fred, the young artist who lives in one of the cabins, has told us how to find this spot. Under the trees, in thick woods, on shaded mossy ground, a bed of calypso orchids. We count twenty-three: pink, exquisite, and quiet. It is most unusual to find this many in one spot. This is just one of thousands of memories of spring in the river bottom.

—Margaret Murie, *Wapiti Wilderness*, 1966

The road past the golf course follows and crosses the Gros Ventre River then heads through still unspoiled **Spring Gulch** and its fine ranches. On top of the big butte east is another resort Shangri-la, the **Amangani,** at 1535 Northeast Butte Road, adjacent to **Spring Creek Ranch**. **The Granary**, a Spring Creek restaurant, has one of the most astounding views of the valley and peaks in the Hole. The restaurant is worth the trip, particularly at sunset or when there's live music. *1800 Spirit Dance Road; 800-443-6139 or 307-733-8833.*

Returning to Gros Ventre Junction and to real life, the main highway continues north, past the airport, and back to Moose.

JACKSON HOLE

■ MOOSE TO THE EAST GATE   *map page 223, B/D-3/5*

The road from Moose to Moran Junction follows along the top of the bench above the Snake River, with turnoffs all along. Here is probably the most spectacular series of roadside views of the Tetons, across the river and the flats beyond, each with its slightly different aspect of the mountains. Little dirt roads take you down to the river and boat landings at various points. Fishing is popular here. Guides lead rubber raft floats down the river. People still sometimes drown trying to do it on their own.

Along with the view of Mount Moran reflected in Jackson Lake, another famous photograph of the Tetons, this one by Ansel Adams, shows the pointed peaks rising over the bend of the Snake River at **Deadman's Bar**. Unlike Death Canyon, the story behind the sinister name is local common knowledge. A group of German strangers came to the bar, a flat place in the curve of the river on the west side, looking for gold. They dug sluices, traces of which still remain, kept to themselves, and then suddenly disappeared. Grisly remains of three of the gold seekers were found in the river. The fourth was eventually arrested in southern Wyoming, and in one of the most notorious miscarriages of justice, even for Wyoming, was set free due to "lack of evidence." He was never heard of again.

Now the view over Deadman's Bar is internationally familiar. A giant blowup of the scene has even appeared as an advertisement over Times Square, in New York. Things sure have changed from the days of the murdered gold miners.

North of Deadman's the road descends, leaving the bench to curve through hay fields and meadows, and crosses Spread Creek and Buffalo Fork. At **Moran Entrance**, the official east gate of the park, the highway splits, with one road returning to Jackson Lake and Yellowstone. This guide, however, follows U.S. Route 287 (and 26) east over Togwotee Pass, and down into the Wind River Basin.

(above) Christmas lights dress up the famous elk antler arches of Jackson's town square.

■ Postscript

The tourist season in Jackson Hole lasts from early summer into fall (fishing, hunting, climbing, boating, biking) and resumes in winter (skiing, snowmobiling, winter mountaineering, ice climbing). In late fall and early spring, the natives get a chance to catch their breath.

In the old days, those who wanted to stay in the valley for a long summer would check into one of the many area dude ranches. Starting with the JY, and growing over the years to include a group of others, the Hole was one of the principal centers of dude ranching. In those days, visitors came by train to Victor, and stayed for weeks. Teton Pass was the only safe way in, and even that wasn't too safe. The valley was nearly empty above Menor's Ferry, the lakes pristine and unvisited, fishing in the Snake world-famous (for a few), and the surrounding hills ideal for pack trips. Everybody who wasn't on a dude ranch was a cattleman or worked in Jackson.

Then, beginning in the late 1920s, came the automobile, and what were derisively known as "tin can tourists." The automobile did not really take over until World War II, however, and the dude ranch world still dominated the thoughts and feelings of visitors until the 1950s. Now, the great flood of car travel has pushed the earlier way of life and conception of Jackson Hole into a reclusive, but still active, corner. The remaining dude ranches still flourish. Many of the long-time settlers and ranch owners were once dudes, but the new Jackson Hole, south of the park, is for the most part ignorant of that whole way of life and feeling.

Golf courses, fancy restaurants, and condominiums were not part of that bygone era, and these amenities were and are despised by those who once loved and still love the old Jackson Hole. A good dude ranch still remains the best way to get away from that brand-new way of life and the explosion of summer tourism, and to find out what Jackson Hole used to be like. The moral in back of this, however, is universal. A day's drive through the Hole or any part of Wyoming is just a glimpse, a taste. However you manage it, you have to stop and stay and poke about and discover for yourself (or with the help of experts) what you can never see from a passing automobile.

(opposite) Paragliders on Rendezvous Peak.

WEST-CENTRAL
WIND RIVER & STAR VALLEY LOOP

◆ **HIGHLIGHTS**

	page
Dubois	262
Lander	265
St. Stephen's	267
South Pass	274
Wind River Vista	278
Snake River Canyon	287
The Periodic Spring	291

Map page 259

•Jackson

◆ **AREA OVERVIEW**

The rugged nature of the Wind River Range poses a special problem to the traveler. There's no real way to get through it, because there's no direct road between the Wind and Green River Basins.

These two sides of the Wind River Mountains are directly accessible for most travelers from the south, through Rawlins or Rock Springs, across vast stretches of semi-desert. Far more beautiful and impressive is a round-trip starting and ending in Jackson Hole: a great loop going over Togwotee Pass to Lander, around the south end of the mountains up to Pinedale, and back. It's better done as a two-day trip. From Moran Junction to Lander is 128 miles, a morning's drive. Once you're settled at Lander, the afternoon can be spent on the Wind River Indian Reservation. After Lander, the trip back up to Jackson Hole via South Pass and Pinedale is rewarding. From the end of the loop you can either continue onto Star Valley or back to Jackson.

Weather: Wyomingites often refer to the area from Lander to Dubois as the "banana belt" because the climate is warmer than the rest of the mountainous areas. On the opposite side of the Wind Rivers and around Pinedale the summer is hot, but thunderheads can form within minutes. Nighttime temperatures can fall to the 40s and snow is a possibility at any time of year.

Food & Lodging: Eating establishments are straightforward. Hudson has two excellent steakhouses. Lodgings are comfortable. Pinedale also has great restaurants and hotels.

WEST-CENTRAL

■ TOGWOTEE PASS TO DUBOIS   *maps page 183, B-3, and page 259, B-1*

Togwotee ("toe-ga-tee") Pass crosses the Continental Divide between Jackson Hole and the Wind River Basin. The pass was used first by Indians, then (in about 1810) by Colter and fellow trapper-guide John Hoback, and later by numberless other trappers and explorers. After the period of the trappers, it was more or less forgotten and not really rediscovered until 1873. Then, an army surveyor recommended it as a possible military road, but Congress was not interested. In 1898, however, a military road was finally built. It was declared by its builders to be a "model road," but since wagons had to be let down the west side by ropes and winches, one wonders what was meant by "model." It wasn't till 1922 that a barely passable auto road evolved from the wagon trail. Until very recently, the pass was famous for corkscrew curves, steep grades, and exciting views west. Now you can sail over it without a thought—or you will be able to, once a major reconstruction is complete, in five to seven years. Call 877-WYO-TRAIL for road reports. The lush meadows at the top are often decorated with snowbanks into July and with wildflowers well into August. There are fine views of the Tetons to the west, and a big pull-off at the top, with a sign indicating that this is the Continental Divide—9,658 feet high.

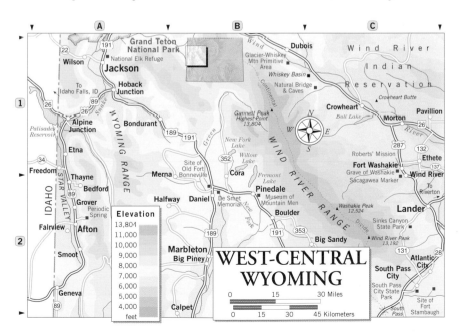

A brief detour to the left, as you go down the east side, takes you to secluded **Brooks Lake**, surrounded by odd, steep-sided, white mountain mesas and green vales. Site of the once-famous Diamond D dude ranch, Brooks Lake Lodge offers cozy rooms and fine meals June to September and December to March for hikers, cross-country skiers and snowmobiliers (307-455-2121.) Continuing east, with a wide panorama of the valley ahead and startling views north of the white, pinnacled Palisades, you pass the Falls Campground, eventually leaving the timber and crossing the infant Wind River.

Before reaching Dubois, you pass a conspicuous monument celebrating the tie-hackers of the Wind River Basin. The monument has a fine view down the valley from its site on a roadside hillock. Tie-hackers were lumbermen who cut track ties for the railroads—the forests to the west were the scene of their activities from 1914 until the 1950s. The peak year was 1947, when some 700,000 ties were cut; but with the decline of the railroads, the tie-hacking business died, too. It is now romanticized as a special, macho John Bunyan–sort of profession. At the time, ranchers and conservationists looked at it all with dismay—the slaughter of trees and choking of mountain streams, including the Green River, with lumber float-

Sharply folded beds of purple and black shale create a lunar landscape behind the lush Wind River west of Crowheart.

Guest Ranches, Food & Lodging in Dubois

◆ Guest Ranches

Absaroka Ranch. Rustic cabins and sauna; fine food and wine. Horseback riding, fishing, whitewater rafting trips, pack trips, hunting. *16 miles northwest of Dubois near Ram's Horn Peak; 307-455-2275.*

CM Ranch. Log cabins with baths. Heated pool, square dances, cookouts. *6 miles from Dubois, 2 miles from U.S. 26/287; 307-455-2331 or 800-455-0721.*

Lazy L & B Ranch. Log cabins, heated pool, meals with homemade breads. *Open June–Sept. Between Absaroka and Wind River Mtns.; 800-453-9488 or 307-455-2839.*

Togwotee Mountain Lodge. Excellent food; unbelievable Western furniture in bar. Horseback riding, fishing, cookouts, hikes. Cross-country skiing, snowmobiling. *U.S. 26/287 between Dubois and Moran; 307-543-2847 or 800-543-2847.*

Triangle C Ranch. Sixteen cabins with showers. Horseback riding, hunting, fishing, pack trips, snowmobiling. *In Wind River Mtn. area, west of Dubois; 307-455-2225.*

◆ Food & Lodging

Cafe Wyoming. Exotic and elegant menu. Highly recommended by locals. *106 E. Ramshorn, Dubois; 307-455-3828.*

Dubois Drug and Sundries. Historic drugstore boasts the best huckleberry shakes in Wyoming. *126 E. Ramshorn, Dubois; 307-455-2300.*

Geyser Creek Bed & Breakfast. Two rooms with private bath in ranch house. Pets boarded; dogsled tours. *151 Bald Mountain Road, west of Dubois; 307-455-2702.*

Jakey's Fork Homestead Bed & Breakfast. Delightful home with great views, many animals; filling breakfasts. *13 Fish Hatchery Road, east of Dubois; 307-455-2769.*

Rustic Pine Steakhouse and Tavern. Housed in a turn-of-the-century building at *119 E. Ramshorn. 307-455-2772.*

Twin Pines Lodge & Cabins. Authentic hunting lodge is historic landmark; 6 rooms with bath, 11 cabins. *Open May–Nov. 218 W. Ramshorn, Dubois; 307-455-2600.*

ing down at flood time toward the Union Pacific. Now, however, tie-hacking has become part of the historical heritage of the upper Wind River valley.

◆ **DUBOIS**   *map page 259, B-1*

Dubois ("DEW-boys") is the first town on the drive from Jackson, and another Western cow town raped by highway expansion through its main street. Yet it still retains some of its old quality as a center for the cattle and dude ranches scattered about a wide area of the mountain-bordered valley.

The **Dubois Museum—Wind River Historical Center,** on the western out-skirts of town, celebrates the tie-hacking profession and other aspects of local and natural history. The displays provide colorful, instructive, and amusing historical detail. Almost every town of any size in the state now has a historical museum, but this museum in Dubois is especially nice. *909 West Ramshorn; 307-455-2284.*

Also in Dubois is the **National Bighorn Sheep Interpretive Center** with exhibits on these magnificent animals, along with directions to nearby viewing areas. *907 W. Ramshorn; 307-455-3429 or 888-209-2795.*

■ WIND RIVER RESERVATION: HISTORICAL OVERVIEW

Southeast from Dubois, the country opens and dries up progressively as the highway travels downstream through spectacular red badlands, with high peaks in the distant

background. Soon the road enters the Wind River Indian Reservation, one of the largest reservations in the West, and the only one in Wyoming. It covers a flat green valley that gradually broadens out into the central plains of the state.

The Wind River Reservation differs from some others, notably the Sioux reservations of the Dakotas, in that it was more of a reward than a punishment. It was given to the Shoshone in recognition of their great Chief

Chief Washakie, longtime leader of the Shoshone and a friend of the U.S. government. (Courtesy, Wyoming State Archives)

The dramatic badlands country in the Wind River Indian Reservation's western section.

Washakie's friendship with the white settlers. Sioux chiefs like Red Cloud were shipped to the Dakotas as a punishment for their wars with the whites. Washakie saw the future, and though he didn't necessarily like what he saw, he decided to cooperate instead of fighting the U.S. government. Whether, in the end, he and the Shoshone fared much better than the warlike Sioux will always be a matter of dispute. It is impossible to get a truly impartial opinion on any matter of any kind involving Indian-white relations. Bias inevitably emerges. Suffice it to say that Washakie was the U.S. government's favorite chief in Wyoming, and that in giving his tribe this passably fertile and well-watered land, officials believed they were rewarding him.

◆ **WHISKEY BASIN**   *map page 259, B-1*
Approximately five miles east of Dubois a sign directs you to Whiskey Basin. Follow this gravel road several miles along Torrey Creek to a string of four small lakes. With a bit of exploring, you'll discover quite a few Indian pictographs on large boulders opposite the lakes. Some of the elaborate figures are otherworldly creations with horns and headdresses, seemingly representations of ancient shamanistic ceremonies. They are believed to be more than 2,000 years old, and of Athapaskan (a Canadian tribe) rather than Shoshonean origin. During the winter months, Whiskey Basin contains

the largest population of Rocky Mountain bighorn sheep anywhere in the world. At times, more than 1,200 sheep congregate here because of the mild winters and the lack of deep snow.

◆ CROWHEART BUTTE   *map page 259, C-1*
Along the river, 10 miles farther south, is a striking butte with a flat top, called Crowheart Butte. This was the site of a single-combat fight between the Shoshone and Crow chiefs. The Shoshone Chief Washakie won, and celebrated his victory—the story goes—by eating the heart of his enemy. This was not too outrageous by Indian standards, since eating the heart of something brave, say a bear, was believed to give you the victim's courage. Everyone in the region was brought up on this story, and it is an excellent example of the superiority of memorable myth over fussy facts. Unfortunately, the fussy facts—the probable facts, as prominently presented by a detailed historical marker on the road opposite the butte—confirm these details: the battle took place in March 1866, with the Shoshone and Bannocks fighting the Crows over the perennial issue of hunting rights. Chief Washakie sure enough conducted the battle and won, and the battle was in the neighborhood of Crowheart Butte, near Black Mountain. But nobody fought on top of the butte; indeed it would have been a scramble to get up there (although teepee rings show that people did reach the top). And nobody ate a heart. Chief Washakie merely "displayed a Crow warrior's heart on his lance at the war dance after the battle."

But Wyomingites have always been prone to telling tall tales. And people like the myth; it's unforgettable, and appropriate for this striking landmark. At sunset, the butte is a mythical blood-red; at noon, a factual drab tan. Take your pick. (It may be that the myth is true. Washakie himself never denied the story. In fact, when quizzed about the incident by an old-timer, he replied cautiously, "When you are young and full of life, you do strange things.")

◆ FORT WASHAKIE   *map page 259, C-1/2*
After you pass an irrigation dam (and the resulting Bull Lake), the road forks. Continue on U.S. Route 287 toward Lander. Fort Washakie, 16 miles from the junction, is reservation headquarters, named for the great Shoshone chief "in whose teepee never hung the scalp of a white man."

The Shoshone were by no means blindly loyal to the whites. There was an uprising in 1861–62, but most of the country was then involved in the Civil War, so the government appeased the tribe with vague promises of huge grants of land—most of southwest Wyoming. In 1868, out of friendship for Washakie, the tribe was promised the entire lower Wind River Basin, at that time called the Popo Agie after the river flowing across the southern border. (Opinions on pronunciation vary widely, but you won't go wrong with "po-PO-zhia.") This was the richest, wettest land in the whole area, so the Shoshone were gradually pushed north by eager, illegal settlers. Sioux, Cheyennes, and Arapahos kept invading, and in 1869, Red Cloud killed 30 Shoshones (and two white women), and stole their horses. In protest, Washakie refused to occupy the area without U.S. military protection. He eventually trekked south to the Green River area, and wouldn't come back until a treaty was signed in 1872. However, he settled for less than what he wanted, giving up some 600,000 fertile acres of the Popo Agie valley for $25,000 and a promise of protection. The reservation was now confined to the north part of the basin, spilling over eventually into the Bighorn Basin, and the government established Fort Brown for protection. The name was changed to Fort Washakie in 1878.

After a defeat by the joint forces of the Shoshone, Crows, and U.S. troops in 1876, the Arapahos were forcibly settled on the east side of the Shoshone Reservation, an act that was vociferously opposed by Chief Washakie. There was a long history afterward of suits and counter-suits by both tribes. By now, the two tribes are more or less blood brothers in the common cause of protecting Indian rights and resources on the reservation. The ancient hatchet appears to have been buried.

The U.S. government wanted to abandon Fort Washakie, along with its other old Indian war forts, at the end of the 19th century. But Washakie was still alive to object until 1900, and out of respect, the post was not closed till 1909. Now, the fort's many buildings have been turned into the tribal agency headquarters. Instead of being a carefully embalmed but empty historic site, it's full of activity and probably gives a truer idea of what such a living fort may have been like in earlier days.

■ LANDER   *map page 259, C-2*

Just four miles south of the reservation border on Highway 287 is Lander, the seat of Fremont County. With a population of 7,000, it's a prosperous-looking, settled, civilized place—old cattle, old oil, and residential sections more like an older New Jersey suburb than anything Wild West, much less Shoshone. Smaller and much more homey than nearby Riverton, Lander is undergoing a rebirth as younger folks move in to raise families and open shops, restaurants, and small businesses oriented to those who love the outdoors. The relatively mild winters make it an attractive place to retire, too, and Lander's proximity to the Popo Agie Wilderness Area makes it a

jumping-off place for treks into the Wind River Mountains. The town is also home to the nation's premier outdoor education program, the **National Outdoor Leadership School (NOLS)**, offering courses all over the world; *307-332-5300.*

The **Pioneer Museum** is full of souvenirs from the good old days, which in Wyoming means almost any time before 1920. The museum first opened in 1915, but a grand new home is expected to debut in 2008 on East Main. It's worth visiting for its impressive Indian collection, which preserves buffalo robes, beaded gloves, painted buffalo hides, and a squaw saddle. For something completely different, peek in the tiny wedding chapel, a popular place for spring nuptials. Most bizarre is the skull of a local farmer killed in 1870—a 10-inch wagon bolt is driven through it. Another room, the One-Shot Antelope Hunt Memorial Room, is devoted to this rather bizarre sport with its own celebrities. Out front is the obligatory sheepherder's wagon, an older version of the RV, still used by those who spend months at a time alone with their flocks. *630 Lincoln Street; 307-332-4137.*

A circle tour is the best way to take in the sights of the reservation, if you can make camp in Lander early enough to have a free afternoon. A visit to Fort Washakie and the three missions—St. Stephen's (Arapaho and Catholic), St. Michael's (Arapaho and Episcopalian), and Roberts' Mission, or the Shoshone Episcopal Girls' School—will give you a survey of this special and curious area.

A popular hangout, **The Lander Bar** (126 Main Street; 307-332-7009), is housed in a 1907 building that has been everything from a hotel to a bordello. The staff swears that ghosts haunt the corridors. The bar serves excellent food and microbrews and live bands play every weekend. Stop by the **Magpie Cafe** (159 N. Second Street; 307-332-5565), for the best coffee and pastries in town. Local artisans display their work and often poets and songwriters will perform.

■ ST. STEPHEN'S   *map page 112, A-4*

Big, wide Wyoming State Highway 789 crosses the Popo Agie on the south end of Lander and heads northeast to Riverton, passing some messy old oil works. In **Hudson**, a quaintly derelict cow town, you'll find two famous old restaurants that folks from all over the state come to: **Club El Toro** (132 S. Main; 307-332-4627) and **Svilar's** (175 Main; 307-332-4516), both specializing in beef. Leaving Hudson, turn left on State Highway 138, clearly marked, which takes you directly to the St. Stephen's Catholic mission.

(opposite) A dancer sits on the sidelines at Fort Washakie's Eastern Shoshone Indian Days Powwow.

St. Stephen's is a big establishment, with rather grandiose Victorian and early 20th-century buildings and a proper air of some papal pride and grandeur. Its old school is now gone, but as you drive up the long entrance road south from Highway 138 to the mission itself, you pass an almost equally grandiose new public school, its gymnasium peaked with a teepee-shaped roof. This impressive new building keeps to the spirit of not only St. Stephen's, but of the reservation as a whole. Quite a few striking, modern buildings, most of them devoted to various aspects of the agency's public business, are equally impressive. They contrast with the modest private dwellings on the reservation.

St. Stephen's was started in the 1870s by Jesuits and nuns (German and Irish), who ran the school for boys and girls and began a long tradition of preserving Indian arts and crafts. Most of the religious personages have left since the schools were secularized (with the establishment of public education). The

big Victorian nunnery is now vacant. The pride of the mission today is its relatively new (1928) church, combining Catholic ritual with Indian decor. Vivid Indian patterns decorate the church inside and out. Special details—like a huge log-stump support for the christening font, a small teepee for an altar tabernacle, and Indian figures in the Stations of the Cross—give the airy, handsome building a special atmosphere.

But probably the most interesting and exciting aspect of the present-day mission is the continuing work in local craft and art,

Sunday service at St. Stephen's Catholic Church, on the Wind River Indian Reservation.

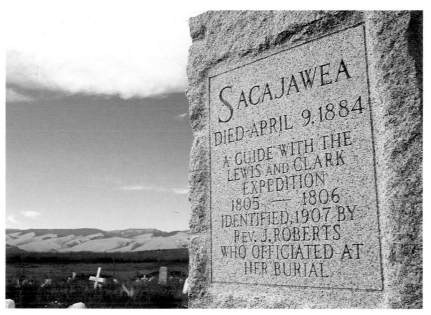

Sacagawea, the Shoshone girl who served as a guide on the Lewis and Clark expedition, has a grave marker on the Wind River Reservation; it is believed that she actually died in 1812.

reflected in the excellent museum and store. Such products are displayed, along with some wonderful old photographs of Arapahos, in the main church office building. An older building east of the church shows further evidence of this renaissance. Local Arapaho artist Bob Spoonhunter is actively promoting the rebirth of reservation arts and crafts, combining tradition with sophisticated modern styles and techniques. It's hard to resist purchasing some of the beautiful jewelry and other artwork.

■ ETHETE TO FORT WASHAKIE *map page 259, C-1*

Saint Michael's Episcopalian mission is in Ethete, right in the center of the southern, settled part of the reservation, between Riverton and Lander. It was the principal school for Arapaho children, and consists of red stone buildings, most of them built around a circle by Bishop Nathaniel Thomas of Wyoming, beginning in 1913. The most famous and attractive building is the mission church, **Our Father's House**, a log building, dark and rather low, in direct contrast to the church at St. Stephen's, but also full of Indian motifs—a big drum for an altar, an elk-horn bishop's chair, and more. Behind the altar is a picture window with a view of the Wind Rivers, celebrating the glory of God in nature as being especially appealing to the Indian parishioners. (This idea was copied in the Chapel of the Transfiguration at Moose, in Jackson Hole.) The once flourishing school is now used as a community and mission center.

◆ ROBERTS' MISSION   *map page 259, C-1*
Driving west on State Highway 137, cross over U.S. Route 287 at the tiny settlement of Wind River and continue west to the Roberts' Mission, founded in 1889 as a girls' school and religious center for the Shoshone. The founder, Reverend John Roberts, was a Welshman and Oxford graduate who came in 1883 and did not die until the 1940s. Chief Washakie urged Roberts to concentrate on the young, whose ears were open, since the old were set in their ancient ways. Ironically, Washakie himself was converted just before he died. This mission school, like the others, was absorbed into the public school system, and the charming old pink Victorian building is shut. But there is a small, active church (also with picture window) and a busy parish hall. The atmosphere on the edge of town is that of a peaceful, old, somnolent, and neglected English country churchyard. On weekdays, the shady, green garden is silent and nostalgic.

◆ GRAVE OF SACAGAWEA   *map page 259, C-1/2*
What some claim is the **grave of Sacagawea** lies up the small road north of the Roberts' Mission school grounds. A Shoshone, Sacagawea was kidnapped in an Indian raid and sold as a wife to Toussaint Charbonneau, a fur trader along the Missouri. The two were then engaged by Lewis and Clark as guides for their expedition. Sacagawea, with her infant son, Baptiste, survived the 3,000-mile trek to become a heroine of historical romance. According to some, she eventually returned to her Shoshone people and was buried here when she died in 1884. It is more widely believed, however, that she died in 1812, her remains lost. The graves of relations flank the handsome tombstone-monument (which spells her name with a "j"—a spelling derived from an 1814 narrative; it is now generally agreed that the correct spelling is with a "g," as Lewis and Clark recorded it, reflecting her own pronunciation). A memorial to Baptiste also stands here, though his actual burial site is uncertain.

The graveyard is dominated by a small log building, where one of the first Episcopal services and baptisms of the area was held, in 1873, by Bishop Randell of Colorado, Wyoming, and New Mexico—a sizable diocese. Many graves are adorned with fancy bedsteads, and the Indian names are more authentic than those at the nearby Fort Washakie military cemetery, where Chief Washakie himself lies.

Sacagawea has become one of Wyoming's great heroines (along with Calamity Jane and Esther Hobart Morris), and there are memorable statues of her—notably, the one in the Buffalo Bill Historical Center garden, and another on the campus of Central Wyoming College, in Riverton. Like most who lived on the reservation, Sacagawea and Washakie were eventually converted by one of the missions.

◆ **GRAVE OF WASHAKIE** *map page 259, C-1/2*

The **military graveyard** where Washakie is buried is located just outside the Fort Washakie compound. Like the civilian graveyard where Sacagawea may or may not lie, this graveyard is not a place of grace and charm. Both are totally bare and indiscriminately covered with bouquets of artificial flowers, with no attempt at planting. But behind Sacagawea's tomb is the grand swell of the Wind Rivers, while the military cemetery is framed by trees and nearby buildings. Still, the atmosphere is evocative, if desolate.

Many of the plain wooden crosses are without dates, but some stone monuments were erected as late as the 1970s. Washakie's memorial is the most substantial: a gray granite oblong with inscriptions. Washakie was nearly 100 years old at the time of his death in 1900; his tombstone gives his birth as 1804. His youngest son, Charles Washakie (1873–1953), is buried just behind the chief. Other, older monuments of flaking yellow stone mark the graves of soldiers stationed at the fort, along with graves of their family members. There are almost no Indian-sounding names, except for Raymond Shoulderblade and his kinsman Raymond S. Blade.

It can't be said that the reservation gives a sense of great individual prosperity. Most ranch and farm houses are small, and some rather derelict; others, however, are spic-and-span new. But the collective bustle and impressive new buildings at Fort Washakie seem to indicate communal prosperity. The contrast is interesting and provocative.

■ LANDER TO SOUTH PASS *map page 259, C-2*

The only way to get around the Wind Rivers without returning to Jackson Hole is by way of South Pass. One route from Lander is via U.S. Route 287 and Wyoming State Highway 28—a wide, easy, rather scenic thoroughfare across the final foothills of the Wind Rivers. The more adventurous and picturesque road is Wyoming State Highway 131, which heads across the southern tip of the mountains. It's not a time-saver

(top) Hidden away throughout the Wind River Reservation are countless petroglyphs of unknown origin and age. (bottom) Harvey Morgan was murdered in 1870 by Indians, one of many casualties of the battles between invading whites and the Indians. (Photo by Dr. George Gill)

by any means, but will give a glimpse of the forest and lake country of the Wind Rivers that you won't otherwise get by car.

Well-marked State Highway 131 leads west from Lander's center, following the Popo Agie River upstream for nine miles to the chief natural curiosity of the region, a phenomenon called **the Sinks**. The Popo Agie, dashing down from the mountains in its rugged canyon, is suddenly swallowed up by a sinister black cave at the bottom of a cliff. A half-mile farther down at **the Rise**, the water oozes out from the bottom of another cliff into an equally sinister, big, dark, calm pool. The whole is preserved and protected by a well-kept state park with a visitors center.

Just below the Rise is a tiny sample of **prehistoric pictographs**. A big ditch flows along the north side of the road. There's a little gravel pull-off, and what looks like a steep little spillway of white concrete. This path, or scramble, leads up to the edge of the ditch, across which you can clearly see the two small, red, vaguely animal-like designs. Since pictographs are so hard to get at, even such a tiny, though vivid, sight of them is worthwhile.

Up the canyon beyond the west boundary of the park, past the road to nearby Popo Agie Falls, the paved highway turns into a sometimes-rutted gravel road. Soon leaving the rush of the river, the road zigzags up the bare side of the mountains. There's plenty of room to pass, and the view down into the valley becomes increasingly spectacular. This road is easy to drive in ordinary weather conditions, but be sure to check at the visitors center before you start up (307-332-6333).

Once you get to the top, you're on a great, forested plateau studded with small lakes (Frye, Fiddlers, Christina, Louis), the goal of campers and fishermen. **Louis Lake**, the most popular, is shadowed by some peculiarly foreboding, tall, rocky cones that look like piles of coal. On its shore is the pleasant Louis Lake Lodge (888-422-2246), which rents overnight cabins, horses, canoes, and boats.

All along State Highway 131, you'll get occasional glimpses of great, snow-capped peaks to the west. Shortly beyond Louis Lake, the road emerges at last from the almost continuous timber of **Shoshone National Forest** (marred by extensive lumbering operations) onto open, hilly, sagebrush range, with scattered pine copses and queer, piled-up castles of gray-brown rock, much like the Vedauwoo near Cheyenne.

After crossing Wyoming State Highway 28, turn left up the gravel road that dead-ends at Atlantic City, passing en route the gigantic open pit of the Atlantic City Mine Company's iron ore mine (now closed).

■ SOUTH PASS   *map page 259, C-2*

The South Pass area, with its two little towns, is yet another memorial to one of Wyoming's boom-and-bust cycles: the state's only significant gold strike. Tales of gold were circulating as early as the 1840s, but were not confirmed till 1867. The population of South Pass City suddenly leaped to 2,000. Stages ran north from the distant, brand-new Union Pacific railroad. The town boasted five hotels, 13 saloons, bowling alleys, beer halls, lawyers and doctors, and a school that was rated one of the best in the state.

◆ ATLANTIC CITY   *map page 259, C-2*

Atlantic City was once a mining suburb of South Pass City. Although the iron and gold mining have stopped, Atlantic City is no ghost town. Its picturesque remains are still inhabited, and there are signs of arts and crafts, and a certain bohemian touch. On the road west of town, a handsome old two-story log cabin, the **Miner's Delight Bed and Breakfast** (290 Atlantic City Road; 307-332-0248) continues its tradition of hospitality from the days when Atlantic City was a solvent gold town. At **Atlantic City Mercantile** (100 E. Main Street), you can order an inexpensive but savory burger and wonderfully grilled fish and meats in an old pioneer setting, an adobe-brick building from 1893.

It's called Atlantic City not because of the ocean, obviously, but because it's on the Atlantic side of the Continental Divide, over which South Pass crosses. On the other side, Pacific Creek flows down toward the Green River, accompanying the Oregon Trail onward.

◆ SOUTH PASS CITY   *map page 259, C-2*

The former boom town of South Pass City lies a few miles west along a big, dusty road. Like Atlantic City, it is nestled in a bare, open canyon, with rugged brown hills about it; but unlike Atlantic City, South Pass City is now primarily a restoration, though some folks still live here.

South Pass was the county seat of the new, now-extinct Carter County, which took up most of western Wyoming, within the Dakota Territory. When the present Sweetwater County was finally created in the 1880s, South Pass was already well on the decline. South Pass tried valiantly to retain the honor of county seat, but the Wyoming territorial government peremptorily threatened suit and transferred the seat to the city of Green River. South Pass and its surrounding mines, bowling alleys, and bars simply died out altogether. What's there now is a small, evocative restoration—a street of fixed-up or reconstructed buildings (business and residential). The restored buildings give you a strong flavor of what the town might have been like; except, of course, for the now-missing crowds and bars, the bustle and excitement. Particularly nice is a law office that acted as the town hall and now has information on the complicated issue of the South Pass City bid for county seat. Also notable is the choicely decorated cabin of Esther Hobart Morris. It was here, in the palmy days of the gold strike, that Esther Morris—whose memorial stands in front of the capitol in Cheyenne—was sworn in for eight months as the first woman justice of the peace in the nation.

But here again, one of Wyoming's good myths takes a beating. A marble memorial slab from the 1930s proclaims Esther's involvement in the Woman's Suffrage Act, passed by the territorial legislature in 1869 as the first of its kind. Next to the marble monument is a later myth-destroying marker, indicating clearly that Esther had nothing to do with this seminal legislation, though she was undoubtedly justice of the peace in 1870.

So be it. It's certainly seems fitting that a woman should be remembered in this nationally important first. But the true bill-proposer, South Pass saloon-keeper William Bright, and another man active behind the scenes, Edward Lee, have been unjustly ignored, although a historical marker along the road describes Bright as "a force for suffrage."

The restored South Pass City is a state park, with a nice place to picnic in back of the houses, alongside the aptly named Willow Creek. You are very likely to see someone panning for gold here, for people are still at it. The park is the splendid result of a commendable state effort, but it's hard to imagine 2,000 people crammed into this narrow, now peaceful valley. The **South Pass City State Historic Site** can be reached at 307-332-3684.

The gravel road continues north and west to rejoin paved Wyoming State Highway 28.

Of all the many remnants of the Oregon Trail heyday, **South Pass** is the most significant. From the earliest days of trapper exploration, the pass was famous as the one truly open and easy way to cross Wyoming, avoiding the unbroken belt of mountains north and south, with good water along the way. South Pass thus became a goal of all pioneers along the trail.

As a pass, it's certainly not very impressive—nothing to compare to Teton, Togwotee, or Hoback. But it's a pass that historians pause at with reverence. Now the area is open range, and it's almost impossible to tell exactly when and where you cross the divide.

WEST-CENTRAL

But the pass was key to the whole settlement of the northern Far West. The dry soil of the barren sagebrush-dotted hillside is visibly scarred with wagon tracks made by thousands of emigrants who crossed here over the years.

■ Entering Trapper Land

Wyoming State Highway 28 gradually descends the Wind Rivers from South Pass, with the brown cliffs of the Antelope Hills appearing to the south. Ahead lies nothing but vast rangeland. At the southwestern foot of the Wind Rivers, a rigorous gravel road (Wyoming State Highway 353) takes off to the north along one of the tributary forks of the Sweetwater, toward a dot on the map called Big Sandy. This is the road for more adventurous travelers; it joins up with U.S. 191 in Boulder, just south of Pinedale.

State Highway 28 zooms down some 40 miles alongside the invisible Pacific Creek to another dot on the map, **Farson.** North of Farson lies the Big Sandy Reservoir and Recreation Area, a most unlikely water resort in the desolation of this basin. Water from the reservoir is used to irrigate the area around Farson and Eden (a bit

(above) Big-sky country near the tiny settlement of Big Piney.
(opposite) The Wind River Mountains rise more than 7,000 feet above the sagebrush-covered plains to the west.

farther south). These are the only civic centers of any size between Rock Springs, in the south, and Boulder, in the north. **Eden** has pretty, tree-shaded picnic nooks and gurgling ditches. If you need gas, groceries, or a huge ice cream cone, stop at Farson, which consists of a fine, rather derelict brick building of oddly distinguished architecture, and nothing much else. Then, our route heads north.

■ WIND RIVER VISTA   *map page 259, B-2*

Now begins one of the truly great mountain-viewing experiences of the Far West. For over 60 miles, U.S. Route 191 takes you north along the western flank of the tremendous Wind Rivers, the highest and most rugged mountains in Wyoming and the whole Rocky Mountain West, except for the great congeries of 14,000-foot peaks scattered across central Colorado. This view—one of America's most bleak yet sublime panoramas—displays the entire west side of the range, lined up for inspection at one glance.

For miles and miles, there's nothing between the road and mountains except areas of rolling range with sheep, cattle, and evasive antelope. Every time the road rolls and rises to a yet higher crest, the mountains approach and loom larger. The major peaks are, from south to north: **Wind River Peak** (13,192 feet), **Washakie Peak** (12,524 feet), **Fremont Peak** (13,745 feet), **Downs Mountain** (13,349 feet), and **Gannett Peak** (13,804 feet)—the highest in Wyoming. True, the Wind Rivers don't have the jagged edges and individual outlines of the Tetons. But as you come closer and closer to them, they grow in grandeur and solemnity.

Meanwhile, other lower mountain ranges begin to crowd in: the tail end of the Absarokas in the north, the top end of the Wyoming Range far to the west. It's a magnificent vision whichever way you come, but it's much more exciting heading north, particularly when there's lots of snow.

■ GREEN RIVER RENDEZVOUS   *map page 259, B-2*

Highway 191 takes you right on up to Pinedale and constantly closer to the mountains. At the risk of breaking that gradual mountain-range crescendo, a detour along Wyoming State Highway 351 is highly recommended. It goes smoothly due west across this northern apex of the Green River Basin, to a point above the settlements of Marbleton and Big Piney, an old cattle town that hasn't much to offer. The attractive heights of the **Wyoming Range** tower straight ahead. The road crosses two big rivers: the New Fork (of the Green), and then the **Green River** itself. Turning north on U.S. Route 189, through varied country of rangeland, pink badlands, white alkali flats, and ubiquitous cattle and sheep, you approach Daniel, 19 miles north of the Big Piney junction.

Daniel itself lies in a broad cottonwood valley where Horse Creek and the juvenile Green River meet and mingle. Horse Creek was the site of many of the most important rendezvous of the 1830s and 1840s—annual meetings of trappers, Indians, and mountain men who gathered for days or weeks at a time to barter, buy, and sell skins, guns, and supplies, and also to swap stories, drink, and renew old acquaintances.

On the still-bare heights, before you descend into this valley, is the **Prairie de la Messe**, where the indefatigable Father De Smet celebrated the first Roman Catholic Mass in the state, in 1840. A historical marker on the right side of the road gives no indication of where the De Smet monument is. Next

to the marker, however, a big sign reads "Daniel Cemetery," and a little gravel road goes east up the bank to a high, deserted, sagebrush plateau. (The road goes straight ahead to the cemetery, despite a rather misleading arrow that seems to point leftward.) A bit beyond the cemetery, you come to the **De Smet Memorial**, a pretty little shrine, not much taller than a man, on a promontory with magnificent views over the river valley and to the numberless mountains. The shrine may not be grandiose, but its location is exotic.

Beside the shrine is an odd, small gravestone dedicated to Pinkney Sublette, one of the many

Jim Bridger is buried in Kansas City's Mount Washington Cemetery (left), but his spirit remains in Wyoming. (Courtesy, Buffalo Bill Historical Center, Cody)

brothers of the famous fur trader William (after whom Sublette County is named). What Pinkney is doing here one can't imagine. He was supposedly killed by Indians after the rendezvous of 1828, and what remained of him was interred on this high bench. He was then removed and taken east, but by an act of Congress, a plaque says, he was brought back and reburied in 1936. William shed brothers like leaves. Another fell sick at the more permanent shelter of Fort Laramie, but suffered so from his infections from an amputated leg that he doped himself with liquor and is said to have died of delirium tremens.

Down at **Horse Creek** stands a stone memorial to Narcissa Whitman and Eliza Spalding, the first white women to cross the American continent. The memorial and a big historical highway billboard are absolutely all there is on this site, except lots of nice, big cottonwoods. But for those interested in Western history, the memories are as thick as the cottonwoods.

The untiring Narcissa, with her husband and the Spaldings, attended the trapper rendezvous here in 1836. On arrival, as soon as Narcissa alighted from her horse, she was "met by a company of mature native women, one after another shaking hands and saluting me with a most hearty kiss." Present at this particular affair were Jim Bridger, who managed to make almost every one of the rendezvous, and also Capt. Nathaniel Wyeth, an active fur trader and ancestor of famous illustrator N.C. Wyeth (prominently represented in the Cody Museum), father of the famous painter Andrew Wyeth. Doctor Whitman, Narcissa's husband, had removed an old Indian arrowhead from Bridger's back at the rendezvous the previous year, so Bridger greeted him with special warmth. On July 9, the local Indian tribes gave a final parade for the ladies, singing, dancing, and cavorting. All the participants were painted and dressed in bright animal skins. In fact, the warriors wore little else but paint, and gave a startling equestrian performance. On July 18, the quartet left, accompanied by a Mr. Drips, and went on to many excruciating adventures.

Another festival in honor of ladies was much less well received. Four missionary wives of a less amiable sort were serenaded at the Popo Agie Rendezvous of 1838. One of the serenaded wrote, "Last night disturbed by drunkards. A large company arrived under the command of Capt. Bridger. A number of them came to salute us. One man carried the scalp of a Black-foot. The music consisted of tambourines accompanied by an inarticulate sound of the voice. They fired guns and acted as strangely as they could." A companion, Myra Eels, was even more shocked. "Twelve white men...dressed and painted Indian style... gave us a dance. No pen can describe the horrible scene they presented. Could not imagine that white men, brought up in a civilized land, can appear to so much imitate the devil." So much for hospitality, trapper style. Victorianism came West with the ladies.

The last rendezvous was held in 1840. The American Fur Company, sponsor since 1836, closed them down. During the 16 years of these rendezvous, Jim Bridger seems to have missed only a couple. One of the more memorable was in 1837, when Sir William Drummond Stewart, the itinerant Englishman, presented him with a suit of ancient English armor (Jim wore it at the rendezvous). Most of the rendezvous, from the first down on Henry's Fork of the Green (in 1825) to the 1840 Horse Creek affair, were held in Wyoming. Of these, six were held at Horse Creek. The well-known 1833 rendezvous, with some 250 whites and 250 Indians in attendance, was described by Washington Irving in his *Adventures of Captain Bonneville* (1837). Though Irving himself never attended a rendezvous, Captain Bonneville gave him detailed descriptions. William Sublette was at the 1833 affair; so were Bridger, Wyeth, and many others.

Horse Creek is handy and accessible, and it's a pity something more isn't done with the site to memorialize these raucous but significant affairs. The best contemporary tribute is the annual rendezvous celebration held every July in nearby Pinedale, which celebrates most, but definitely not all, of the characteristic events.

Daniel, the small community immediately north of Horse Creek, retains a good deal of Old West cow-town charm, despite the best efforts of the highway department.

■ PINEDALE   *map page 259, B-2*

Unfortunately, the same can't be said of Pinedale. The scene along its wide central street seems to encourage you to speed through. The town's old-time charm, like Dubois (Pinedale's "twin city"), is being obliterated, with ready help from an influx of riches courtesy of another round of oil and gas drilling.

Still, it would be a pity not to stop, since the town has a lot to offer. Pinedale is the most accessible starting and provisioning point for a trip into the Winds. With shopping and entertainment, it's Wyoming's smallest county seat (population 1,400 in the year 2000, but surely much greater than that once you add in roughnecks and others attracted by the energy boom), and the highest, at 7,128 feet. The elegant **Western McGregor's Pub** (21 N. Franklin Street; 307-367-4443), in the 1905 Pinedale Hotel building, is one of the best country restaurants in the state.

Pinedale and its neighbor to the south, **Boulder**, stand out among modern Wyoming towns for their deliberate attempt to keep the tradition of the log cabin going. New log cabins are still being built there; they're very good-looking and appropriate, too. There are small, squeaky-clean motels and cafes, and the whole town offers a refreshing sense of peace and order compared to frenetic Jackson, the next major stop on the road west.

■ Wind River Excursions

Pinedale is above all a center for excursions into the formidable but gorgeous Wind River Mountains. The more adventurous can pursue an infinite variety of horseback riding, backpacking, mountain climbing, skiing, and snowmobiling opportunities. A series of foot and horse trails leads through the entire length of the range. The fishing on the outskirts of Pinedale is famous, and the local chamber of commerce (on the main street) will be glad to help you make arrangements.

One easy excursion from Pinedale takes you to Fremont Lake, practically in the suburbs of town. The road starts at the east end of the main street, passing near the large new **Museum of the Mountain Men**, full of souvenirs not only of trappers but of local life, particularly as portrayed in some wonderful early photographs of Wyoming. *700 E. Hennick Street, Pinedale; 307-367-4101.*

Back on the road to **Fremont Lake**, you pass over a summit, where you get a stunning view up the long lake to the mountains, 16 miles away. That, unfortunately, is about it. You can get the same view from the lake shore, where a cut-off leads left to the pleasant log Lakeside Lodge (307-367-2221), with a marina, cabins, and food. From there you can arrange for a boat to take you to the far end; there are no direct roads. The east shore is bordered by a popular, tree-shaded campground. The opposite shore is occupied by a grim, bare butte, whose cliffs slope precipitously into the water. A roundabout road takes you to the north end of the lake; it's not very inviting country around the south end, a dreary and gray stretch of badlands. But that one grand vista looking to the north is worth the trip.

A longer excursion from Pinedale takes you to the **Green River Lakes**, reached by Wyoming State Highway 352, which takes off from the west side of town. **Cora**—a quaint old log store, a post office, and a restaurant-bar called "The Place"—is the only settlement on the road. Don't try to find Cora city center or you'll just bump into ranch gates. The highway continues north over rolling sagebrush range, with the magnificent Wind Rivers visible to the east. Crossing a

(opposite) Cirque of the Towers in the Popo Agie Wilderness of the Wind River Mountains.

Casting into the Winds

The Green River quietly flows out of the heart of the imposing Wind River Range and into the memory of anyone lucky enough to cast a fly into the clear, rich water. Fishing for a crafty brown trout just below Lower Green River Lake north of Pinedale is a constant struggle; a struggle to keep your eye on your fly. The drive from Pinedale along "the Cora Highway" (Wyoming 352) rolls along the river and beside a ridge that hides the Winds. About 30 miles from Cora it turns in a long, lazy U around the point of the ridge. The granite rises and jaws drop. The menacing presence of Square Top Mountain demands reverie. The massive peak stands apart from the surrounding mountains and the prairie-flat summit seems impossibly wide and level. Other peaks surrounding the lakes display obvious fault lines at crazy angles, sharp corners, and broken edges that contrast with Square Top to produce an effect that recalls cubist sculpture in the middle of emptiness. For the moment, the fish are forgotten… but not for long.

Standing beside the fluid, generous, soothing river and occasionally seeing widening concentric circles spread across the surface reminds one of great art. The beauty of the scene is both sublime and maddening. Maddening to fly fishers because they know exactly what causes those mesmerizing circles. A closer look reveals healthy brown trout leisurely feeding. The ultimate joy for fly fishers is watching a strong fish swimming slowly up to slurp the imitation fly tied to his or her line. The contest is far from over once the hook has been set. Brown trout are known to be the smartest of the Salmonid family. Browns learn fast and will try to tangle the line in weeds, try to break it by wedging it under rocks and running fast and far, reeling it out to full length. If you are lucky enough to get one of these beauties in your hands the feeling is addictive. Be careful not to stare too long at these creatures: they have bewitched many a fisher for the remainder of a lifetime. You have been warned.

The Great Outdoor Shop. *332 W. Pine Street, P. O. Box 787, Pinedale, WY 82941; 307-367-2440.*

High Country Flies. *185 N. Center Street, P. O. Box 3432, Jackson, WY 83001; 307-733-7210.*

— John H. Clark

The Great Divide Mountain Bike Route

Peter L. Bower, a retired educator and bicycle tourist, recalls his bicycle travels in Wyoming with poetic abstractions and concrete detail. "Perhaps the wind, if there is any, will remind me of days in Wyoming. Perhaps the sight of clouds will remind me of how they would build to large masses and reach great heights above the mountains. Perhaps it will be so cold that I have to wear a jacket and gloves, which will bring me back to ascending many a mountain pass." Non-motorized travel has been a part of life in Wyoming for thousands of years. The Crow and later the Sioux followed the plentiful buffalo herds on foot. The horse was unknown in the area until the mid–1700s. All peoples of Wyoming famously took to the horse and to this day riding is often preferred to driving by many Wyomingites. The expression "vast silence" is no mere cliché in the high plains and mountains of the Continental Divide, where vehicles can be few and far between. A great way to experience the openness and stillness of the expanse is by bicycle on the Great Divide Mountain Bike Route.

The Great Divide Mountain Bike Route, completed in 1997, is an epic tour, a worthy successor to the traditional seasonal movements of the ancient natives and the great stagecoach migration throughout Wyoming. The route covers nearly 500 miles through the state and 2,465 miles all told. From the Port of Roosville, on the Montana-Canada border, it follows the Continental Divide, passes through five of the largest states in the union and terminates at the Mexican border near Antelope Wells, New Mexico. Many sections of the route in Wyoming require that cyclists carry food, medical supplies, and foul weather gear for days at a time. Other sections are pleasant and on quiet county or Forest Service roads. A great many of the empty vistas, towering mountain barriers, and seemingly endless plains are exactly the same as when the Crow, Sioux, French trappers, English cattlemen, Basque shepherds, and homesteaders of the 1800s crossed or settled on them. Today, there's a Great Divide Mountain Bike Route race in which über-athletes complete the course in as little as two weeks.

Wilson Backcountry Sports. Fish Creek Center, 1230 Ida Lane, Wilson, WY 83014; 307-733-5228.

— John H. Clark

minor pass, you enter a broad valley of the Green River. All the way along are the gates of the big ranches that fill the valley.

At a scattering of summer cabins, where the Bridger-Teton National Forest begins, the paved highway turns into a white gravel Forest Service road, at first wide, then gradually narrower, alternating between smooth and tooth-shattering. The road veers east as the valley narrows, following the delightful Green River all the way up its open, pleasant course. Along the way are off-road campsites and historical markers, one describing the tie-hacking that flourished here. Another points out the site of the Gros Ventre Lodge, a hunting camp that opened as early as 1897 and closed in 1906. It catered mostly to Eastern and English big-game hunters, but folded when game laws became more strict. Though there's no sign of the lodge now, it may have been the state's first unofficial dude ranch.

The end of the line is the beginning of the Bridger-Teton Wilderness Area, where you can camp for a fee. Trails lead up to the nearby Green River Lakes. The lower lake, long, blue, and dominated at the end by the striking monolith of **Square Top Mountain** (11,670 feet), is without doubt one of the state's most beautiful lakes. Totally unspoiled, although much visited, it's certainly worth the long drive to get there, and the trek itself is beautiful, too. This end-of-the-lake spot is ideal for a picnic. Nearby is a small, coarse-sand beach. Trails continue on both sides of this lake to the upper lake. Fair weather, however, is crucial. The road can be difficult in wet weather, and the lake gloomy under clouds. Fishing is choice all along the upper Green River.

The oddity of the river is that it comes into life full-grown, so to speak; a wide, smooth, clear stream from its very beginning, it flows unchanged all the way to Pinedale (or its vicinity) with the same width, depth, and character, gliding or gamboling over stones on its long way toward the awesome Flaming Gorge and, eventually, the Gulf of Mexico. In the days before the Flaming Gorge was dammed, the trip down its rapids was considered very dangerous indeed.

The expedition to the lakes is beautiful and rewarding, but it is something of a relief to get back to the paved road again.

■ PINEDALE TO JACKSON HOLE *map page 259, A/B-1*

The highway between Pinedale and Hoback Junction, at the south tip of Jackson Hole, traverses 64 miles of increasingly exciting scenery. First, open sagebrush range stretches toward low, pine-topped ridges, surrounded by distant peaks. The timber and hills soon close in, and you cross a divide with wide, wonderful views into the watershed of the Hoback River. The road then travels up the Hoback Valley, open and green, with big hills about, and mountains to the north. **Bondurant**, a small summer-cottage and ranching center, lies in the middle of this valley. Then, the walls of **Hoback Canyon** struggle to contain the increasingly rough water of the river.

This spectacular canyon is named after trapper-guide John Hoback, who guided W. P. Hunt's company through the region as early as 1811. Hoback Canyon and the Togwotee Pass have long been the two main east entrances to Jackson Hole.

Wyoming religion got an early start here, too. On August 23, 1835, the Reverend Samuel Parker preached the first Protestant sermon in the state near the river's banks. Parker was an associate of Dr. Whitman. These religious firsts seem to have had little effect on the later moral scruples of the region.

Along the canyon, some ten miles before the Hoback joins the Snake River, the sizable **Granite Creek** comes down from the north. A road follows it through an especially beautiful valley to **Granite Recreational Area** and a hot spring open to the public. Bathing hours are posted at the junction.

The highway gradually emerges at the south end of Jackson Hole, where the Hoback joins the Snake as it rumbles off into the grand Snake River Canyon, and Idaho. **Hoback Junction** offers a rash of tourist facilities and traps. Just north, at Horse Creek, a large sign advertises the **Teton Mystery**, but it's closed (word is it's up for sale on eBay). Horse Creek Station, however, is not, and offers good steaks, fish and fowl and local color.

This ends the big circular tour of the Wind Rivers. You can either return to Jackson, 13 miles north, or head south into Star Valley.

■ STAR VALLEY OVERVIEW

Still a stronghold of proud, hard-working Mormon farm and ranch families, Star Valley is becoming a bedroom community for Jackson Hole workers. Star Valley is peaceful rather than awe-inspiring—though the surrounding mountains are grand enough. Its appeal, however, is its small town rural agricultural character, and its locally famous cheese. The trip south from Jackson Hole begins with the grandeur of the 3,000-foot-deep **Snake River Canyon**, a gorge of white water, where early attempts (like those of the Hunt party) to raft down into Idaho met with trouble. A spectacular, recently widened road runs in the canyon alongside the river to Alpine Junction and Palisades Reservoir, where a right-hand turn takes you into Idaho.

Alpine Junction is growing, with hundreds of new houses and a clump of tourist facilities at the point where the Snake River roars out of its canyon and comes to an abrupt halt in the big **Palisades Reservoir,** most of which lies over the state line, in Idaho. Alpine's principal attractions are water sports: white-water rafting in the canyon or calm-water playing on the reservoir. You can go riding, hiking, hunting, and fishing in the mountains roundabout and partake of all kinds of winter sports. To cater to this, motels have congregated. Most striking is the immense and elegant neo-Swiss hotel called the **Alpen Haus** (junction of U.S. 89 and U.S. 26; 800-343-6755 or 307-654-7545), obviously built with Swiss winters in mind. It is beautifully done up with luxurious quarters and dining and lounge rooms. Walls are decorated charmingly with Swiss-style painting, mottoes in German, and 18th-century peasant touches. A fancy, terraced esplanade in front, with a fountain, carries on the illusion. It's all very spectacular, if somewhat peculiarly out-of-place.

■ ALPINE JUNCTION TO STAR VALLEY   *map page 259, A-1/2*

From Alpine Junction, U.S. Route 89 heads straight south, first through a low, wooded pass, and then through the pastoral and Mormon-settled farmlands of bucolic Star Valley. It could be called a "hole" like Jackson's—it's totally surrounded by mountains. But it isn't so called.

The chief occupation of the valley was dairy farming, and products like cheese and butter are produced by ranchers, handled by cooperatives, sold to tourists, and shipped out over the whole Northwest.

A most pleasant vacation from purposeful, big-highway travel can be had by just wandering back and forth on the small roads crisscrossing the valley, admiring the mountains from one side and another, and letting the peaceful farm greenery soothe you. There's nothing else in Wyoming quite like this valley for spacious, pastoral greenery and sheltering hills.

Though the first non-Indians to see Star Valley were trappers and a rather off-course trickle of Oregon Trailers trying a shortcut northward, the area was deliberately colonized by Brigham Young in the late 1870s. His delegate, the Apostle Moses Thatcher, is supposed to have exclaimed on his first overview, "I name thee Star Valley because it is the star of all valleys." This is contradicted by a tale that it was originally called "Starved Valley," because of the hard winters endured by the first settlers—hard to believe, now.

(opposite) Bridger-Teton National Forest is one of the largest in the lower 48 states, with hundreds of lush mountain meadows popular for pack trips.

WEST-CENTRAL

Settlement was accelerated by Mormon reaction to the Edwards Anti-Polygamy Act of 1882. Star Valley was a remote refuge, far enough away to be beyond any attempts to enforce the anti-polygamy law, since Idaho police couldn't cross the state line, and Wyoming lawmen didn't care. Settlers arrived with their plural families and have created many more families since. The valley is 80 to 90 percent Mormon, and the general feeling is that, a century after settlement, all the descendants of the older families are at least second cousins.

Unlike most of Wyoming (except around equally farm-oriented Torrington), Star Valley is studded with little old farming villages (Etna, Freedom, Thayne, Bedford, Auburn), most of which have either been eviscerated by Highway 89 or have dwindled away, in the age of the automobile, losing residents to larger centers like Afton. **Freedom**, south of Alpine and right on the state border (one side of the principal street is in Wyoming, the other in Idaho) is the oldest settlement in the valley. The name celebrates the joy of immigrants in 1879, who escaped to the safety of Wyoming from persecution in Idaho. Unfortunately, there's nothing much left of the town except the usual substantial, red-brick, Latter-day Saints church, as well as the world-famous **Freedom Arms Factory**, where the most powerful handgun—the .454 Cassull—is manufactured.

Bedford is an exception. It lies off to the east, in a separate, secluded nook of the valley, the most beautiful part of it. The town is very small, but it's famous for flower gardening. It's well worth a detour.

Another specialty of the valley can be found at the **Star Valley Cheese Cafe** in **Thayne**, north of Afton. Here you can sample and acquire a bewildering variety of the native Star Valley Swiss Cheese and other products. It's crowded with tourists, but the cheese is good. You can eat, drink, and buy many a postcard. **Dad's** is a hit locally even though the steakhouse is only open on Friday and Saturday nights. The bar is open seven days a week.

■ AFTON   *map page 259, A-2*

Afton was casually named by some poetic wanderer after the old British song about a stream: "Flow gently, sweet Afton / Among thy green braes." The Salt River does indeed flow softly among its green braes through Afton, Wyoming.

Afton was a marketing center for dairy and farm products, and also for religion. Moses Thatcher, the founding father, supposedly struck the ground with his cane and said (more or less), "This is the place!" The town is still dominated by the high steeple of the unusually original and handsome big LDS mother church of the valley. (LDS or Latter-day Saints is the name most Mormons prefer for themselves.) Built of yellow stone sometime around the beginning of the 20th century, it has been remodeled most tastefully in a style that blends a touch of New England severity with Mormon solemnity. It is surrounded, like a hen by chicks, with up-to-date school and church edifices. Impressive, beautiful, interesting, dominant.

A surprising early phase of the town's history was its use as still another hideaway for outlaws such as the ubiquitous Butch Cassidy. The outlaws holed up in this rustic sanctuary between jobs, and patronized a barroom reputed to have been papered with stolen bank notes. Nothing like that in town nowadays.

Afton is anything but decadent. It's a spic-and-span community that any state could be proud of. It has the air of a county seat, but it isn't. Kemmerer down south still dominates Lincoln County. One suspects that the people of Star Valley wish it were otherwise. The wide main street, Washington, is spanned by an **elkhorn arch** and lined with well-kept stores. You could probably eat off the sidewalks. Flawless lawns and neat flowers surround the snug houses on the east side of town, along streets named after the earliest U.S. presidents, from Washington to Monroe (only one Adams St., since two might be confusing). If the town has a fault, it is that those fine streets are too wide and handsome—good for traffic, but producing a sort of lonely, empty effect that is at odds with the cozy households on either side. This is a general fault of Wyoming towns: there's already enough wide-openness all around, and towns ought to try for a more intimate compactness. Afton has motels as spic-and-span as everything else in town—notably the neat, pleasant, log-cabin **Corral Motel** (161 Washington Street; 307-885-5424) and equally spic-and-span eateries, such as the spacious **Elkhorn Restaurant** (461 Washington Street; 307-885-9401), right at the elk-horn arch.

■ THE PERIODIC SPRING   *map page 259, A-2*

The principal sight of Star Valley, in the mountains east of Afton, is a phenomenon called the Periodic Spring. When it's functioning properly (late summer and early fall), it gushes out of a cliff face for 18 minutes, then shuts down for an equal length of time. This particular oddity is caused by a subterranean water chamber behind the cliff face. In dry seasons, the flow stops each time the chamber is emptied; then subterranean springs refill it and the overflow begins again. Supposedly there are only two other such phenomena in the world. This is the only one in America. All very curious. During the spring months, the spring flows constantly; but there are other reasons for going to see the spring.

The trip there is half the reward. From the north end of town, head east on Second Avenue. The street becomes an unpaved road that goes into the hills along **Swift Creek**, in its rugged canyon. Never was a stream more aptly named. It dashes down between high, serrated cliff walls studded with peculiar yellow towers and pinnacles. It's slightly macabre, but most arresting; the **Balancing Rock**, which teeters over the road to the left, seems about to crash onto the passing car. To the right, the almost hidden, delicate **Shawnee Falls** streaks the high cliff face. Lush vegetation and massive, leaning firs and spruces line the creek; there's also a modest pipeline, which conveys water to Afton. The road permits a speed of only about 5–10 mph, so you get plenty of time to admire the scenery.

From the ample dirt parking lot 5.5 miles up the creek, the trail to the spring takes off along the north side of the towering heights. The trail is well marked, tended, and graded, but definitely designed for horses, not for pedestrians. It proceeds for three-quarters of a mile up the canyon, and the scenery becomes more and more wild and glorious. This trail leads farther into the mountains, and to a view of the Periodic Spring's white cascade of water foaming down the high cliff (in season, of course). But to get down to the spring's outlet, you have to take one of two slippery little cutoffs (sliding on one's bottom is sometimes appropriate), until you reach the rushing creek.

At the bottom of the canyon, and past a small concrete tank with odd water spouts coming out of it (this is *not* the Periodic Spring), rustic bridges lead across the roaring water to the trail that takes you up to the spring itself. Early in the year, when there is nothing periodic going on anyway, a big, picturesque arch of frozen snow blocks the way up, with the cascade roaring down through the center—a grand enough sight in itself.

The spring's setting is as romantic as anything in the Alps. In fact, there's a curious Germanic fairy-tale quality about the whole canyon, its sheer cliffs, magic springs, wild waterfalls, and great, leaning, shaggy spruces—a setting for gnomes and water sprites.

An added spectacle is a tall, narrow landslide down the opposite cliff wall, downstream from the springs. It makes a sinister gash in the cliff and forms a sickly, poisonous-looking lake at the bottom.

(opposite) Roger Preston bags wool on the Preston Ranch in Bedford.

■ GREYS RIVER ROAD DETOUR   *map page 259, A-2*

Greys River Road is a far more adventurous, alternate route south to lower Star Valley from Alpine Junction. Well marked by a Forest Service sign, the road takes off in an easterly direction, and before you know it you are in Bridger-Teton National Forest. Check at the nearby ranger station for road conditions before you go.

For the first 35 miles, the highway is wide, two-lane, and gravel. After a junction with the road east to Merna, Daniel, and Pinedale, things get rougher. The principal danger all along the route is the big logging trucks that command the highway and raise great clouds of white dust in dry weather. In wet weather, don't go. In any case, go slow, stay alert, and pull to the side when the trucks hurtle by, then wait for the dense dust cloud to subside.

There are all sorts of delightful picnic turnoffs along clear, rushing Greys River, which is a fisherman's delight as well as a constant refreshment to the eye (except in dusty conditions). Being an open and easy passage from the Green River to the valley of the Snake, Greys River was a favorite route for early trappers.

Greys River exactly parallels the Salt River. Between them are the also-parallel Salt River Mountains. The Wyoming Range is on the eastern side. Both ranges are rugged enough, especially the Salt Rivers; but the total effect of the scenery is cheerful and comfortable, rather than stunning like the Tetons or grim like the buttes and breaks farther south along the Green River. The only habitations are some tucked-away guest ranches and hunting lodges.

After the junction with the Merna-Pinedale road, marked with a big sign, the road first passes through a wide, willowy meadow where elk sometimes graze, then it goes into logged, burnt timberland. Big cliffs frown overhead. The road is a single-lane, dirt logging road. But once past this area, the scenery gets more attractive, and the road easier. The river begins to shrink into a brawling creek, the timber opens up, and sagebrush hills and ridges emerge; farther south, the country gets drier. Finally, you come to a wide, handsome, empty valley that stretches southeast toward La Barge, on the Green River.

You can return to Star Valley via a good side road that peels off southwest then heads north to Smith's Fork Pass. Gradually the road descends, along water and willows, to the valley. You'll get memorable views looking north to the valley: truly a glimpse of a "promised land of milk and honey," sheltered by friendly hills. When you strike busy Route 89, you can return to Afton (to the north) through **Smoot**—named for a famous Mormon senator and apostle—or turn south toward Kemmerer.

(opposite) Ron Hawks at Fort Bridger Rendezvous.

SOUTHERN WYOMING
FOSSIL COUNTRY, GREAT BASIN & COPPER COUNTRY

◆ **HIGHLIGHTS**

Map pages 302-303

Rock Springs • Rawlins •

◆ **AREA OVERVIEW**

You've now left Wyoming's northwest corner, with its peaks, lakes, streams, forests, and numberless beauties. Entering the southwest corner, you are back once more in the world of dry, open spaces. But Wyoming's southwest corner is not really plains. Bits of national forest encroach on it, and there are lots of irregularities—plenty of cliffs, buttes, ridges, and breaks—but no real mountain ranges. (The massive Uintas loom to the south, but they're in Utah.) Although the Bear River crosses through the far corner of the state, watering farms and ranches en route, the prevailing colors of this part of Wyoming are tan and gray, with dashes of red. The area is chock-full of fossils.

It's an important area for stock raising, intensive coal mining, and oil drilling. Still, it seems largely uninhabited outside its valleys and towns. The principal attractions for visitors are Fossil Butte National Monument, Fort Bridger State Historic Site, Green River, and Encampment.

Weather: In southern Wyoming expect it to be sunny, not too hot, and windy in the summer; cold, snowy, and windy in the winter. Of course, expect wintry conditions in the high mountain passes over the Sierra Madre or Snowy Mountains as early as October and as late as May or even June.

Food & Lodging: Restaurants and lodging are mostly confined to Green River, Rock Springs, Rawlins, or Encampment, but there are some nice resorts and lodges around Flaming Gorge. Camping can be found all over Sweetwater County and the Great Basin.

■ SOUTH FROM STAR VALLEY   *map page 302, A-1*

As you come down from the lush, secluded, picture-postcard Star Valley to all this dryness, the contrast becomes more and more vivid. Trees become sparser. **Cokeville** (pop. 500), in the wide, green, almost treeless Bear River valley, is one of the foremost stock-shipping centers in the state. During World War I, Cokeville boasted that it was the richest town per capita in Wyoming. Not many capita, however. How a place so obviously not devoted to coal got the name Cokeville is explained by a humorous story. The Oregon Short Line of the Union Pacific goes right up the middle of the valley, and some confused railroader is said to have mixed up his station signs for Sage and Cokeville. Sage was supposed to go here, and Cokeville was supposed to go down toward the coal-mining town of Kemmerer, but he switched them by mistake.

■ FOSSIL BUTTE   *map page 302, A-2*

Fossil Butte is a noted quarry of ancient sea creatures. During the Eocene Age, some 50 million years ago, the butte was the sediment-covered bottom of a tropical freshwater lake. Ancient fish and plants died and settled in the mud on the lake floor. Over the course of geologic time, the lake dried up, and the dry bed was thrust up and then eroded. Now the lake bottom lies on top of 1,000-foot-high buttes, and the fossils are preserved in incredibly delicate detail on easily detachable, flat slabs of fragile oil shale.

Founded in 1972, the 8,198-acre **Fossil Butte National Monument** is still in its infancy. The modern Fossil Butte Visitor Center houses a variety of displays on the area's geology, paleontology, and natural history, including a 13-foot crocodilian critter and the oldest known bat. During the summer, visitors can learn how the experts prepare fossils and can visit the quarry on weekends. Picnic tables overlook the colorful butte, and several trails provide access to old fossil quarry sites and other attractions. A two-mile foot trail leads up onto the bare, grand Fossil Butte. There's a deserted quarry on top from which fossils were once crudely dredged, and a fine view over the desolate, rugged landscape. 307-877-4455.

Far more interesting and rewarding is a private establishment down closer to the road and on the south side of the railroad tracks. This is **Ulrich's Fossil Gallery**. Started in 1947, this by-now famous gallery displays and sells fossils that Carl Ulrich and his assistants dig up from private quarries on high buttes to the south. The process involves clearing off the topsoil and rubble to reveal the flat substratum of oil shale. Carefully extracted, the fossils are taken to Ulrich's three-story wooden castle, a contemporary, romantic, irregular structure with laboratories below, display area above, and living quarters behind. Properly salvaged and mounted, the fossils are presented not just as specimens, but as natural art objects. They range from tiny to enormous, and are in museums, galleries, and private collections all over the world. The gallery also sells many other useful and ornamental objects and books. Other private quarries in the area—such as Severn's and Tynsky's—offer similar services, as well as chances to participate in excavations.

Observing the actual digging-up of one of these fossils is an emotional experience. Imagine standing on top of a steep butte with a panorama of the august country roundabout, antelope skipping across the slopes, and even an eagle nesting in the canyon nearby, as workers carefully lift out a slab of fragile, brown stone with a 50-million-year-old black fish perfectly preserved in it. Almost anything else in the area seems anti-climactic by comparison.

■ KEMMERER   *map page 302, A-2*

About ten miles east on the antique U.S. Route 30 is the only really sizeable town in the area: Kemmerer (pop. 3,000). The names of the city streets—Pearl, Emerald, Diamond—reflect the town's basic interests, and those of its satellite towns—Diamondville, Opal, and Cokeville—testify to Kemmerer's origins as an old-time mining center. Most of the original mines have been exhausted, but the old **Pittsburg & Midway Mine**, said to be the nation's deepest open pit coal mine, still extracts 4.2 million tons a year, and it's said there's enough of the stuff in these high plateaus to keep the operation going for a hundred years. The area was once full of ghost towns—Cumberland, Ham's Fork, Sublette, Fossil, Blazon, and Brilliant—but even these have, for the most part, vanished. Nowadays, there's oil here, though coal still persists. Many people are employed at a huge nearby natural gas processing plant, along with the coal mine.

A coal vein was opened near Kemmerer in 1897, backed by a Mahlon S. Kemmerer, of Mauch Chunk, Pennsylvania (the town was later renamed Jim Thorpe, after the famous Indian football player). Mauch Chunk was also a coal-mining area. Kemmerer's right-hand man was an Irishman, Patrick Quealy, whose name is dotted about the area (a small town on Sweetwater Creek, south of Rock Springs, is one such namesake), and whose descendants are still prominent in town. Kemmerer was yet

(opposite) The cliffs of Fossil Butte National Monument contain countless numbers of fossil fish.

another Wyoming boom town, settled, like Newcastle, by a polyglot influx of miners. Nowadays Kemmerer seems into the role of regional shopping center and county seat of extensive Lincoln County. Its claim to fame is that a resident, Mr. James Cash Penney, opened his first store here and went on to father the once ubiquitous chain store that carried his name all over the globe.

Kemmerer is oddly picturesque, with remnants of big old houses on the upper slopes, and a lush, triangular city park at town center. In the middle of this oasis is a small log-cabin visitor center and the **Fossil County Frontier Museum**,preserving a variety of art, mining, and archaeological materials central to Lincoln County history, including a replica coal mine, bootlegging stills, a dino footprint, and the interesting story of Annie Richey, cattle rustler. *400 Pine Avenue; 307-877-6551.*

Not far away are the principal stores, the old hotel (now closed), and a reminder of Kemmerer's peculiar claims to national prominence—the **J.C. Penney Mother Store and Home**. Penney arrived in Kemmerer in the spring of 1902 at the age of 27, specifically to start a new business founded on the principle of doing unto others as you would have them do unto you (hence the name of the business, the **Golden Rule Store**). Within a decade, he had a chain of 34 stores, and in 1913 the business took the name J.C. Penney's. Unfortunately, the store is not preserved in its original form, except on the outside. Inside, it's just an ordinary shop, not worth visiting unless you need to buy something. But the house—a restored six-room cottage that is a National Historic Landmark—is full of memorabilia of Penney's extraordinary rise to success. The by-one's-bootstraps tale that all started here, in an isolated corner of Wyoming, is thoroughly documented and illustrated by souvenirs and photos in the homestead. It is open in the spring and summer.

Another object of interest, farther up the hill above the triangle, is the **County Courthouse**. The domed building is rather special: it was designed in a combination Native American–Art Deco style. It's very original and colorful, and well worth the walk up the hill. A meal at **Luigi's**, a splendid Italian restaurant in Diamondville, should complete your appreciation of this odd, curiously pleasant, and quirky area, a remnant of Wyoming's early coal days. If you're looking for more, come by in March for the town's annual **History Festival**. July brings the fine **Oyster Ridge Music Festival** to town, with a full weekend of bluegrass, folk, and more rocking acts.

For many people, visiting Wyoming means a long drive across the state on Interstate 80.

■ EVANSTON   *map page 302, A-3*

The next logical destination on this tour of Wyoming is Evanston, tucked down almost in Utah, in the very southwest corner of the state. The drive from Kemmerer goes through an almost empty landscape: there's not a settlement of any kind on this 50-mile stretch of U.S. Route 189. Of course, the land is range for cattle (and antelope), and many oil roads lead off the road into the surrounding hills.

The trip begins with a grand panorama of the great Uintas far to the south—including Kings Peak, Utah's highest point at 13,528 feet—but the hills around Albert Creek soon enclose the road and block this mountain view. Beautiful spaciousness again takes over, in this case enlivened early in the summer by a surprising sight along the edges of the highway for miles and miles: swatches and pools of brilliant, violet-blue flax flowers, and some good bird-watching, too.

Then you come to Interstate 80, unavoidable this time. To go either east (to Rock Springs) or west (to Evanston), you have to take it whether you like it or not. It's as truck-choked here as everywhere, but the scenery—though not as handsome as the stretches around Laramie —is rather impressive for Interstate 80: great rolls of land swooping up and down, rocky prominences, groves of odd, stunted, wind-combed aspens, and occasional stirring vistas of the Uintas to the south. Evanston, 11 miles west, is the gateway to the Uintas and their camping and fishing opportunities. It's also the westernmost Wyoming settlement on Interstate 80.

Evanston (pop. 11,500) is a farming center along the Bear River. It's on the Union Pacific Railroad line to Salt Lake City, but that doesn't mean what it once did. Like its sister cities along the line to the east, Evanston was settled by the U.P. railroad-building crews in 1868. Some 600 Chinese workers were brought in to break a strike in the late 1870s. In Rock Springs, a similar action caused an infamous, bloody riot, but nothing that violent happened in Evanston. A Chinese temple, called Joss House, was erected, but unfortunately burned down in the 1920s. A replica was built later in the old depot square. One famous citizen named Chinese Mary survived all sorts of vicissitudes and lived to be well over 100. By the 1930s, all the Chinese natives and their descendents had died or moved on, although a few signs of their passing remain, including an annual Chinese New Year's celebration, complete with Chinese dragon.

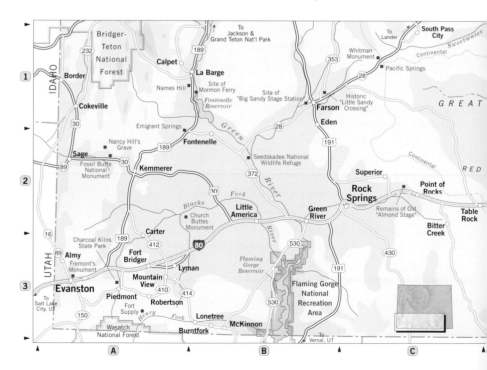

Evanston is the seat and hub of Uinta County, which between 1869 and 1872 stretched right up to Montana. Then Yellowstone National Park was cut out of it. In 1911, Lincoln County broke off from Uinta; and in 1921, Teton from Lincoln. There even have been rumblings about Star Valley threatening to secede from Lincoln.

Like other up-and-coming Wyoming cities, Evanston has two faces. One, reached by Exit 6, is an area of unbridled commercialization—garages, motels, shopping centers. It's very dreary, though useful. A bridge then crosses the Bear River to Old Evanston, which can be reached directly from Exit 7. Up a slight rise behind the center of town lies the shady, pleasant, old residential section. It's altogether a model small Wyoming city.

Old Evanston has a central shopping area, concentrated along Front and Main Streets, the latter lined with trees. **Bear River State Park**, with nice foot and bike paths, is right on the river here. The chief attractions of this part of town include the Uinta County Courthouse and the depot area. The old, original **courthouse** at Ninth and Main is not at all distinguished, but around it has been wrapped,

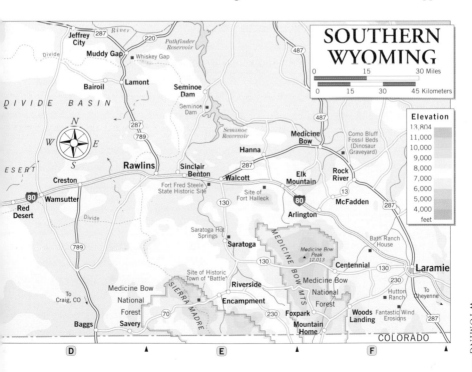

with marvelous architectural ingenuity, a brand-new section of very modern construction, where most of the civic offices now are located. The courthouse, completed in 1874, was built by one Harvey Booth, who was also credited with erecting the first "building" in Evanston just six years earlier, appropriately enough, a canvas-tent saloon. Behind the hybrid building, a courthouse separated by a planted walk elevated over parking spaces, is one of Wyoming's most spacious and well-organized public libraries.

The depot area, near Tenth and Front, has a prime chamber of commerce–information center and a two-level museum combined under one handsome roof; the building was once the Carnegie Library, built in 1906. The restored Union Pacific depot (1901) itself is quite handsome, but not functional. Evanston seems to be full of such substantial, turn-of-the-19th-century civic buildings, no doubt expressing the former status of Uinta County and Evanston's grandiose ambitions to be the capital of western Wyoming. Today, the depot area also includes the rebuilt Joss House with historical photos and artifacts. Also nearby is another restored historic structure, the Beeman-Cashin Implement Depot, now used for community events. The Blyth and Fargo Building on Main Street celebrated 100 years in Evanston in 1972.

Other points of interest include the ghost town of **Almy** to the north, a rich coal mining area in the late 1800s and site of several accidents in which many lives were lost. There is still an old cemetery there. **Bear Lake** is 60 miles north of Evanston, offering many recreational opportunities. **Sulphur Creek Reservoir** offers great fishing and windsurfing 15 miles south of Evanston. And the **Piedmont Kilns** and ghost town of **Byrne** lie about 25 miles to the southeast. Folks enjoy Thoroughbred and quarterhorse racing at **Wyoming Downs**, 8 miles north of Evanston on Highway 89, between Memorial Day and Labor Day, and there are a number of folk and mountain man festivals that take place during summer.

■ FORT BRIDGER   *map page 302, A-3*

This tour now turns eastward for good. Before you leave Uinta County, Interstate 80 takes you past the **Fort Bridger State Historic Site** (307-782-3842), the interesting historic center of Wyoming's southwestern corner. This is some 34 miles east of Evanston, and adjacent to the modern town of Fort Bridger.

Fort Bridger was established not as a military fort but as a trading post. It's along the Black's Fork of the Green River, one of the few green, shaded areas of lower Uinta County. The fort is not too far from the site of the first annual trappers' rendezvous, held on Henry's Fork in 1825, and it was built by and bears the name of the most consistent attendee of the riotous rendezvous, which developed into real extravaganzas and attracted as many as 1,500 Indians, traders, trappers, and travelers. Trappers often went for months alone or with only a few companions, so they had lots of steam to let off. Gorging, drinking, dancing, singing, fighting, games, sex, story-telling, and athletics went on for days. In the whole West, there were no gatherings more famous at this time.

The old system of using military or trader forts as gathering places for fur trading proved inconvenient, since the forts weren't near fur-trapping regions. General William Ashley instituted the tradition of holding annual rendezvous in various locations, a practice continued by later fur-trading companies.

In 1843, as the fur boom died, mountain man Jim Bridger established his so-called fort as a trading post for the swelling flood of emigrants on the Oregon and Overland Trails. All routes converged at the crossing of Green River, funneling west past Fort Bridger. The business flourished for a while, but trouble began when Mormons established their own Fort Supply on Willow Creek near present-day Robertson, 12 miles to the south, founding the very first agricultural settlement in Wyoming. Unfortunately for neighborly harmony, they opened a rival trading post. Bridger claimed the Mormons were driving him out of business, and sold his post. A Mormon eventually purchased the fort, but tension between Mormons and others evolved into a miniature war, during which the original fort was burned, the Mormons were driven back to Utah, and U.S. troops occupied Salt Lake City. The Willow Creek settlement was also destroyed. In 1857, Bridger's fort was rebuilt to serve as a military base. The army closed it in 1890.

Now preserved and refurbished, Fort Bridger is perhaps not as authentic as Fort Laramie, as naturally evocative as Fort Fetterman, or as beautiful as the site of Fort Phil Kearny. It is, however, more completely and elaborately restored than any of the others, and its site in a lush valley, with willows and grass, is in itself a relief after so many miles of semidesert.

As at Fort Laramie, one is astounded by how big these military installations were. Working quarters, offices, horse corrals, a blacksmith shop, a guard house, and other structures give you a complete picture of the activities of such a place. During the summer, staffers dress in period costumes. The original **commandant's house**, on the east side of the parade ground, is stylishly furnished in 1880s decor. Nearby is a low log house with the bachelor officers' quarters, amusingly

(following pages) Sheepherder Pedro Gonzalez watches over 1,800 sheep in the Firehole Canyon section of Flaming Gorge National Recreation Area.

restored as though occupied by two very different officers. Their contrasting characters are portrayed through furnishings and decor. One is an earnest young post–Civil War science buff, neat and full of high thought, his bedroom dominated by portraits of his stern parents. The other is an older, raffish Civil War veteran, whose bed is unmade and whose dining table is littered with the debris of last night's poker and drinking party. The restored **trading post** was originally managed by a sutler named William A. Carter, who went on to become a successful entrepreneur and judge. The original (now extinct) Carter County, with its seat way up in South Pass City, was named after him. He is much memorialized here, and is buried in a pleasant little family graveyard next to the commandant's house. Bridger's own old log-palisaded post, where all of this started, is reconstructed and is open during the summer.

The fort's center of attraction, at the western edge of the parade ground, is a large **museum and store** full of Indian, trapper, and military information. Prominent displays discuss Chief Washakie and the complicated creation of the Wind River Reservation. On Labor Day weekend Fort Bridger comes alive with Wyoming's biggest modern-day Mountain Man Rendezvous, a three-day blowout that attracts hundreds of participants; living-history demonstrations take place throughout the year.

Altogether, Fort Bridger is an oasis of historical interest and greenery along the grimness of Interstate 80.

■ FLAMING GORGE   *map page 302, B-3*

Unless pressed for time, one can avoid the interstate in favor of taking a long, worthwhile detour south to Flaming Gorge and back, via either Green River or Rock Springs. This trip is one of the most spectacular of Wyoming's happy surprises.

From Interstate 80 near Fort Bridger, Wyoming State Highway 414 heads south to Mountain View, which initially doesn't have much of a view, since it is down on the flat bottomland. Farther on, the Uintas are indeed beautifully visible. The scenery changes continually and is always handsome. You go through pink-and-white badlands, broken-up range country, and several tiny dots on the map—Lonetree, Burntfork, McKinnon—and lots of ranches. Wider vistas open as you near the semidesert country around Flaming Gorge. Black timberland topped by distant snowy peaks encroaches on the southwest, and the road finally crosses the state line into Utah.

WHICH GREEN RIVER BASIN?

There was a Green River Basin in Wyoming that was not to be confused with the Green River Basin in Wyoming. One was topographical and was *on* Wyoming. The other was structural and was *under* Wyoming. The Great Basin, which is centered in Utah and Nevada, was not to be confused with the Basin and Range, which is centered in Utah and Nevada. The Great Basin was topographical, and extraordinary in the world as a vastness of land that had no drainage to the sea. The Basin and Range was a realm of related mountains that all but coincided with the Great Basin, spilling over slightly to the north and south. To anyone with a smoothly functioning bifocal mind, there was no lack of clarity about Iowa in the Pennsylvanian, Missouri in the Mississippian, Nevada in the Nebraskan, Indiana in the Illinoian, Vermont in the Kansan, Texas in the Wisconsinan time. Meteoric water, with study, turned out to be rain. It ran downhill in consequent, subsequent, obsequent, resequent, and not a few insequent streams.

—John McPhee, *Basin and Range*, 1980

At Manila, in Utah, you can recoup with gas and food, if necessary, and make a choice of return routes north. Directly up from Manila, Utah State Highway 44 almost immediately recrosses the state line and becomes Wyoming State Highway 530. It proceeds along the west side of the Flaming Gorge Reservoir to the town of Green River. This is an interesting if somewhat bleak trip. It provides glimpses of the blue reservoir, with its striking red-cliff shores, and gives easy access to marinas and campsites near the water. Information is available at Manila.

A far more exciting motor trip detours through Utah around the south end of Flaming Gorge and up the other side to Rock Springs. This is one of the more breathtaking drives in the state. The climax of it, however, belongs to Utah, not Wyoming.

Utah State Highway 44—a fine, wide road—heads south from Manila, beginning a long, rather hair-raising but exalted ascent. It eventually reaches a forested plateau that broods high over Flaming Gorge, to the north. Unfortunately, insatiable lumbering operations in the Ashley National Forest have devastated the looks of this entire section of the Flaming Gorge National Recreation Area. Evidently the designation "national recreation area" does not provide for the same protection afforded national parks and monuments.

GEOLOGY

Wyoming's geology and topography are the result of geological processes that uplifted land into hills and mountains, while concurrently washing them away, depositing the sand and silt into lake bottoms and rivers. These processes took place over about three billion years. Most of Wyoming, though, began forming about 250 million years ago, when the area was covered intermittently by a shallow inland sea. Into this sea great depths of sediments were deposited. Around 70 million years ago, part of this land began to rise, forming the Rocky Mountains, while large rivers eroded the mountains away, depositing vast areas of sedimentary rocks.

Thirty-five million years ago, Wyoming was covered by huge deposits of volcanic ash carried eastward by the prevailing winds from the violent volcanic activity to the west. The ash and debris were so copious they obliterated valleys and mountains. Today this vulcanism is still active in the Yellowstone area. About six million years ago, the old mountains began to rise again and rivers eroded the landscape, washing away much of the volcanic ash deposits and exposing the older rocks underneath.

While all this was taking place, valuable minerals were slowly deposited in the rock formations. As a result, the state has petroleum and natural gas deposits and many operating mines that produce gold, uranium, iron, soft coal, and phosphates. Wyoming also mines important industrial and construction materials, such as gypsum, bentonite, sand gravel, and some marble. In several areas, gem-quality agate is found, and Wyoming is famous for its jade.

Dinosaur remains have been found in abundance in several areas, notably at Como Bluffs. The Green River Formation is world-famous for its 50-million-year-old fossil fish preserved in remarkable detail in a fine silt deposit. Not only fish are found there, but an occasional insect, a tiny frog, and the oldest known bat. In the Absaroka Mountains, there are whole forests petrified *in situ* by the slow process of mineral grains replacing the wood.

Parts of Wyoming took millions of years to form, but not all of its geological phenomena were so slow in developing. Well-known landmarks, such as the Devils Tower and the geysers and hot springs of Yellowstone, result from long-term volcanic activity. At the other end of the spectrum, on June 23, 1925, a gigantic landslide dropped 37 million cubic meters of rock down Gros Ventre Mountain, creating that huge scar on the landscape in less than three minutes.

—Peggy Cross

The Powell expedition of the Green River in 1870. (Photo by E.O. Beaman, U.S. Geological Survey. Courtesy, John Wesley Powell River History Museum, Green River)

Halfway along Highway 44, you come to a short, well-marked road leading north to a series of sensational viewpoints. From the top of the 1,000-foot cliffs above the reservoir, you can look dizzily down the flaming red cliffs to the jade-green water below. "Spectacular," "sensational," "awe-inspiring"—all these well-worn words inevitably come to mind.

Flaming Gorge Reservoir was created by the construction of the 502-foot-high Flaming Gorge Dam, begun in 1958 and completed in 1964. Congress declared the 42,020-acre reservoir and about 160,000 surrounding acres a National Recreation Area in 1969, and folks come here from Wyoming, Utah, and Colorado to boat, fish, water-ski, and hike. Prehistoric petroglyphs testify to the presence of Indians in the region for thousands of years, and the geologic history of the area is laid bare with interpretive signs helping visitors to understand the story. The dam generates an average of 429 million kilowatt hours each year.

The road then proceeds east to join U.S. Route 191. Here it goes across the dam at the end of the reservoir, past a camp area with the picturesque name of Dutch John. Shortly thereafter you are back in Wyoming, and bowling along on yet another of the state's happy surprises, a smoothly paved and beautifully engi-

(preceding page) Devil's Kitchen, near Greybull.

neered highway that swoops through and alongside some of the state's most color-ful and intimidating scenery. You are now on the east side of Flaming Gorge, but too far away to see it. What you do see is the desolate and marvelous expanses of Sweetwater County, a great, empty country, mostly uninhabited and more or less impenetrable except to those who know what they're doing. Stock graze here and pipelines cross the area, but mostly it's all bare wilderness. To the left, a paved road leads west through Firehole Canyon to the remote east shore of the reservoir.

The dam and reservoir at Flaming Gorge are together one of the most conspic-uous, famous, popular, beautiful, and intensely controversial of Wyoming's many water-management projects. The reservoir provides a great source of pleasure and recreation in an area that has precious little of the kind. However, the waters engulfed one of the most spectacularly famous gorges in the West: the canyon of the Green River. Furthermore, the agricultural gain went not to Wyoming, but to Utah. The fact that this natural wonder was practically inaccessible to anyone but hardy rough-water boaters (like John Wesley Powell, who navigated it more than once, the first time in 1869) hardly lessens the seriousness of the environmental crime. The harm is done now.

■ GREEN RIVER   *map page 302, B-2*

The town of Green River, which you will miss if you take the long detour from Fort Bridger to Rock Springs, is the first real civic center along Interstate 80 since Evanston. Though very much a mining town, it has an attractive site on the river under a dominating Castle Rock and other whimsically named formations. It is in a way older than any other southern Wyoming town, since at this site, or near it, all the covered wagons came together to camp and celebrate their passage across the plains.

Green River is a typical railroad city, laid out in 1868. By September of that year it had 2,000 settlers. It now has about 11,800, down from 14,000 during the mid-1990s, which by Wyoming standards qualifies it as a city. It claims to have one of the mildest climates in the state.

Green River may be a mining town, but it's a bit unique because the treasure is neither coal nor oil, but something called trona, a relatively rare mineral from which white soda ash is produced. Green River seems to have a monopoly: over 90 percent of the soda ash produced in the United States and 15 percent of the world's supply is natural soda ash from Sweetwater County. White soda ash is used to make products as varied as glass and baking soda, so trona is a good thing for Green River. A remnant of the 20,000-square mile inland lake that covered this region 50 million ago, trona is today mined by five companies in Green River, together producing over 15 million tons of trona and over 8 million tons of soda ash each year. Geologists say there's 100 billion tons of the stuff in the 1,000 square miles around Green River, enough to last the world a thousand years. On May 21, 1997, celebrating the county's 50th year of soda ash production, Governor Jim Geringer officially proclaimed Sweetwater County the Trona Capital of the World. The city is lightly powdered with white dust.

It's sort of a nice town, too. The complete story of Green River and its county is told at the **Sweetwater County Museum,** located near the county courthouse. Displays include dinosaur stuff, Indian artifacts, exhibits about pioneer days and the westward migration, history related to the old Chinese community of the region, and historic mining photographs. *3 East Flaming Gorge; 307-872-6435.*

Some nice natural areas worth exploring are **Expedition Island,** the **Green Belt Nature Area,** and the **Scotts Bottom Nature Area,** all found along the river. Expedition Island was the point where John Wesley Powell began his expedition down the Green and Colorado Rivers. The Green Belt and Scotts Bottom Nature Areas contain riverside paths and wildlife.

Not far to the north, wildlife watchers can scope for more than 200 species of birds and animals at the 14,000-acre **Seedskadee National Wildlife Refuge,** about 37 miles north of Green River on U.S. Highway 191. Its unusual name comes from a Shoshone word for the Green River: *Seeds-kee-dee-Agie,* meaning "River of the Sage Chicken." The refuge also contains several historic sites: The Oregon, Mormon, Pony Express, and California National Historic Trails pass through here; and from about 1843 into the early 1900s, the Lombard Ferry was a much-used route across the Green River. 307-875-2187.

■ ROCK SPRINGS *map page 302, B/C-2*

Rock Springs is 15 miles east of Green River and the real metropolis of southwest Wyoming. It's big, for Wyoming, with about 19,000 people, putting it in a class with Laramie and just below Cheyenne and Casper. Nobody ever described it as a nice town. It's a place that is, and always has been, devoted to energy—first coal, then oil, then uranium—and it has always been a rough, tough town, as rocky in its character and situation as its name implies. Not cowboys, but miners, prospectors, engineers, and entrepreneurs have roamed its streets and filled its bars, and even the look of Rock Springs is not a bit like the wide-open grids of most of Wyoming's townscapes.

Though only a short distance from Green River, Rock Springs is quite opposite in character. Green River has scenery, the river, and Castle Rock looking benignly down from above, not to mention stability (trona). Rock Springs doesn't. It's in a grim gorge, where the railroad was put through, and trees struggle to survive.

Like Green River, Rock Springs began as a stage station, but along the Overland (rather than Oregon) Trail. This Overland Trail was created in an effort to avoid Indian attacks, but though safer, it was never a real success. The country was rough, arid plains, lacking in water. The railroad made the town Wyoming's first great coal-shipping depot, controlled by and dependent on the Union Pacific. It was the urban center for miners from the nearby pits.

The usual polyglot population of such mining centers settled here in exaggerated diversity. Some 56 different nationalities and ethnic groups are represented, a figure about which signs along the highway boast even today. French bakeries, Greek confectioners, Chinese restaurants, and German beer gardens have been traditional in the town since it started, and the mixed atmosphere still lingers. Since 1924, an international festival has been celebrated by all these different groups.

Lunchtime at the FMC trona mine near Green River, the largest trona mine on earth.

COLD LARAMIE DAWN

Shortly before daylight that morning the train stopped somewhere west of Laramie, and I got off and went up to the front end of the cattle cars to look at our steers. Before I had time to start back to the caboose the train began to roll. By the time the caboose came along I figgered the train would be going too fast for me to get back on so I climbed up on top of the car next to the engine, thinking I could walk the top of the train back to the rear end.

By then we were heading down the east slope of the mountains and, for the first time that night, that train was getting up some speed. I'd tied my bedroll and saddle on top of one of our saddle cars and by the time I got to them those cars were swaying and bucking along so rough that I couldn't stay on my feet any longer. I got down behind my bed and saddle and hung on. A cold east wind was blowing and the smoke and cinders was something fierce up there. When the train pulled into Laramie at nine o'clock I was about froze to death.

—A. B. Snyder, *Pinnacle Jake*, 1953

◆ ROCK SPRINGS HISTORY

This does not mean that the history of Rock Springs is one of unblemished tolerance. As in Evanston, Chinese workers were brought in by the railroad to break a miner's strike in 1878. By 1885, over a thousand were living in the segregated, close-packed, shanty complexes characteristic of these railroad "Chinese company towns." A mob attacked the Chinese workers, considering them strike-breaking scabs. Thirty Chinese were killed, and an attempt was made to drive the rest out of town. Troops were called in to protect them and stayed until the end of the 19th century. Chinatown was rebuilt after being gutted by fire, and carried on life and customs for decades, including an annual dragon procession with firecrackers. Nowadays, this has all disappeared—except for the modern Chinese restaurants.

The name of the city was derived from a spring discovered in 1861, which became an oasis and stopover for the Pony Express and stagecoaches. The random construction of miners' houses and the excavation of mine pits right in the middle of the town caused the streets to wander and to be built up densely, so that the confusion of a European street plan exists downtown, unlike the monotonously

(opposite) A cold morning near Elk Mountain, between Laramie and the Red Desert.

rigid pattern of most settlements west of the Alleghenies. Nobody can claim that Rock Springs ever was "charming" or "quaint." But it is picturesque in its rugged way, with nice residential streets scrambling up the heights south of the city, and lots of life in the crowded downtown. In later years, while there was still an energy boom, various intellectual, collegiate, and even artistic plans were made on a large scale, but the oil collapse of the 1980s has rather dimmed these bright prospects. When you went into a public place in the 1970s, it was full of wild, rugged characters, male and female, who looked like extras in a TV shoot-'em-up spectacle: handsome but desperate. Things are quieter now.

Green River and Rock Springs are by general consent (except for their chambers of commerce) not really tourist meccas. They are, as has been noted, of special interest as centers for the production of energy and the study of geology that goes with it. In *Rising from the Plains* (1986), John McPhee gives a vivid and somewhat horrifying picture of what's been going on around this area in the last years: enormous mining and energy-producing developments, none of which is visible from any of the roads recommended or mentioned here.

In fact, the great energy development and spoliation of the state is something of a hidden secret. This is probably just as well, at least from a tourist's point of view. Still, the energy industry is an important part of modern Wyoming life. The boom of the 1970s and its partial collapse in the 1980s had a traumatic impact on the whole state. In recent years, boom times have returned. We'll just have to see.

■ GREAT DIVIDE BASIN   *map page 302–303, C/D-1/2*

From Rock Springs to Rawlins, it's Interstate 80 all the way for 110 straight miles of the most desperate scenery in the state. If you can think clearly about what you're seeing as the trucks rush by, however, it's certainly curious enough.

The Great Divide Basin, through which the interstate passes for much of this journey, is a huge depression where all the streams sink into the ground and the continental divide makes a big corral around the 6,000-foot-high total desolation. No trees, no farms, no people—in an area about 100 miles from east to west, and 50 miles north to south.

Except for little dots on the highway, relics of old U.S. Route 30, or defunct railroad stations, there is not a habitation north or south, except some ranches, from the Colorado state line to the central belt mountains— Crooks, Green, Ferris, Seminoe, and Shirley, roughly following the long and rather lonely northern boundary of Sweetwater County. Point of Rocks (an old stage station and railroad stop), Bitter Creek and Table Rock (old Union Pacific stops), Red Desert (a big service station), Wamsutter (which actually has 260 people in it), and Creston Junction (which does not)—these are the names that try to fill up the empty map.

This stretch of Interstate 80 has given all Wyoming a bad name. The typical, snide crack, that "Wyoming is nothing but Yellowstone and Grand Teton, and Rock Springs in the rearview mirror," comes from the unimaginative tourist exposed to this almost unavoidable stretch. More cross-continental travelers pass over it during the year than through any other part of the state—even Yellowstone. Most of them, of course, are on their way somewhere else.

Sweetwater County, which contains almost all of this landscape, is the largest county of the state, and most of it is not only the least inhabited, but the most completely uninhabitable section of Wyoming. No name could be more ludicrously inappropriate than "Sweetwater." For one thing the Sweetwater River, that savior of emigrants, is located north, across the central belt mountains in Fremont County. In the second place, once east of the Green River and its few tributaries, Sweetwater County has hardly any water at all.

The basin is generally dismissed as a wasteland and the mining industry has been allowed to pretty much do with it what it wants. There are, however, those who love it—absolutely uninhabited space—and even those who live off it. It's considered good winter sheep range. Geologists love it passionately. And the Bureau of Land Management has been encouraging more camping, hiking, mountain biking, and other appropriate uses of the vast area; visit the bureau's field office in Rock Springs (260 U.S. Highway 191; 307-352-0256) for maps and other information. It's full of game: antelope in great numbers, of course, and one of the largest herds of wild horses in the country, carefully watched by the government. The inevitable inbreeding caused by isolation is cured by periodic importation of new, vigorous stallions from other herds. Their numbers are managed to limit competition with other range-mates; excess wild horses are rounded up and put up for adoption or are shipped to a wild horse sanctuary in Oklahoma, where they live out their lives. Spring and early summer are the best times to watch them with their shaky-kneed foals. The White Mountain herd area on the west side of U.S. Highway 191 north of Rock Springs is the best place to go look for them. More recently, a movement has been afoot to preserve its treasures.

Historically, many of the old pioneer trails passed through this arid region. The Cherokee Trail ran north of Baggs to the old Emigrant Trail, east of U.S. Highway

191 across the Green River just above its confluence with the Black's Fork River, and on to the Lone Tree Station. The Overland Trail stretched from Bridger Pass in Carbon County all the way to Fort Bridger. Remnants of stage stations along the trail can be found with easy access at Point of Rocks (along I-80) and Granger (a short distance north of I-80). Petroglyphs and ancient Indian sites can be found, and the harsh desert ecosystem offers plenty of opportunities to be pleasantly surprised and fascinated by life's ability to gain a foothold even here.

■ COPPER COUNTRY

By the time you reach Rawlins you have almost made a complete tour of Wyoming—if you had the pertinacity to follow along the path laid out by this particular guide. When you cross the Sweetwater County line, some ten miles west of Rawlins, you are back in Carbon County and the southeast corner of Old Wyoming again.

For anyone heading east, the normal and natural thing to do would be to speed right along Interstate 80 back to Laramie and Cheyenne. Since this guidebook has so far not included this particular piece of highway, it would presumably be new territory; and it happens to be the best-looking part of Interstate 80 in all of Wyoming. It skirts the northern edge of the Medicine Bows and Elk Mountain. To the northeast, the Laramie plains stretch out grandly, and it is altogether a splendid change from the preceding Great Divide Basin. But this is Carbon County, named none too subtly for its rich coal deposits. The third largest county in the state, created in 1868, Carbon County is traversed by the Overland Trail, Oregon Trail, Mormon Trail, Union Pacific Railroad, Lincoln Highway, and now I-80. The train stopped along the way for the snow-capped mountains—rising to 12,000 feet—and for tiny towns scattered across desert prairie. A cursory glance will reveal little more than a few sites of minor historical interest and a lot of cows—this is one of the most productive livestock-raising areas in Wyoming—but get off the interstate for a closer look.

■ RAWLINS   *map page 303, E-2*

Rawlins, with a population of about 8,500, is a frontier town on the edge of that long stretch of desolation to the west. As you head east, the area is increasingly settled. Despite its fairly dour surroundings, Rawlins itself is a nice, clean, well-watered town, rather on the order of such old railroad cities as Laramie or Evanston. It was named after a Gen. John A. Rawlins, who in 1867 dispatched a

WRINKLES ON CATTLE HORNS

We had noticed with a great deal of anxiety that the wrinkles had commenced to accumulate on our cattle's horns, as a new wrinkle grows each year after an animal is two years old, and we had been advised by several cattlemen who had been in the habit of taking their cattle by rail to market in place of driving them, to procure files and rasps and remove these  wrinkles before we got to Omaha. So we secured a lot of rasps and files at Cheyenne and had Jackdo carry them for us, and when we caught up with the train we went to work to take off the sign of old age which had come on our stock since shipping them, as the Nebraska corn-raisers only want young stock to feed. When we first loaded our cattle we were informed that they were a little bit too fat for the killers, but, of course, the next day, they was about four pounds too thin for the killers, but too fat for the feeders. However, by this time they were nothing but petrified skeletons, and Dillbery Ike wanted to leave the wrinkles on their horns and sell the entire outfit for antiques. But the more we discussed it, the more we made up our minds that as this railroad done a large business hauling stock, the antique cattle market must be overstocked. So we finally concluded to take off the wrinkles that had grown since we started and sell the cattle on their merits. We arranged to run two day shifts and one night shift of six hours each and to commence up the engine and work back. So getting in the first car we climbed astride the critters' necks and commenced to file. Day after day, night after night, we kept at this wearisome task, and when our files and rasps became worn we sent Jackdo (who wouldn't work, but who didn't mind tramping) to the nearest town to get fresh files and rasps. Sometimes we became discouraged when we saw the wrinkles starting again that we had removed to commence with, and our eyes filled with bitter tears when we thought how much better it would have been to have trailed our cattle through, or even sold them to some Nebraska sucker and taken his draft on a commission house.

—Frank Benton, *Cowboy Life on the Sidetrack,* 1903

crew to go in search of a spring to aid his and his detachment's thirst while protecting a railroad survey crew. The unit located a spring nearby, which was named "Rawlins Springs," later shortened to its current name. The town was incorporated in 1886 and designated the seat of Carbon County. Its chief claim to fame is not a capitol or a university, but a jail. In such a way were territorial and state plums parceled out when these railroad towns were young. From 1903, when the prison was built, till 1981, when a new one went up south of Rawlins, the handsome, castellated old prison was the town's chief attraction—though in some cases the visits were not voluntary. The **Frontier Prison and Museum** is indeed a fine castle, pretty well-aged for Wyoming, surrounded by nice planting. It's now on the National Register of Historic Places, and is open to visitors in summer, with various historic programs and activities taking place there now. Many old-timers in the state spent vacations there in former times. *Fifth and Walnut; 307-324-4422.*

Like all these southern belt towns, Rawlins was a Union Pacific creation of that busy year, 1868, and went through the obligatory Hell-on-Wheels stage. Criminals were not only hanged, it seems, but some actually skinned. That's what happened to the town's most serious outlaw, "Big Nose" George Parrott, at least. Various items made of his hide were available as souvenirs and as a warning to other malefactors; some of them are even on display at the Frontier Prison and Museum. As usual, things quieted down. Today, Rawlins is a generally prosperous center for stockmen and the various surrounding energy producers, though its downtown has been designated a national historic district. A self-guided walking tour takes visitors past all the important structures, including **Ferris Mansion**, a Queen Anne–style Victorian mansion built near the turn of the 19th century by the widow of mining pioneer George Ferris.

If you do happen to stop in Rawlins don't miss **Rose's Lariat** (410 E. Cedar). The Mexican food here has earned this place a great reputation; folks make special trips to Rawlins just for Rose's enchiladas.

■ EAST OF RAWLINS

From Rawlins, Interstate 80 takes you back to Laramie. Just east of town, and a bit off the interstate, are three very different sites of some interest.

◆ SINCLAIR   *map page 303, E-2*

Sinclair (once called Parco, pop. 423) is a town that was built all at once during the oil boom of the 1920s, in the then-popular Spanish style. Its many pseudo-adobe cottages surround a handsome 80-room hotel resembling a Spanish mission. In fact, the hotel is modeled on the monastery of Montesion in Barcelona. In its palmy days, it was a welcome refuge for motorists coming along the Lincoln Highway. Long in decline, it is by now pushing its 80th year, and if it survives it will no doubt be rescued as "historical." Eighty is *old* in Wyoming. Sinclair is still home to one of the largest oil refineries in the U.S. Seminoe State Park, with the largest reservoir in the state park system is just 34 miles north on County Road 351. The North Platte River lies just a few miles beyond, including Wyoming's "Miracle Mile," actually a 5.5-mile stretch of the river known for good fishing.

◆ BENTON   *map page 303, E-2*
Nearby, to the southeast, is the site of Benton, a mushroom town on the Union Pacific. In 1868, it was considered the first real city west of Laramie. The railroad brought its usual hectic prosperity and high jinks. Within two weeks of its founding, Benton had a population of 3,000. The great institution of Benton was the Big Tent—100 by 40 feet, covered with canvas (as were most of the buildings of Benton), and floored for dancing. The usual end-of-the-line rabble rejoiced, drank deep, shot one another, and departed. Nothing remains of Benton except the faint, rancid perfume of its rowdiness.

◆ FORT FRED STEELE   *map page 303, E-2*
By contrast, Fort Fred Steele, farther east along the highway and beside the North Platte River, is now in pretty good shape—what's left of it. It is surrounded by a well-kept picnic area and a small, restored, historic site by the water. As early as 1843, blood was shed here, by accident. Cheyenne Indians saw Lieutenant Frémont and his group camped here, drying buffalo meat, and thought they were an enemy tribe. The Indians attacked, but quickly made peace when they saw their mistake. The army established a fort here from 1868 to 1886, to safeguard Overland Trail emigrants. The ruins that persist provide a lingering sense of the isolation the soldiers of yore must have felt here.

■ OVER THE SIERRA MADRE   *map page 303, D/E-2/3*

There is a long, beautiful alternate route from the Great Divide Basin to Laramie, which takes you away from this last mad dash eastward, and into a whole separate region of southern Wyoming that includes some of its most fascinating country and history.

(following pages) Moonrise over the Medicine Bow Mountains east of Encampment.

SOUTHERN WYOMING

The detour begins 27 miles west of Rawlins off Interstate 80, from a no-place on the map, Creston Junction. Almost as soon as you turn due south on wide, smooth, straight Wyoming State Highway 789, things begin to change for the better. For another dozen miles the road runs through the Great Divide Basin, but the landscape begins to ameliorate. It's still vast, wide-open rangeland, but gradually you perceive the emergence of the Sierra Madre Range. There is, once more, that typically Wyoming excitement of unobstructed plain and approaching mountains.

Crossing the imperceptible Continental Divide, you strike an actual water course, Muddy Creek. When it does have water in it, the creek flows into the Little Snake River, crosses into Colorado, slips into the Yampa, then the Green and the Colorado, and on to the Gulf of California. It's glamorous in a way—the thought that such rivers, often so paltry in Wyoming, find their distant ends in the Pacific and the Atlantic Oceans. Muddy Creek needs all the glamour it can get.

There's no settlement for 50 miles. Ranch houses are visible; gravel roads stray off on either side; cattle, sheep, and antelope (your by-now familiar travel companions) appear, as usual. Eventually you get to Baggs.

◆ **BAGGS**   *map page 303, D-3*
Baggs (pop. 348) is an old cow town, once totally isolated from any other settlement of any size. It's still pretty lonesome. Nothing up north except Interstate 80 and the Great Divide Basin, and nothing west until you reach Flaming Gorge, 100 miles away. Craig, Colorado, is closer—only 40 miles south—but there's nothing between Baggs and Craig. In the old days, Baggs's isolation made it a favorite resort for bad guys. Butch Cassidy (where *didn't* he go?) came to Baggs to celebrate a $35,000 haul he pulled off in Winnemucca, Nevada. He and his group stayed in the Gaddis-Matthews Cabin, still standing, and took over the town, such as it was. Bullets and money flew around, much to the gratification of the inhabitants, who dodged the former and bagged the latter.

Nowadays, Baggs is a quiet little place, somewhat forlorn. Once it had nice examples of old-time, rustic, cow-town architecture, but the sweeping highway improvement has totally destroyed the town's atmosphere, and most people wouldn't think of stopping except to get gas. The road that was supposed to bring visitors just takes them right through.

◆ **THE SIERRA MADRE**   *map page 303, E-3*
Wyoming State Highway 70 leaves Baggs, heading east. Now paved all the way, it gradually rises to a pass across the Sierra Madre and on to the once-active copper-

mining town of Encampment. It's surely one of the most handsome stretches of road in the state of Wyoming.

The first section east from Baggs, through Dixon, on to Savery, and then up into the foothills of the Sierra Madre, takes you along the beginnings of the Little Snake River (no kin to the big Snake), through an idyllic, remote, green valley of small ranches, with increasingly close views of the peaks to the south. These Sierra Madre (the only mountains with a Spanish name in the state) are shaped like pagoda roofs: exotic blue silhouettes that eventually disappear as the road climbs and enters an enormous forest of aspens. This fairy-tale forest, unbelievably colorful in fall, culminates in a breathtaking viewpoint overlooking Battle Mountain and Battle Lake and the valley below.

This region does, of course, have a typically bloody Wyoming history. A group of trappers, led by Henry Fraeb, camped in the valley in 1841. A small party from the group, out to reconnoiter and look for furs, was attacked by Indians and saved in the nick of time by rescuers from the main camp. In revenge, the frustrated Indians set fire to the forest, which may possibly account for the great growth of aspen in the vicinity. (Aspens often take over after a fire.)

Another story about Battle Lake tells how a visiting camper named Thomas Edison conceived the idea for the electric lightbulb filament. Dubious.

After this spectacular viewpoint, the road climbs still higher, through shaggy firs and under the frown of Bridger Peak (11,007 feet) to the north—the highest in the Wyoming section of the Sierra Madre Range. After going over Battle Pass (9,955 feet), the road, paved once more, descends into the valley of the North Platte, and to the former boom town of Encampment.

■ ENCAMPMENT   *map page 303, E-3*

Along with Centennial, Atlantic City, and South Pass City, Encampment is one of Wyoming's more famous "ghost towns." Unlike those others, Encampment has no glorious relics of the past. It does have a living population of about 450 people. It is a small, quite ordinary village on the lower slopes of the mountains, a bit above the valley floor, with a scattering of old houses and store buildings from its great days, but nothing conspicuously curious. Even so, Encampment's great days were great indeed. The town once claimed to be the copper capital of the United States, and the region was a scene of action and ecological destruction unmatched in the state until modern times.

Encampment derives its name from an 1851 trapper rendezvous on the fur-rich spot, but nothing much happened here until 1896, when Ed Haggerty found an outcrop of copper near Bridger Peak, in the northwest corner of the Sierra Madre Range. A mine was started the same year with the excruciating name of Rudefeha, derived from the names of the four original partners: (*Ru*msey, *De*al, *Fe*rris, and *Ha*ggerty). The Rudefeha was bought out in 1897 by Willis George Emmons, novelist, lawyer, politician, and promoter, who changed the name to the more sober North American Copper Company. He persuaded the Union Pacific to build a spur down from the main line at Walcott, and started a boom that riddled the mountains with mines, leaving the slopes gouged up to timberline.

By 1901, there were more than 260 companies at work in the area. Emmons's attorney, Charles P. Winter (who has claims to being Wyoming's first native-born author), cashed in by writing half a dozen novels set in the area. Ten million dollars worth of ore was extracted, but the bubble burst in 1908 when the price of copper fell below the cost of mining it. The company was also involved in scandal involving fraudulent stock and over-capitalization. Within a year, the populations of Rudefeha, Dillon, Copperton, Rambler, Battle, and Elwood had emigrated, and the smelter was shipped to South America. Ranchers in the North Platte Valley bought the railroad spur and then gave it back to the Union Pacific on condition that they keep it running.

The highway passes the scene of all this short-lived riot, but everything is thoroughly overgrown now. For years, one log building marked the site of Copperton, near Haggerty Gulch, where it all started. Of the town of Dillon, only the privies endured, having been built to withstand blizzards. Dillon was founded when the company town of Rudefeha banned saloons. Tired of trying to pronounce the name, as well as thirsty, everyone deserted Rudefeha and moved the short distance to Dillon. A paper, the *Double Jack*, was founded here. Rather like Bill Nye's Laramie *Boomerang*, this newspaper also had its nationally popular star: editor Grant Ives. Ives invented mythical monsters said to inhabit the area—such as the Cogly Woo, the Backaboar, and the One-eyed Screaming Esu—which caught the fancy of the public and made the Sierra Madre temporarily notorious. But Ives died in 1903, shortly after his arrival. Nothing remains now except totally forest-hidden scars on the mountains. Surely one of the most peculiar aspects of this copper boom was its literary tinge, a reputation that persists today.

Encampment keeps the memory of all this alive with its mines, its towering smelter, and a 16-mile hydro-powered aerial tramway (largest in the world) that brought ore across the mountains. The marvelous **Grand Encampment Museum,** an official repository of U.S. Forest Service memorabilia, stands on the southwest edge of the town's small grid, at Seventh and Barnett Streets. Around a green lawn with mountain views stands a row of more than a dozen old buildings, all moved from elsewhere, then preserved and refurnished. Included are a false-front store, an ice cream parlor, a schoolhouse, a fire lookout tower, a blacksmith shop, a historic stage station, and a properly furnished rancher's log-cabin home. Especially note-worthy is the two-story outhouse: the lower level was for summer use, while the upper level became necessary in winter, when heavy drifts of snow piled up. The museum is a special delight for sheer nostalgia's sake, and for a glimpse into the rather active past of this now retired village. Whatever the actual town may lack in atmosphere, the museum possesses. *807 Barnett; 307-327-5308.*

Then there's also fishing and floating, 365 miles of snowmobile trails, cross-country skiing, easy access to the Medicine Bow National Forest, and the annual **Woodchoppers Jamboree** to recommend the area, too. This last event takes place in late June and includes contests that test the traditional tools and talents of tie-hacks and cow hands (also see page 343).

The tiny town of Riverside lies another mile up the road, where a fork leads either south to Colorado or north to the road over Snowy Range Pass or to Saratoga. From there, the route back to Laramie repeats in reverse the journey through Old Wyoming described in the beginning of this book.

This last leg of the journey from Rawlins is a proper grand finale to the whole great circle around the state of Wyoming. By itself, this leg of the trip covers plains and mountains, rivers and forests, and quite a bit of history—all the essential ingredients that give Wyoming its characteristic flavor. The tour ends at Laramie, like a snake biting its tail: after weaving around through all of the state's counties and countrysides, with their enormous distances and great variety, the persistent traveler arrives back at the pleasant starting point. It might be presumptuous to think that anyone would actually follow the route determinedly in one direction, from start to finish, but it could be done. The route does give a panorama of all the state's more accessible beauties, and can serve at least as a foundation for one's travels in wonderful Wyoming.

(following pages) A train rolls across the barren winter landscape near Kemmerer.

PRACTICAL INFORMATION

◼ State Information

Bureau of Land Management. *Box 1828, Cheyenne, WY 82003; 307-775-6130.*
Road & Travel Information. *307-WYO-ROAD.*
State Parks & Cultural Resources. *Barrett Building, 2301 Central Avenue, Cheyenne, WY 82002; 307-777-6306.*
Wyoming Arts Council. *2320 Capitol Avenue, Cheyenne, WY 82002; 307-777-7742.*
Wyoming Dept. of Commerce (Wyoming Recreation Commission). *Herschler Building, 2 West, 122 W. 25th Street, Cheyenne, WY 82002; 307-777-7695.*
Wyoming Game & Fish. *5400 Bishop Boulevard, Cheyenne, WY; 307-777-4600.*
Wyoming Geological Survey. *Box 1347, University Station, University of Wyoming, Laramie, WY 82071; 307-766-2286.*
Wyoming Internet Information. *www.state.wy.us/state/welcome.html*

◼ Area Code and Time Zone

The area code for the entire state is 307. Wyoming is in the Rocky Mountain time zone.

◼ Getting There

◆ By Air

The three major airlines serving the state are United, Delta, and American. Although there are major airports in Casper, Cheyenne, and Jackson, and smaller ones in Cody, Gillette, Laramie, Riverton, Rock Springs, Sheridan, and Worland, travel to the state usually requires a Salt Lake City or Denver connection.

◆ By Land

Most folks traveling on land arrive by car (or RV or pickup), but Greyhound does travel along Interstate 80 in southern Wyoming. Wind River Transportation serves the Lander-Riverton area, and Powder River Transportation covers the rest of the state.

■ About Wyoming Food and Lodging

Many lodging and some food establishments in Wyoming close down for part of the year, so it is always advisable to call ahead.

There are two kinds of hotels: mostly modern ones that cater to conventioneers or business travelers, and mostly older ones that still retain a whiff of the Old Wyoming grandeur and character. The principal chains are represented in every town of any size, especially Cheyenne, Casper, and Jackson. For winning examples of the state's classic inns and lodges, see "Historic Wyoming Hotels," page 334.

Other options for tourists are historic bed-and-breakfasts, found in many Wyoming towns and villages. Still another option, and an old Western lodging tradition, is the dude ranch, and its more luxurious variant, the guest ranch.

In Wyoming, accommodations are usually booked up pretty early in the day during the height of the tourist season. Without reservations, a weary motorist may be scrambling for a bed long after bedtime.

Wyoming is not a state known for its snooty city-slicker haute cuisine. This is cattle country, the land of the free and the home on the range, where juicy steaks and the finest prime rib can be found in every podunk town in the state (the best steakhouse may well be in the don't-blink-or-you'll-miss-it town of Hudson, between Lander and Riverton). For breakfast, it's pretty much standard all-American fare, accompanied by the dark brew that folks in these parts call coffee. Real cowboy coffee, made only over a smoky open fire and not available within 20 miles of any town, is a potent medicine, not advised for children and the weak-kneed. Check local outfitters for the prescription.

■ Dude and Guest Ranches

Probably the most attractive, intimate, and characteristic accommodations in Wyoming are guest ranches, which are concentrated in the northwest corner of the state, especially around Cody and Jackson. Some are real dude ranches, which never (or never used to) take anyone off the road without an introduction. Things have changed, however, and many dude (and all guest) ranches now offer overnight accommodations for tourists. All conform to the pattern of the dude ranch—a main log cabin for dining and socializing, and separate log cabins for sleeping.

Dude ranches are the best way to get back into the country and the available fishing, game-spotting, and scenery. They are usually set in beautiful locations, and

Historic Wyoming Hotels

◆ Grand Teton National Park

Jenny Lake Lodge. Cozy and luxurious in a simple, Old West way, these romantic log cabins (no TV, radio, or phone) are set right at the base of the Tetons, on the shore of Jenny Lake. Prices include horseback riding, cycling, breakfast, and a six-course dinner at the excellent restaurant. The lodge dates from 1922 and was part of the Tony Grace dude ranch. *Open mid-May–early Oct. Jenny Lake Road; 800-628-9988 or 307-733-4647.*

◆ Yellowstone National Park

For the following park hotels, call **Yellowstone Central Reservations,** *307-344-7311.*

Lake Yellowstone Hotel. Built in 1889 on the northern shore of Lake Yellowstone, this 194-room lodge features stately Greek Revival columns and giant lakefront windows; it's really more Great Lakes–style than Western. Wander into the lobby in the afternoon to hear chamber music, then into the restaurant for a sophisticated dinner. In addition to the main building's cherrywood-furnished rooms, over a hundred simple, pine-paneled cabins are also available. *Open mid-May to late Sept.*

Mammoth Hot Springs Hotel. Less crowded—because farther from the park's main attractions—are this hotel and its 140 cabins, a few with hot tubs. One restaurant serves well-executed regional cuisine, while the other spacious dining room offers faster, cafeteria-style food. *Open summer and winter; closed spring and fall.*

Old Faithful Inn. Built in 1903 and still one of the world's largest log buildings, this spectacular lodge features an open, six-story hall with deep, beautifully wrought balconies up to the ceiling. The dining hall contains a volcanic stone fireplace. More expensive rooms are decorated in antique cherrywood and face the geyser; others are motel-style. *Open mid-May to mid-Oct.*

Roosevelt Lodge Cabins. Close to beautiful Lamar Valley and Tower Fall, these 86 simple cabins were initiated by TR himself. The lodge has retained its rough-and-ready hunting, or dude-ranch, feel. The restaurant serves Western-style dishes like "Roosevelt beans" and barbecued ribs. *Open June–Aug.*

◆ Throughout Wyoming

Hotel Higgins. This hotel, on the National Register of Historic Places, has been beautifully restored as a bed-and-breakfast with two suites and four rooms, all with private baths. Antiques are everywhere, from the sewing machine sink in the lobby ladies room to the glamorous lampshades in the Highlander Bar. The hotel's dining room, the Paisley Shawl, attracts people from throughout central Wyoming. *416 W. Birch Street, Glenrock; 800-458-0144 or 307-436-9212.*

Irma Hotel. When he built this inn in 1902, Buffalo Bill Cody named it for his daughter; it was one of three hotels Buffalo Bill intended to house tourists en route to Yellowstone. This one boasts brass beds, period furniture, a huge restaurant, and an elegant cherrywood bar given to Buffalo Bill by Queen Victoria. In summer, locals stage gunfights on the porch. Breakfast in the restaurant is a gathering place for local ranchers. Ask for historic rooms. *1192 Sheridan Avenue, Cody; 800-745-4762 or 307-587-4221.*

The Plains Hotel. Built in 1911 and refurbished in 1986, this hostelry and bar were for years the real political center of the state. Take note of the mosaic of Chief Little Shield on Central Avenue just outside. *1600 Central Avenue, Cheyenne; 307-638-3311.*

The Virginian Hotel. The striking yellow stone rectangle, built in 1911, was named for *The Virginian*, the popular Owen Wister novel set in Medicine Bow. Guest rooms at this fashionable hotel, on the National Register of Historic Places, are decorated in an early 1900s style, and fine meals are offered in the intimate dining room. Ask for the Owen Wister Suite. *409 Lincoln Hwy., Medicine Bow; 307-379-2377.*

Wolf Hotel. Built in 1893 by German Frederick Wolf, this old brick hotel was for years heavily frequented by stagecoach passengers, especially miners headed for the Sierra Madre. Refurbished with antiques and now on the National Register of Historic Places, this small downtown inn gives guests a peak into the past. Fine dining is available in the restaurant, where chicken and beef are especially well prepared. Four suites and five rooms. *101 E. Bridge Street, Saratoga; 307-326-5525.*

Wort Hotel. Though dripping with history, this brick Victorian feels oddly up-to-date. A fireplace in the lobby keeps loungers toasty. Those looking to be warmed from the inside can visit the Silver Dollar Bar for a whisky. *50 N. Glenwood (at Broadway), Jackson; 800-322-2727 or 307-733-2190.*

though not exactly luxurious, have a personal and genuinely Wyoming character that no mere motel or hotel can match.

At the turn of the century, the term "dude" was universal American slang for any dressed-up young man. In the West, it settled down to mean any newly arrived, unadjusted, and dressed-up Easterner. Nowadays, it is pretty much confined to guests at dude ranches. Contemporary dudes need not dress up. If anything, dudes tend to dress down, sometimes to the point of squalor. (Real Westerners don't dress dirty on purpose.)

Though Wyoming can honestly lay claim to the world's oldest dude ranch, the honorable tradition of regular catering to dudes actually started in North Dakota, where the hospitable Eaton brothers—Howard, Alden, and Willis—kept a horse ranch near Medora (they were neighbors of Theodore Roosevelt). As more and more of their Eastern friends came to stay for the summer, the Eatons found that whatever money they were making on horses, they were losing on guests. The idea of charging guests for their board and keep was encouraged by the visitors themselves—and so the idea of the dude ranch was born.

In 1904 (two years after the publication of *The Virginian*), the Eatons moved to Wolf Creek, on the edge of the Big Horn Mountains, west of Sheridan. Their ranch still continues under family auspices as the oldest surviving dude ranch in the world. It has served as a model for all the others: a family ranch, often actively engaged in cattle or horse raising, that takes in friends as paying guests for summer riding, fall hunting, and winter skiing. The idea of the dude ranch spread from Sheridan through Wyoming and the whole West. In the Big Horns, the Hortons' HF Bar Ranch, the Paradise Guest Ranch, and the Bones Brothers' Ranch near Birney, Montana, are almost as long-established as the Eatons'. In Jackson Hole, the JY Ranch began a few years after the Eatons' Ranch, in the first decade of the twentieth century, and dude ranches have flourished there ever since.

Dude ranches are definitely not hotels or lodges. They are closer to sporting clubs—basically, a group of friends of the owner out for a holiday visit, in simple surroundings. Active outdoor participation in ranch life and a developing intimacy among the guests are the basis for this kind of community life.

This ideal of dude ranching was easy to maintain before the days of the automobile, when dudes perforce took a six-day train trip from the East, and a wagon or truck trip of a dozen or more hours from the nearest depot. In the twenties, as the automobile gradually made its way into Wyoming, a change began. Shorter stays were practicable. The dudes became less and less a close circle of friends of the family.

Basically, however, the tradition of intimacy manages to persist. Families still come back year after year, and children grow up on the same ranch summer after summer.

The boom times of the 1920s were the golden age of dude ranching, when dudes were flush and automobiles were scarce. The depression of the thirties and the Second World War devastated the dude ranch business. Many ranches failed. After the war, the automobile and the plane changed their character. No one could pretend that most of the older establishments were really remote any more. The intimacy of dudes with the owner and one another came less naturally. The surrounding wilderness on which the ranches depended for riding, fishing, and camping became increasingly less wild. The small towns that provided weekend nightlife for dudes and hands became less local and more sophisticated.

The end result of these outside changes has caused a gradual blending of the dude ranches and the tourist courts. Some real old-line dude ranches now call themselves "guest ranches" and cater to drop-in travelers off the road. For these, introductions and friendship with the owners aren't necessary. Dude ranches that don't advertise would still require some sort of introduction. Your chances of just dropping in during the summer months at any of these places and getting a bed are minimal.

Price designations are not given, as rates vary according to activities, packages, etc. Keep in mind that because many amenities (meals, outings) are included in the price, staying on a ranch can cost more than staying at a luxury hotel.

◆ Big Horn Mountains

Deer Haven Lodge. Six-unit motel and 12 rustic cabins with fireplaces; dining room, lounge. Pack trips, winter sports, fishing. Extensive cross-country trails nearby. *Open year-round. U.S. 16, 18 miles east of Ten Sleep; 307-366-2449.*

Eatons' Ranch. Historic working cattle ranch on 7,000 acres next to Bighorn National Forest. Horseback riding, fishing, hiking. *Open seasonally. 270 Eaton Ranch Road, Wolf; 307-655-9285.*

HF Bar Ranch. The second oldest dude ranch in America. Rustic cabins with baths; family-style meals served in ranch house. Horseback riding, pack trips, fishing, hunting; clays course, as well as shoots on private bird preserve. *Open June–Sept. Saddlestring, 15 miles northwest of Buffalo; 307-684-2487.*

Kedesh Ranch. Sixteen cabins with baths. Dining in main lodge; trail rides, fishing, hayrides, wildlife walks, square dances. Pack and hunting trips. *Open June–Nov. 1940 U.S. 14, Shell, 20 miles east of Greybull; 307-765-2791 or 800-845-3320.*

Meadowlark Lake Resort. Rustic mountain setting; 28 units: condo, cabin, motel. Dining room, lounge. *Open year-round. 26 miles east of Ten Sleep on U.S. 16; 307-366-2424.*

Paintrock Adventures. Room for 20 in main lodge and a cabin, near Cloud Peak Primitive Area. *Open June–Nov. In Bighorn National Forest, 23 miles southeast of Shell Ranger Station turnoff; 307-469-2274.*

Paradise Guest Ranch. Deluxe cabins with fireplaces, porches, baths. Sunday to Sunday week stays only; all meals. Horseback riding, fishing, children's program. *Open summer only. Box 790, Buffalo; 307-684-7876.*

◆ **CODY AND WAPITI VALLEY**
See page 190 for dude and guest ranches in this area.

◆ **DOUGLAS**
Cheyenne River Ranch. Working cattle and sheep ranch on 8,000 acres. Seasonal chores: moving cattle, branding, shearing sheep. Family-style meals. *Open May–Oct. 1031 Steinle Rd., Rte. 2; 307-358-2380.*

◆ **DUBOIS**
See page 261 for dude and guest ranches in this area.

◆ **GRAND TETON NATIONAL PARK**
See page 251 for dude and guest ranches in the park.

◆ **JACKSON AREA**
See page 251 for dude and guest ranches in this area.

◆ **MEDICINE BOW NATIONAL FOREST**
Medicine Bow Lodge & Guest Ranch. Renovated log cabins, private baths. Horseback riding, fishing, rafting; cross-country skiing and snowmobiling in winter. Hearty meals. *Medicine Bow National Forest; 307-326-5439 or 800-409-5439.*

Mountain Meadow Cabins. A National Historic Place in Medicine Bow National Forest: 8 modern cabins at an elevation of 10,200 feet. Trail rides, hiking, fishing near cabins; 100 lakes and streams within a 10-mile radius. Gorgeous fall colors on surrounding hills. *Open year-round. 7 miles west of Centennial; 307-742-6042.*

◆ PINEDALE

Big Sandy Ranch. Log cabins with wood-burning stoves and family-style meals. Horse trips, fishing, hunting, snowmobiling. *In Bridger National Forest, near Boulder; 307-537-5675.*

David Ranch. Working cattle ranch. Log cabins with private baths. Cattle drives, branding, chores; max. 10 guests at a time. *Open June–Oct. 40 miles south of Jackson, Daniel; 307-859-8228.*

Green River Guest Ranch. Modern, simple cabins. Horseback riding, snowmobiling. The place has a peaceful atmosphere and delicious food. *Closed Apr. and Nov. It's 15 miles north of Cora on edge of Bridger Wilderness; 307-367-2314.*

◆ THERMOPOLIS

High Island Guest Ranch. Lodge accommodations with shared bath. Working cattle ranch. Cattle drives, branding, wilderness pack trips. Saturday to Saturday week stays. *Open June–Sept. Hamilton Dome, northwest of town; 307-867-2374.*

■ RODEO EVENTS

Steer wrestling, or **bulldogging,** involves leaping from a quarter horse onto the back of a 700-pound Mexican steer running at 25 miles an hour, grabbing his horns and wrestling him to the ground. The event involves two men, a dogger, and a hazer. When the steer hurtles into the arena, the two spur their horses in quick pursuit, with the hazer trying to force the steer to run straight ahead while the dogger gets into position to leap onto the steer's horns, wrestling him to the ground. Good doggers can get a steer down in less than seven seconds. The term "bulldogging" originated in 1903 when black cowboy Bill Pickett (many cowboys in those days were African American) became the first steer wrestler. He'd jump onto the steer, grab its horns, bend over its head, then bite the animal's lower lip like an attack bulldog.

Calf roping originated in the Old West when cowboys had to rope and tie calves for branding. This is the most competitive of all rodeo events today, with big money prizes. Time is of the essence, and the most valuable asset for a roper is his horse.

Probably the most controversial of all rodeo contests is **steer roping,** an event banned from most rodeos because it is so hard on the animals. It's illegal in some states, but is still done at Cheyenne Frontier Days. The procedure is essentially the same as

Saddle bronc rider at Cowboy Days in Evanston.

calf roping, but with a much larger animal. When the 700-pound steer is jerked back by the rope and then thrown down with a thud, you can almost feel the impact.

When you say the word rodeo, many people immediately think of **saddle bronc riding.** The oldest of all rodeo sports, it originated from cowboys' efforts to train wild horses on the range. Rodeo saddle bronc riding is more complex than this, however, requiring a special "association" saddle, dulled spurs, and very precise rules. Broncs are saddled up in the chutes and riders climb on, grabbing a thick hemp rope in one hand and sinking their boots into the stirrups. When the gate opens, the bronc goes wild, trying to throw the rider off. To count as an official ride, the rider must hold his toes forward and out, with the spurs against the horse's shoulders for the first jump. Balance and rhythm are important, and only one hand can be used to hold on. The smooth back-and-forth motion of a good saddle bronc rider makes it look like he is atop a rocking chair. Rides last only eight seconds.

Bareback riding is a relatively recent rodeo sport, arriving on the scene in the 1920s. The rules are similar to saddle bronc riding, but the cowboy rides with only a minimum of equipment—no stirrups and no reins. The cowboy holds on with one hand, an effort akin to trying to juggle bowling pins while surfing on a big wave.

Bull riding is in a class of danger all its own. Unlike broncs, who just want that man off their backs, bulls want to get even. When a bull rider is thrown off (and this is most of the time, even with the best riders), the bull immediately goes on the attack, trying to gore or trample him. Many bull riders are seriously injured and some die when hit by 2,000 pounds of brute force. There are no saddles in bull riding, just a piece of thick rope wrapped around the bull's chest, with the free end wrapped tightly around the bull rider's hand. A cowbell hangs at the bottom of this contraption to annoy the bull even more. When the chute opens, all hell breaks loose as the bull does everything it possibly can to throw his rider off—spinning, kicking, jumping, and running against the fence. If the rider hangs on for the required eight seconds (style isn't very important in this event), the next battle begins—getting out of the way of one very angry bull. Here the rodeo clown comes in. Dressed in bright red-and-white shirts and baggy pants, they use every trick in the book to distract the bull from the fallen bull rider: climbing inside padded barrels that the bull butts against, weaving across the arena, mocking the bull with matador capes, and simply running for their lives in an attempt to reach the fence ahead of the bull.

—Don Pitcher, *Wyoming Handbook*

■ FESTIVALS AND RODEOS

During the summer months, every town in Wyoming has its own celebration, generally centered around a morning parade, an afternoon rodeo, and an evening of country music and dancing. Rodeos are the definitive Wyoming event, reflecting the enduring importance of cattle and cowboys, and on any given night between June and September there's probably a rodeo going on somewhere in the state.

◆ JANUARY

Afton: Cutter Races. Chariot racing on ice; *Jan.–Feb.; 307-883-2759.*

Fort Collins: Mountain States Circuit Finals Rodeo. Top professional cowboys and cowgirls from Wyoming and Colorado compete; *307-778-1291.*

Jackson: Jackson Hole Powder 8s. *Mid-Jan.; 307-733-3316.*

Lander: Wyoming State Winter Fair. Including state horse show, livestock exhibits, dog weight-pulling contests, and dances. *Late Jan. or early Feb.; 307-332-3892.*

Saratoga: Annual Ice Fishing Derby. One of the nation's top such derbies. *Mid-Jan.; 307-326-8855.*

◆ FEBRUARY

Afton, Alpine, Dubois, Jackson, Kemmerer, Lander, Pinedale: International Pedigree Stage Stop Sled Dog Race. A 10-day sled dog race that circles the Wind River Mtns. *Early Feb.; P.O. Box 1940, Jackman, WY 83001; 307-734-1163.*

Casper: Casper College Kinser Jazz Festival. *Early Feb.; 307-268-2100.*

Casper: Cowboy State Games Winter Festival. Winter sports contests (skating, skiing, et al.) over Presidents' Day weekend; *307-577-1125.*

Jackson: Cowboy Ski Challenge. Novelty ski races, cowboy poetry, barn dance, novelty rodeo events. *Late Feb.; 307-733-3316.*

Jackson: Cutter Races. *Mid-Feb.; 307-733-3316.*

Saratoga: Don E. Erickson Memorial Cutter Races. Two-horse teams race down the straightaway. *Mid-Feb.; 307-326-8855.*

♦ **MARCH**
Alta/Grand Targhee: Annual Spring Snow Carnival. Includes Nordic skiing contest. *Early Mar.; 800-827-4433 or 307-353-2300.*

Cheyenne: Laramie County Community College Rodeo. Some of the best collegiate rodeo around. *LCCC Arena, early Mar.; 307-778-5222.*

♦ **APRIL**
Cody: Cowboy Songs and Range Ballads. Cowboy poets and singers at the Buffalo Bill Historical Center and the Wynona Thompson Auditorium. *Early Apr.; 307-587-4771.*

Douglas: High Plains Old Time Country Music Show & Contest. Guitars, fiddles, and banjos play 'til the cows come home; *307-358-5622.*

Jackson Hole: Pole, Pedal, Paddle Race. Competitors cross-country ski, cycle, and kayak or canoe in this strenuous rite-of-spring triathlon. *First Sat.; 307-733-6433.*

Meeteetse: Annual Arts Festival. *Late Apr.; 307-868-2423.*

Rock Springs: Cowgirl Classic Women's Pro Rodeo. *Late Apr. or early May; 307-362-3711.*

♦ **MAY**
Green River: Lake Flaming Gorge Fishing Derby. *Mid-May; 307-875-5711.*

Lusk: PRCA Rodeo. *Late May–early June; 307-334-2950.*

Rock Springs: Cowboy Poetry and Music Festival. *Mid-May; 307-362-6212.*

◆ JUNE

Casper: Cowboy State Games. An Olympics for Wyomingites—track, basketball, swimming, more. *307-577-1125.*

Casper: Ft. Caspar Rendezvous & Skills Competition. *Mid-June; 307-235-8462.*

Chugwater: Chili Cook-Off. Bring your appetite and some Alka-Seltzer to this all-you-can-eat spicy bean-and-meat eatfest. *Late June at the Diamond Guest Ranch; 307-422-3345.*

Cody: Cody Nite Rodeo. Nightly rodeos; this event is usually more family-oriented than the state's other big rodeos, with music and food and much more. *June–Aug.; 800-207-0744.*

Cody: Plains Indian Powwow. Native Americans come from the Rockies and Canada to participate in this well-known and acclaimed event. The traditional dances are held at Buffalo Bill Historical Center. *Mid-June; 307-587-4771.*

Encampment: Woodchoppers' Jamboree & Rodeo. The weekend following Father's Day, thousands of people flood this tiny settlement for lumberjack contests as well as dances, rodeos, and other family activities. Wonderful food and drink and merriment abound; *307-326-8855.*

Fort Washakie: Eastern Shoshone Powwow & Shoshone Stampede Rodeo. *Late June; 307-332-9106.*

Green River: Flaming Gorge Days. *Late June; 307-875-5711.*

Lander: Popo Agie Rendezvous. *Mid-June; 307-332-3892.*

◆ JULY

Casper: Central Wyoming Fair and Rodeo. *July–Aug.; 307-235-5775.*

Casper: Governor's Cup Regatta. Biggest regatta in the state, held at beautiful Lake Alcova. *Late July; 800-852-1889 or 307-234-5311.*

Cheyenne: Cheyenne Frontier Days. A 10-day blowout established in 1897 and certainly one of the top four rodeos in the world. More than 1,000 contestants, with events beginning at 7 A.M. daily. Morning parades, country-music concerts, Indian dancing, chili cook-offs, and free pancake feeds—but rodeo is the main attraction for the 300,000 visitors. *Frontier Park, late July; 307-778-3133.*

Cody: Cody Stampede. Three days of parades, entertainment, barbecues, and an all-around chance to party, including a popular rodeo south of town. *Fourth of July weekend; 800-207-0744.*

Cody: Yellowstone Jazz Festival. World-renowned jazz artists perform outdoors. *Mid-July; 307-587-9669.*

Jackson: Teton County Fair. Family events, rodeo. *Late July; 307-733-5289.*

Jackson/Teton Village: Grand Teton Music Festival. All-star orchestras and chamber ensembles present classical repertoire five days a week. Walk Festival Hall. *July–Aug.; 307-733-1128.*

Lander: International Climbing Festival. *Mid-July; 307-349-1561.*

Lusk: Legend of Rawhide. This outdoor play, held every July since 1947, is based on the 1849 murder of a Sioux girl by a white gold-seeker, and the Indians' skinning-alive of the protagonist. *Early July; 307-334-2950.*

Pinedale: Green River Rendezvous. Begun in 1936, this annual event, complete with historical pageantry and a feast of pit-roasted buffalo, relives the rendezvous of trappers, Indians, and mountain men of the mid-1800s. *Mid-July; 307-367-2242.*

Powder River: Sheepherders' Fair & Mutton Cook-off. Sheepdog trials, sheep roping and hooking. *Mid-July; 307-472-7055 or 307-876-2778.*

Sheridan: Sheridan WYO Rodeo. Professional rodeo cowboys, parade, dancing. *Mid-July; 307-672-9715.*

◆ AUGUST

Throughout Wyoming: County fairs in nearly every Wyoming county throughout Aug.

Alta/Grand Targhee: Bluegrass Festival. Rain or shine, 3 days of music, arts and crafts, food booths. *Early or mid-Aug.; 800-827-4433 or 307-353-2300.*

Cody: Buffalo Bill Festival. Art fair, chili cook-off, headliner concert, rodeo finals, cowboy poets. *Mid-Aug.; 307-587-2297.*

Douglas: Wyoming State Fair. Ten days of carnival rides, livestock shows, arts and crafts, C&W concerts, and "sheep-to-shawl" contests. PRCA rodeos the last three days. *Mid-Aug.; 307-358-2950.*

Pine Bluffs: Trail Days. Four-day festival with teenage rodeo, mud volleyball, parade, crafts. *307-245-3695.*

Rock Springs: Great Wyoming Polka Festival. *Late Aug.; 307-352-6789.*

Thermopolis: Gifting of the Waters. Re-enactment of 1896 passing of Wind River Reservation hot spring to U.S. government; *first weekend in Aug.; 307-864-5183.*

◆ SEPTEMBER

Cheyenne: Western Film Festival. Growing in size and stature. *307-638-3388.*

Evanston: Labor Day Weekend Celebration & Cowboy Days. *307-789-4900.*

Fort Bridger: Mountain Man Rendezvous. The state's biggest rendezvous. Participants dress up in handmade costumes, live in tepees and old tents, attempt to outshoot others with black-powder rifles, bake bread over a fire, and mug for the clicking cameras of tourists. *Labor Day Weekend; 307-782-3842.*

Jackson: Fall Arts Festival. Concerts, dance, theater, open galleries, workshops. *Mid-Sept.; 307-733-3316.*

Kaycee: PRCA Deke Latham Memorial Rodeo. Best small-town pro rodeo in America. *Early Sept.; 307-738-2444.*

Riverton: Cowboy Poetry Roundup. *Mid-Sept.; 307-855-2000.*

Sheridan: Big Horn Mountain Polka Days. Several thousand enthusiasts come to this polkathon. *Labor Day weekend; 307-672-2485.*

◆ OCTOBER

Casper: PRCA Rodeo. *Late Oct. or early Nov.; 307-235-5775 or 888-225-2600.*

Douglas: Halloween Parade. *307-358-2950.*

Jackson: Quilting in the Tetons. *Early Oct.; Call Mary Martin, 307-733-3087.*

Pine Bluffs: Halloween Carnival. *307-245-3695.*

Rawlins: LeClare Square Dance Festival. *Jeffrey Center; 307-324-4311.*

Rock Springs and Wheatland: Oktoberfest. German food, German music, and a good excuse to drink beer. Call visitors bureaus for dates. *Rock Springs: 307-362-3771; Wheatland: 307-322-2322.*

◆ NOVEMBER

Cheyenne and Rawlins: Christmas Parades. Floats, horses, marching bands, just after Thanksgiving. *Cheyenne: 307-778-1407; Rawlins: 307-324-4111.*

◆ DECEMBER

Alta/Grand Targhee, Buffalo, Laramie, Torrington: Christmas Torchlight Parades. *Grand Targhee: 800-827-4433; Buffalo: 307-684-5544; Laramie: 307-745-7339; Torrington: 307-532-3879.*

Jackson Hole: Christmas and New Year's Eve Torchlight Parades. *307-733-2292.*

RECOMMENDED READING

■ HISTORY AND MEMOIRS

Burt, Nathaniel. *Jackson Hole Journal.* Norman: University of Oklahoma Press, 1984. Takes off from where the senior Burt's *Diary of a Dude Wrangler* ends. Reminiscences of 60-odd years of the valley's lives and times.

Burt, Struthers. *Diary of a Dude Wrangler.* New York: Scribner's, 1924. The earliest autobiographical and local account of Jackson Hole, the dude ranch business, and the stories that accumulated about both. Also author of *Powder River, Let 'Er Buck* (New York: Farrar and Rinehart, 1938). In the voluminous Rivers of America series, this book gives you all the mythology that historians like T. A. Larson, editor of the Wyoming WPA guide, eschew. It is no longer in print, but every Wyoming public library will have it. The book cultivates the colorful aspects of Wyoming's history, based on the activities along the Powder River, and gives you plenty of stories.

DeVoto, Bernard. *Across the Wide Missouri.* Boston: Houghton Mifflin, 1947. This classic—the most famous modern account of the trappers and their Far West—won a Pulitzer prize and remains the best account of the trappers' era.

Larson, T. A., ed., and the Works Progress Administration. *Wyoming: A Guide to its History, Highways, and People.* Lincoln: University of Nebraska Press, 1981. This is a reprint of the now-classic WPA guide of 1941, first and foremost among the great mass of literature on Wyoming. As an actual guide, it's half a century out-of-date, but as a depository of fact and myth it remains invaluable. Oddly enough the basic road structure of Wyoming has not changed, except for the intrusion of Interstates 80, 25, and 90. No other main routes have been added. Flaming Gorge has been created, Grand Teton Park has been extended, various historical sites have been refurbished, and towns have grown—but that's about it. If you buy one book about Wyoming, this should be the one.

Larson, T. A. *The History of Wyoming.* 2nd Edition. Lincoln: University of Nebraska, 1978. Another bible. This is the second edition of Larson's monumental work, first published in 1965 and still available. If you find its nearly 700 pages a bit too too hefty, look for a condensation of it, Larson's *Wyoming: A Bicentennial History,* in your local library. This shorter version, part of the Bicentennial State Histories series, is more convenient and up-to-date, and it tells you all you want to know about the whole span of Wyoming's past, with plenty of picturesque detail. Larson is one for the facts, and you'll get plenty.

Parkman, Francis. *The Oregon Trail.* Boston: Little, Brown, 1886. First published in 1849, this first and most vivid account of Wyoming—when nobody knew about it except Indians, trappers, soldiers, and a few adventurers like young Parkman—is the classic account of that early time.

Roosevelt, Theodore. *Ranch Life and the Hunting Trail.* New York: Hippocrene, 1985. A rather detailed and sobersided, but still romantic, account of TR's ranch life in the Dakotas during the great cattle days of the 1880s. The illustrations are by Frederic Remington. Not quite Wyoming, but might as well be.

Saylor, David. *Jackson Hole, Wyoming.* Norman: University of Oklahoma Press, 1990. This thorough, rather detailed account of the history of the valley, from trapper to tourist, also conveys the history of the state as a whole.

■ NATURAL HISTORY AND GEOLOGY

Blackstone, D. L., Jr. *Traveler's Guide to the Geology of Wyoming.* Laramie: Geological Survey of Wyoming, Bulletin 67, 1988. A comprehensive guide to the state's geologic past and today's evidence of it.

Hager, Michael W. *Fossils of Wyoming.* Laramie: Wyoming Geological Survey, Bulletin 67, 1988. A concise, illustrated digest of the state's interesting paleontological past.

Largeson, David R., and Darwin R. Spearing. *Roadside Geology: Wyoming.* Missoula, MT: Mountain Press, 1987. This guide handily takes you along the major roads of the state, with geological explanations of what you see. Designed not for experts but for average travelers, the book can be enormously rewarding.

McPhee, John. *Rising from the Plains.* New York: Noonday Press, 1986. A contemporary picture of Wyoming, based on a trek across the state on Interstate 80. It describes the geology and modern energy development en route, with many picturesque diversions into other eras and areas. Some of the rock-work, however, is fairly dense for non-rock-lovers. While too young to be a "classic," it may well become one in the future. McPhee is also the author of *Basin and Range* (New York: Farrar, Straus & Giroux, 1981).

Murie, Margaret, and Olaus Murie. *Wapiti Wilderness.* Boulder: Colorado Associated University Press, 1985. The Muries present a charming autobiographical account of a conservationist couple's life, including their experiences with elk, during summers and winters in Jackson Hole.

■ TRAVEL GUIDES

Fodor's Travel Publications. *The Rockies.* New York: Fodor's, 2002. A brief section on Wyoming gives good advice on ski resorts, lodges, and restaurants.

Hunger, Bill. *Hiking Wyoming.* Helena, MT: Falcon Press, 1997. A good overall guide to hikes in the state. Falcon Press also has a number of other hiking guides to specific parts of the state, including Yellowstone and the Wind River Mountains.

Pitcher, Don. *Wyoming.* Chico, CA: Moon Publications, 2000. A thorough town-by-town guide to Wyoming's main attractions, accommodations, restaurants, and special events. Interesting topical pieces.

■ FICTION

Nye, Bill. *Bill Nye's Western Humor.* Lincoln: University of Nebraska Press, 1985. Some of the humorist's most wry essays.

Proulx, Annie. *Close Range: Wyoming Stories,* New York: Scribner, 2000. This collection of short stories by the Pulitzer Prize-winning author of *The Shipping News,* who now lives in Wyoming, has been cited for capturing "the brutal loneliness and magnificent beauty of the Wyoming landscape."

Wister, Owen. *The Virginian.* New York: Penguin, 1988. First published in 1902, this novel fits right in with the Roosevelt-Remington picture of the Far West (as given in *Ranch Life and the Hunting Trail,* see page 348) of that same period.

■ WYOMING LIVING

Anderson, Susan, and Zbigniew Bzdak (photographer). *Living in Wyoming.* Oakland, CA: Rockridge Press, 1991. A visual introduction to modern Wyoming scenes and people. Bzdak's photos are captivating.

Ehrlich, Gretel. *The Solace of Open Spaces.* New York: Penguin, 1985. Accounts of the tough lives and the wide and wild landscapes that fill Wyoming. *A Match to the Heart* (New York: Pantheon, 1994) is Ehrlich's story of being struck by lightning. In *Wyoming Stories,* (Santa Barbara: Capra Press, 1986) Ehrlich describes life in the state with just the right balance of realism and poetry. Some have called her the "Walt Whitman of Wyoming." Also the author of the novel *Heart Mountain* (New York: Viking, 1988).

(following pages) Old wagons age gracefully at Triangle X Ranch, with the sharp-edged Tetons as a backdrop.

INDEX

COMPASS AMERICAN GUIDES

Alaska (5th Edition)
978-1-4000-0736-3

Alaska's Inside Passage (1st Edition)
978-1-4000-1480-4

American Southwest (3rd Edition)
978-0-679-00646-6

Arizona (6th Edition)
978-1-4000-1265-7

Boston (3rd Edition)
978-0-676-90132-0

California Wine Country (5th Edition)
978-1-4000-1783-6

Cape Cod (1st Edition)
978-1-4000-1310-4

Chicago (3rd Edition)
978-0-679-00841-5

Coastal California (3rd Edition)
978-1-4000-1538-2

Colorado (6th Edition)
978-1-4000-1204-6

Connecticut and Rhode Island (1st Edition)
978-0-676-90492-5

Florida (2nd Edition)
978-0-676-90494-9

Georgia (3rd Edition)
978-1-4000-1617-4

Gulf South: Louisiana, Alabama, Mississippi
(1st Edition) 978-0-679-00533-9

Hawaii (6th Edition)
978-1-4000-1482-8

Idaho (2nd Edition)
978-0-679-00231-4

Kentucky (2nd Edition)
978-1-4000-1661-7

Las Vegas (8th Edition)
978-1-4000-1244-2

Maine (4th Edition)
978-1-4000-1237-4

Manhattan (4th Edition)
978-0-676-90495-6

Massachusetts (1st Edition)
978-0-676-90493-2

Michigan (2nd Edition)
978-1-4000-1483-5

Minnesota (3rd Edition)
978-1-4000-1484-2

Montana (6th Edition)
978-1-4000-1662-4

Montreal (1st Edition)
978-1-4000-1315-9

New Hampshire (1st Edition)
978-0-676-90151-1

New Mexico (5th Edition)
978-1-4000-1393-7

North Carolina (4th Edition)
978-1-4000-1616-7

AUTHOR'S ACKNOWLEDGMENTS

It would be impossible to thank all the people in Wyoming—friends and strangers—who were helpful in my months of touring and writing. Some are those mentioned in the text, such as the hospitable Ulrichs of fossil fame. Others were kind strangers. My largest single debt is to the editor of this book's first edition, Barry Parr. Other friends, especially those in Sheridan, will recognize themselves and their works in the text; likewise inspirational Bob Spoonhunter of St. Stephen's on the Wind River Indian Reservation. I am deeply grateful to all these, and many others, for their hospitality and information. Margot Holiday, also of Sheridan, was particularly kind and informative, as were a number of people at the University of Wyoming in Laramie. I remain grateful to Gene Gressley there for kindnesses past and present. And thanks always to my original publishers, Christopher and Tobias, for encouragement and help along the way.

PUBLISHER'S ACKNOWLEDGMENTS

The publisher thanks Chuck Reher of the University of Wyoming's Department of Anthropology for his helpful advice and assistance; Peggy Cross for her piece on geology; Mike Papciak for his piece on the Vedauwoos; Paul Zimmerman for his contribution on "Big Nose" George Parrott; and Ellen Klages for proofing this edition. Special thanks to Jeanne Ball, Richard Anderson, and John H. Clark, who updated the text of this edition.

Sagebrush near Encampment.

■ About the Author

NATHANIEL BURT was born during a snowstorm on a kitchen table in a log cabin, attended by a psychiatrist on the Bar BC, one of Wyoming's first dude ranches. The son of Struthers and Katharine Burt, themselves famous authors – he of *Diary of a Dude Wrangler* and *Powder River* and she of many romantic novels about the West, several of which became films – Burt grew up in the truly American Shangri-La of Jackson Hole in the Grand Tetons. In his book *Jackson Hole Journal* he tells the story of a life surrounded by his parent's Eastern friends – countesses, writers, and gentle eccentrics – who came to ride, fish, sing Western songs, and write poetry to each other. He also describes the evolution of the frontier town into the resort it has become today. In this guide he shares the secrets of a state he has learned from the idyllic world of his childhood to the rugged realities of a lifetime's experience. He shows us why many people choose to call Wyoming home.

Burt is a writer and composer whose published works include poetry, fiction, and nonfiction. His musical compositions have been performed at the Teton Village Music Festival.

■ About the Photographer

DON PITCHER'S travel photography and writing grew out of his interest in the natural world. After receiving a Master's Degree in fire ecology from the University of California, Berkeley, he worked on bear and owl studies, fire research, and as a wilderness ranger in Alaska, Wyoming, and California. Pitcher is the photographer for Compass Alaska, as well as a coauthor of the *Alaska-Yukon Handbook* and the author of *Wyoming Handbook,* both for Moon Publications. Pitcher's photographs have appeared in books, magazines, and calendars.